CONFESSING JESUS AS LORD

Terry Chrisope has provided us with a wonderful resource. It is biblical theology at its best, showing how the Lordship of God in Christ is the fundamental storyline of the Bible. It is systematic theology at its best, highlighting the offices of Christ as the key to our salvation. It is evangelism at its best, underlining that our rebellious condition can only be addressed by the saving work of Jesus our Lord. And it is spirituality at its best, as Chrisope opens our minds to the glories of Christ's mediatorial reign. It is a clear guide through what has been an unfortunate controversy. I wish it a wide circulation, with the prayer that many would gladly acknowledge Jesus as their Lord through its publication.

Iain D Campbell
Minister, Free Church of Scotland, Point, Isle of Lewis,
Moderator, General Assembly of the Free Church of Scotland 2012

Confessing Jesus as Lord is one of the most timely books to appear in a long time. We are surrounded by false Gospels, confused Gospels, and half Gospels. In this important book, Terry Chrisope lays out the authentic Gospel of the Lord Jesus Christ and clearly identifies what it means to confess Jesus as Lord. The most fundamental affirmation of the church is the lordship of Christ. This new book is both important and powerful.

R. Albert Mohler, Jr.
President, The Southern Baptist Theological Seminary,
Louisville, Kentucky

CONFESSING JESUS AS LORD

TERRY A. CHRISOPE
FOREWORD BY JOHN MACARTHUR

ⅢENTOR

Copyright © Terry A. Chrisope 2012

ISBN 978-1-84550-962-0

Published in 2012
in the
Mentor Imprint
by
Christian Focus Publications
Geanies House, Fearn, Ross-shire,
IV20 1TW, Scotland

www.christianfocus.com

Cover design by Daniel van Straaten

Printed by
Bell and Bain, Glasgow

MIX
Paper from
responsible sources
FSC® C007785

CONTENTS

Foreword

Is the lordship of Christ an essential aspect of the gospel message? The answer to that question should be obvious to anyone who has read the New Testament. 'Jesus is Lord' (Rom. 10:9; 1 Cor. 12:3) is the first, simplest, and most basic of all Christian statements of faith. It is the central truth of Christianity itself and the one confession every tongue will make when the triumph of the gospel is complete (Phil. 2:11).

An absurd notion spread like leaven through the evangelical community for much of the twentieth century. Actively promoted by several well-known evangelical leaders, it was the idea that Christ's lordship is somehow extraneous to the proclamation of the gospel, and therefore this is a truth best suppressed until after a person has first embraced Christ as Savior. Surrender to the lordship of Christ was portrayed as a meritorious work and therefore deemed hostile to the principle of grace.

The result was a doctrine that divided Christ (radically separating His role as Savior from His office as Lord). It eviscerated faith (boiling belief in Christ down to mere assent and thereby making faith a purely intellectual exercise, devoid of any emotional or volitional aspect). It eliminated repentance from the process of conversion. It made assurance cheap and easy while making obedience optional. And in its most extreme versions, it emphatically repudiated the necessity of any kind of spiritual fruit as evidence of regeneration, including (especially) turning from sin, perseverance in the faith, and simple fidelity to Christ.

Proponents of this idea insisted that to proclaim the lordship of Christ was to preach justification by works. Jesus' lordship is advanced doctrine for devoted believers only, they claimed. To mingle the truth of Christ's lordship with a call to trust Him as Savior is to preach heresy, they insisted. They tagged the view they opposed 'lordship salvation'. Their view therefore has fittingly come to be known as 'no-lordship salvation'. For a time, it seemed as if the no-lordship view was on the cusp of becoming the majority opinion among American evangelicals.

I wrote two major books dealing with the lordship controversy. The first, titled *The Gospel According to Jesus* (released in 1988) owes much to the work of Terry A. Chrisope, who entered the fray several years before I did with a wonderful little book titled *Jesus Is Lord* (Welwyn, Hertfordshire: Evangelical Press, 1982). I was given a copy when I was just beginning to collect research material and while planning the outline for my book. *Jesus Is Lord* was barely more than a hundred pages long, comprising just four chapters, but of all the books I read on the lordship controversy, I found it the most helpful, the most rich with insight, the most spiritually uplifting, and the most lucidly clear.

So I was pleased and grateful to learn that Dr Chrisope has developed his earlier work into a much larger volume. The result, even better than the original, is the book you hold in your hands. It is an important installment in the lordship debate, which is by no means over.

No-lordship doctrine has clearly lost much of its luster and some of its popularity. But the defenders of the idea are becoming noisier and more insistent. Popular evangelicalism's disdain for doctrine and polemics has produced a generation of young Christians who are predisposed to spurn precision when it comes to many of the issues underlying the lordship controversy. Among young adults just entering into positions of church leadership, an astounding number seem totally unaware of the previous debates about this issue. Hence in some quarters the issue is coming back into focus as a point of controversy.

Confessing Jesus as Lord is an invaluable addition to the debates and discussions that are already beginning to take place. I'm thankful for the way Dr Chrisope handles the issue. This book is not an arcane and academic discussion of theological technicalities; nor is it a caustic polemical diatribe. It is just straightforward biblical wisdom applied with clarity and simplicity to an issue every Christian needs to understand. I trust you will find it as helpful and as persuasive as I did.

John MacArthur

Preface

The original embodiment of the argument of this book appeared in 1982 (*Jesus Is Lord*, published by Evangelical Press) as perhaps the first book to address the emerging 'Lordship Controversy.' In its current form the argument has been considerably expanded to include the Old Testament and the earthly career of Jesus; the original material has been extensively revised; and the entire book has been reconfigured around the concepts of 'lordship' and 'autonomy,' as explained in the Introduction. The result is that this work may be considered a new book (with a new title), but with lines of continuity connecting it to the older one. The emphasis has not changed (some friends facetiously suggested I call it 'Jesus Is *Still* Lord').

In the meantime a considerable and highly publicized debate broke out between certain figures in evangelical circles (see the introductory paragraphs of Chapter 10). It is not the purpose of this book to provide a history or analysis of that debate or to reply directly to the proponents of the opposing viewpoint (except where their teaching intersects with the concerns of this book), for such would likely be neither helpful nor edifying. Rather, it is the purpose of this book to present a positive and coherent account of the teaching of the Bible concerning God's lordship and the human rebellion against that lordship, with particular focus on the redemptive remedy which God has instituted for dealing with that rebellion, a remedy which is epitomized in the believing confession 'Jesus is Lord.' This purpose has caused me to cast the book into a predominantly positive and expository form, with the polemical element appearing only occasionally, and mostly in Chapter 10 dealing with objections. I hope that this approach results in a book which will be both helpful and edifying in setting forth the purposes of God as expressed in the Bible.

Neither is this book intended as a display of erudition or scholarship. I hope that the documentation which is presented will suffice to show that the position set forth here is supported by respectable and respected scholarship, both from the evangelical world and beyond, but it is not intended to be exhaustive. The book deals with the central message of a great portion of the Bible, and citations could be multiplied on almost every point addressed, as well as contrary positions fully engaged, but such would likely be useless and would unnecessarily extend the length of the book. I trust that the teaching ministry of the Holy Spirit combined with a heart which is in sympathy with the teaching of the Bible will be sufficient to persuade the reader of the truthfulness or falsehood of what is offered here. Nothing else will (or should) prevail anyway.

In some ways, it should seem (and will seem, judging from my reading of the relevant literature) virtually incredible to many observers and serious students of the Bible that a debate over the propriety and necessity of Christians recognizing the lordship of Jesus Christ would even occur, so plainly does the matter lie on the pages of the New Testament. Indeed; but doctrinal controversy may have the beneficial result of promoting helpful discussion of questions at issue, bringing about clarification, increased understanding, and theological correction and growth. I hope that this study contributes to such an outcome.

I owe a debt of gratitude to Arlen Dykstra, Provost and Vice President of Academic Affairs at Missouri Baptist University, for granting me several May Term sessions in which to work on this project; to my colleague Curtis McClain for frequent assistance with computer issues; to First Baptist Church of St. Peters, Missouri, USA, and its pastor Joseph Braden, for allowing me to first write this book as a series of weekly Bible studies for the congregation; and to my wife Linda for her support throughout this writing project. Gratitude is also expressed to the Banner of Truth Trust for permission to quote the material in Appendix 2.

A special word of thanks is extended to Pastor John MacArthur for providing his gracious Foreword to this volume. Pastor MacArthur has been for several decades a veritable 'Mr. Valiant-for-truth' (to use Bunyan's memorable term), and I deeply appreciate his contribution both to this book and to the preservation of the gospel in our generation. I am honored by his presence in these pages.

The practical applications which appear periodically were initially part of the lesson format in which the book originally was written. I was planning to omit them from the book, but was urged by others to leave them in, and thus they are still present. It remains only to be said that I am aware of many of the weaknesses and imperfections of this book, and it surely possesses others of which I will no doubt be made aware in the future. Needless to say, I alone am responsible for its flaws, and for them and for myself I ask the reader's grace, forgiveness, and forbearance, just as God has received us in Christ Jesus (Eph. 4:32–5:2).

Introduction

THE HUMAN CONDITION

We humans live in a world which in many ways is mysterious to us and which evidently has somehow gone awry.

We are born without our consent into a world not of our own making and perhaps not to our liking. We are placed in conditions to which we did not agree and which may or may not enhance the possibility of our survival and flourishing. As individuals we control almost nothing that occurs in the world around us and precious little that occurs in our own lives. Everything that concerns us seems to be contingent and uncertain.

And that is the good part. The world in which we live seems also to be a world of woe. We are confronted with disease, depravity and death both in the observable world around us and within our own selves. A dear co-worker at the institution where I teach spent a year battling colon cancer and was declared free of the dread disease, only to succumb to a massive heart attack. Every day we are treated by the news media to appalling accounts of human wickedness, depravity and cruelty, and when we are honest, we must admit that we perceive the seeds of such qualities in our own souls as well. And I still vividly recall the searing pain caused by the death of my mother nearly two decades ago and my attendant desolate recognition that the world was now a lonelier place for me: I had never lived in a world in which my mother was not present, but now I must. It did not help my grief that my father quite reasonably had his own name engraved on the headstone in anticipation of his being buried beside her. But perhaps that was a salutary reminder to me not only of his mortality but of my own also.

We are left to try to understand all of this. Initially, we receive whatever answers are passed on to us by our parents, our teachers, or our culture, but eventually we have to reach our own conclusions as mature individuals. And when we do come to some kind of understanding, it is often accompanied by unanswerable questions or nagging doubts. Historically, there have been perhaps three modes of seeking understanding and developing a coherent worldview: mythology, philosophy, and revelation. Ancient traditional cultures developed mythology, and one suspects that there are still many who adhere to myths in the modern world. The ancient Greeks invented philosophy, the attempt at a rational understanding and explanation of things on the basis of human reason alone; this approach is still with us but without much agreement as to conclusions, and in some respects has passed into the enterprise which we call 'science.' Various religions have claimed the support of divine revelation, information communicated by a god or gods or God to humans, and of course they are multitudinous in our modern world and often in a state of mutual hostility. Besides these three approaches there are perhaps other cultures which have developed traditions of 'wisdom' for living which fall into one or another of these categories or somewhere between them.

It is not my intention here to attempt a refutation of the alternatives, but simply to affirm that the approach which seems to me to make the best sense of things is the revelational approach of the Judeo-Christian tradition, embodied in the Old and New Testaments of the Christian Bible. If the content of the Bible constitutes genuine revelation from the God who created the universe, then it follows that (1) such revelation is of tremendous importance to us, because (2) we have access to information there which we could obtain in no other way. And the Bible's account of things does indeed provide us with an explanation for the way things are. That explanation is fairly simple: the God who created the universe originally made everything good, conformable to his will and under his lordship; but humans have rebelled against God's lordship, and this rebellion and God's response to it have introduced certain distortions into human life, resulting in the conditions under which we now live.

It is all pretty straightforward, then: the human revolt against God's lordship has produced the dislocations, distortions, and disharmonies, the alienations, aberrations, and abnormalities which now characterize human life. The remedy is also straightforward: the human acknowledgment of God's rightful lordship over all (all persons and all aspects of human life) and the reception of forgiveness which the God of the Bible offers to humans at great expense to Himself. The result of such willing acknowledgment and reception is that 'substantial healing' (as one thinker has called it) is brought into human life and relationships in the present, a healing which will eventually be made complete and perfect one day in the future. This book is about that willing acknowledgment of God's lordship, reception of his forgiveness, and the renewal of human life which occurs as a result.

In particular, this study constitutes an examination of the biblical teaching on the lordship of Jesus Christ and the meaning of the corresponding New Testament confession, 'Jesus is Lord' (Rom. 10:9; 1 Cor. 12:3; Phil. 2:11). This is a matter, it will be argued, which reaches to the very heart of the biblical message and is thus of no small importance.

I. The Argument

The argument set forth in this study may be summarized in the following affirmations.

1. The story of the Bible can be told as one of God's lordship, of humanity's effort to become independent of that lordship, and of God's program to reclaim humanity's submission to his lordship.

The biblical story can be told as a reflection on two Greek words: *kyriotes* and *autonomia*. The first means 'lordship' and refers to God's right to rule; the second means 'living by one's own laws' and describes man's effort to live independently of God. From Genesis to Revelation, the story of the Bible is one of God's assertion of his lordship – his 'right to rule' – over all the universe but more specifically over human beings, and of humans' counter-assertion of their right to live apart from God's rule. Genesis 3:1-7 describes humankind's decisive rejection of God's right to rule and thus the initial expression of human autonomy, while the rest of the Bible describes the disastrous consequences of that action and God's program of redemption to bring humans back under his acknowledged rule, forgiven and willingly submitting to Him.

While a major motivating impulse behind God's program of human recovery may be said to have been love (John 3:16; Eph. 1:4; 2:4; 1 John 4:9-10), and its operating procedure may be said to be grace (Eph. 1:7; 2:5, 8-9; Titus 2:11; 3:7), yet its major outcomes include (along with the reconciliation of humans to Himself) the display of God's glory (his attributes: Eph. 1:6, 12, 14; 2:7; 1 Pet. 2:9b) as well as the rightful submission of his redeemed people to his authority (James 4:7; 1 Pet. 5:6), which suggests that these matters may also have had no small part in the divine motives. And on the human side, while the application of redemption is to result in human love for God and for other humans (Matt. 22:34-40; 1 John 4:19-21), yet the concrete expression of that love is to be found in obedience to God's commands (John 14:15, 21; 1 John 2:1-5; 5:2-3). Thus neither the divine love expressed in the biblical gospel nor the human love which is the result of the operation of the gospel in human lives is a vague, amorphous, contentless sentimentality, but both are intended to result in the concrete acknowledgment of God's authority to rule over human life, expressed in obedience to Him.

2. The agent for the recovery of humanity's submission to God's lordship is Jesus Christ.

The appointed agent for the accomplishing of redemption and the reassertion of God's lordship is the God–man, Jesus of Nazareth. Through Jesus the Messiah: (1) God's claim to rightful dominion over human life is asserted (in Jesus' preaching of the kingdom of God, Matt. 4:17; Mark 1:15); (2) God's provision of redemption from the guilt and power of human efforts to achieve autonomy is accomplished (in Jesus' perfect life and atoning death, Matt. 20:28; 26:27-28), and (3)

God's establishment of a concrete agency through which his lordship is manifested is brought to pass (in Jesus' resurrection and exaltation to supremacy in the universe, Matt. 28:18). Thus the person and work of Jesus of Nazareth become the means for God's recovery of humanity to its proper stance of love for, reliance on, and submission to its Creator.

3. The mechanism for expressing humanity's renewed submission to God's lordship is the confession 'Jesus is Lord.'

The specific and appointed mechanism for humankind's re-entry into this proper relationship is the New Testament confession of faith, 'Jesus is Lord' (used explicitly in Rom. 10:9; 1 Cor. 12:3; Phil. 2:11). The current study claims that:

1) This confession represents a personal acknowledgment of an objective reality. The objective reality acknowledged by this confession is that the eternal Son of God has taken human nature to Himself in a space-and-time incarnation in real human history as Jesus of Nazareth, that He lived a perfect life as a human and died an atoning death representing humans who were in rebellion against God, that He has been raised from the state of death and exalted to God's right hand where He is enthroned as Lord of the universe and agent of God's reign, with the full and open manifestation of his lordship to come about at a future time.

2) This confession involves the personal acknowledgment of a subjective reality. The confessor also acknowledges that he has been engaged in an unjustifiable and culpable rebellion against God his creator, that he trusts in Jesus Christ and his atoning sacrifice as God's appointed means of forgiving his rebellion, and that he willingly places himself under the rightful authority of Jesus Christ as God's agent in governing the universe.

3) This confession thus implies the attitude which the New Testament calls 'repentance toward God' (Acts 20:21). The attitude of repentance is one which is tantamount to the human renunciation of the claim to autonomy and the recognition and acceptance (in principle) of one's rightful place of submission to God's lordship.

4) This confession, sincerely offered, is the beginning of a transformed life.

The new life initiated by this confession is one of increasing holiness, practical obedience to God, and growing conformity to the image of Jesus Christ.

There are other implications of this confession as well (such as the acknowledgment of Jesus' essential deity; the necessity of submission to his authority as exercised through the writings of the New Testament, etc.), but these will be developed in the course of this study.

II. Necessary Clarifications

Because of the possibility of misunderstanding and misrepresentation, it is necessary to insert immediately some important clarifications.

1. This understanding of the confession 'Jesus is Lord' does not overturn the biblical teaching of salvation by grace alone, through faith alone, and by Christ alone.

Opponents of the position advocated here claim that this stance constitutes an abandonment of salvation by grace and introduces the merit and works of fallen human beings as the ground of salvation. Such is not the case. In fact, this position insists on the contrary: that sinful human beings are justified (pronounced righteous by God) solely and entirely on the ground of the imputed righteousness of Jesus Christ, received by faith (1 Cor. 1:30; 2 Cor. 5:21; Phil. 3:9; Gal. 2:16); and that the exercise of such faith (as well as repentance, which is its corollary) is not a product of the unregenerate and unaided human will but is a gift of God, bestowed by his grace (Eph. 2:8-9; Phil. 1:29; Acts 11:18). It is maintained here that the works and efforts of fallen human beings do not enter at all into the ground of their justification before God.

2. This understanding of the confession of Jesus' lordship does not imply perfection on the part of the believer.

This confession does not mean that the individual confessor will fully or perfectly live out the demands of Jesus' lordship over him (see Phil. 3:12-14). The confession simply represents an *acknowledgment in principle* of Jesus' rightful authority over oneself (a former rebel) and a reorientation of one's life toward rendering to God that love, submission, and obedience which is due Him as Governor of the universe (Matt. 22:37; John 14:15). This confession does teach us, however, that the initiation of the Christian life does not occur without the (at least) implicit acknowledgment of Jesus' rightful lordship over the believer (suggesting willing abandonment of one's rebellion against God's government) and the placing of oneself *in principle* under that lordship.

Both of these positions will be developed more fully in later portions of this study.

III. Terminology: Lordship and Autonomy

The terminology utilized here derives from the Greek language in which the New Testament was written.

1. The language of 'Lordship' involves the concept of God's 'legitimate authority'.[1]

The word that is applied to Jesus in the New Testament and to God in the Greek translation of the Old Testament (the Septuagint) is the Greek term *kyrios,* commonly translated 'lord'. Its basic meaning when applied to persons is '*having power* or *authority* over, *lord* or *master of* ' someone or something else. Grammatically, *kyrios* is an adjective which may be used as a substantive (a noun) with the resultant meaning of *a lord, master: an owner, possessor,* which is usually its sense when applied to God or Christ. *Kyrios* derives from the more basic term *kyros,* meaning *supreme power, authority,* and secondarily, *validity, security,* indicating the overtone of legitimacy possessed by the 'lord'. *Kyros* is the root of a whole cluster of Greek words, including the noun *kyriotes,* which means *power, rule, dominion,* and thus it is this latter term that could be translated 'lordship', referring to God's rulership or right to rule, God's reigning or governing activity, or God's

---

1   For a more extensive study of this terminology, see Appendix 1, 'The Meaning of the Title "Lord" (*kyrios*).'

'government,' a term which will often be used in this study.[2]
Kyriotes is used four times in the New Testament (Eph. 1:21;
Col. 1:16; 2 Pet. 2:10; Jude 8): in the first two instances of
lesser or subordinate 'authorities' or dominions than God's,
but the concept can properly be applied as well to God's or
Christ's dominion or lordship, as it may be in the latter two
instances.[3]

2. The language of human 'autonomy' involves the concept of rejection of God's legitimate authority.

The English word 'autonomy' derives from two Greek terms,
autos, meaning 'self,' and *nomos*, meaning 'law.' The combining of
these two terms results in the adjective *autonomos*, meaning *living
by one's own laws: independent*; in the derivative noun *autonomia*,
meaning *independence*; and in the verb *autonomeomai*, meaning
to live by one's own laws, be independent.[4] The definition of the
Greek term captures precisely the sense in which the English
terms 'autonomous' and related words will be used in this study,
as referring to 'living by one's own laws,' and thus in rejection of
God's laws and of God's rightful dominion over his creatures.

At this point, a distinction may be drawn between God's
dominion or kingdom as *exercised*, as *manifested*, and as
acknowledged.

(1) The Bible speaks of God's rule *exercised*. It teaches
that God is a sovereign King, and that his reign is a present
reality that is universal and constant (Pss. 47:8; 93:1; 97:1;
99:1; 103:19; Dan. 4:34-35). This is what we might call God's
de facto dominion; it is an objective reality and it is exercised
whether humans acknowledge it or not.

(2) The Bible also speaks of God's kingdom *manifested*.
This involves the coming of God's kingdom or rule in earthly
history, a complex of events in which God's enemies are

---

2   Henry George Liddell and Robert Scott, *A Lexicon: Abridged from
     Liddell and Scott's Greek-English Lexicon* (Oxford: Oxford University
     Press, 1966), pp. 400-01.

3   On the meaning of *kyriotes* in 2 Peter 2:10 and Jude 8, see Thomas
     R. Schreiner, *1, 2 Peter, Jude*, New American Commentary (Nashville:
     Broadman & Holman, 2003), pp. 345, 456.

4   Liddell and Scott, *Lexicon: Abridged*, p. 117.

overthrown and God's people are blessed with a promised salvation. It is accomplished through the person and work of Jesus Christ (Matt. 12:28), and occurs in three stages, anticipation (the Old Testament era), inauguration (the New Testament era) and consummation (which is yet future). This is also an objective reality (although it will not be recognized by all) and people are called upon to prepare for it (Matt 4:17) and pray for it (Matt. 6:10).

(3) The Bible speaks of God's kingdom *acknowledged*. The kingdom manifested calls for the subjective human response in which humans acknowledge God's kingdom or rule (God's right to command, acknowledged in repentance) and receive the salvation which its historical manifestation brings (received through faith; see Mark 1:15). This involves recognizing what we could call God's *de jure* dominion, his legal right to rule over his personal creatures.

It is the latter two, God's kingdom *manifested* and *acknowledged*, which are the primary focus of the present study.

IV. Why the Issue is Significant

Perhaps some justification of the present study is warranted. The matter is worthy of attention for several reasons.

1. It is a most edifying topic for the Christian to consider.

It is wonderfully encouraging to Christians to be made more fully aware of the victory over death, the exaltation, and the present status of their redeemer, Jesus Christ. It becomes evident through such a study that the New Testament – indeed, the entire Bible – teaches that the redeemer of God's people is not only their Savior but has also been appointed as God's agent to rule over the entire universe. It is in virtue of his investiture with such authority and power that He is called by his characteristic New Testament title, 'Lord,' and that someday all personal beings shall acknowledge Him as such (Phil. 2:9-11). Thus, Christians are granted to know the end of the story, including the final victory of God's kingdom, the defeat of all opposition and the universal acknowledgment of Him who is called 'King of kings and Lord of lords' (Rev. 19:16). This truth can serve to fortify Christians in the face of hostility from the world or outright persecution, and to encourage faithfulness to Him who gave Himself for them and rose again from the dead.

2. This study serves to give a glimpse of the full scope of the biblical concept of salvation.

Such a study informs us that God's purposes in redemption include not only forgiveness of sins but also the bringing of rebellious humans back under God's acknowledged rule and his lordship over them. These purposes involve the renewal of human life and of the universe to the extent that both have been touched by the effects of sin. It is no small thing that God has designed to accomplish, but a large-scale renovation which includes the establishment of his acknowledged government through Jesus Christ, his appointed agent in the exercise of his rule. It was concerning God's rule through the Lord Jesus that Isaiah wrote these words:

> For to us a child is born,
> to us a son is given;
> and the *government* shall be upon his shoulder,
> and his name shall be called
> Wonderful Counselor, Mighty God,
>   Everlasting Father, Prince of Peace.
> Of the increase of his *government* and of peace
>   there will be no end,
> on the throne of David and over his *kingdom*,
>   to establish it and uphold it
> with justice and with righteousness
>   from this time forth and forevermore.
> The zeal of the LORD of hosts will do this (Isa. 9:6-7).

The gospel will not have its full and intended effect until all this has been accomplished.

3. This study helps to clarify the message of the gospel.

In light of the foregoing two points, it is evident that such a study as this must show that God intends in human salvation not only to bestow forgiveness of sins and the status of righteousness before God's judgment seat, but also to bring those who receive this salvation into a stance of willing submission to Jesus Christ as Lord. As Paul expressed it, 'to this end Christ died and lived again, that he might be Lord both of the dead and the living' (Rom. 14:9). If it is God's intention through Christ's death and resurrection to establish Christ's lordship over Christian converts, then that intention must be made clear in the proclamation of the gospel; otherwise, those who proclaim it will be preaching a truncated message and not its full biblical content, and those who receive such a truncated message will not be receiving the biblical gospel but only an abbreviated and thus distorted form of it. Thus such a study helps Christians to be more biblical in their understanding and presentation of the gospel.

4. This study helps to clarify the relationship between conversion and sanctification.

Much recent and current theological controversy (over so-called 'Lordship salvation'; the teaching of theologian Norman Shepherd; the 'New Perspective' on Paul; the so-called 'Auburn Avenue theology' in some American Presbyterian circles) deals with the proper relationship between conversion, justification, sanctification and the final judgment. While these issues cannot all be directly addressed by the current study, it is the author's conviction that much confusion can be eliminated and much clarity gained by understanding the proper place of the confession of Jesus' lordship in genuine biblical faith. I am convinced that this central New Testament confession will be found, upon careful reflection, to have implications for all these issues.

5. This study deals with the eternal well-being of everlasting persons.

If a distorted 'gospel' is in danger of producing a distorted 'faith', then at some point such faith ceases to be a biblical faith in the biblical gospel. Admittedly it is difficult for us fallible humans to discern precisely when such a momentous shift has taken place and a professed 'faith' becomes no faith at all in the biblical sense. Only God can judge the human heart. But it will be one of the conclusions of this study that no one can enter into biblical salvation while consciously rejecting the lordship of Jesus Christ. If this be the case, then it is incumbent on those who attempt to proclaim the gospel to ensure that they have the message straight. Charles Ryrie, maintaining a stance opposed to the conclusions of the present study, once stated that these two opposite conceptions of the gospel 'cannot both be the gospel; therefore one of them is a false gospel and comes under the curse of perverting the gospel or preaching another gospel (Gal. 1:6-9), and this is a very serious matter.'[5] It is perhaps instructive to note that in the very context in which Paul pronounced that curse upon those who preach a false gospel he indicated that 'grace' and 'peace' come 'from God our Father and the *Lord* Jesus Christ' (Gal. 1:3), suggesting at least some of the content of the true gospel which he had in mind.

In summary, it is the thesis of this study that the Fall of Genesis 3 was an assertion of human autonomy, a declaration of independence from God; that the person and work of Jesus the Messiah were intended, in the broadest terms, to overturn that human rebellion and mitigate its consequences, particularly for receptive humans; that faith in Jesus Christ necessarily implies the personal renunciation of one's claimed autonomy along with the acknowledgment of the exalted Jesus Christ as the agent of God's rule over humans; and that the New Testament confession of faith 'Jesus is Lord' embodies that reception, renunciation, and acknowledgment. The question, then, is one of how rebellious humans can assume their rightful stance before their Creator and his government. With both the reputation of the glorious God and the eternal well-being of humans at stake, nothing more momentous could be imagined. Let us approach the matter with all due seriousness and care. Nothing less is required of us.

---

5   Charles Caldwell Ryrie, *Balancing the Christian Life* (Chicago: Moody Press, 1969), p. 170.

PART ONE

THE OLD TESTAMENT: ANTICIPATION

1

Beginnings:

God's Lordship and the Human Rebellion

The lordship of Jesus Christ, which is revealed clearly in the New Testament, rests on foundations which are laid in the Old Testament. Just as, in a real sense, the gospel begins in the first chapter of Genesis, so it is with the lordship of Jesus Christ. This being the case, we must turn to the opening chapters of the Bible in order to discern there the nature of God's lordship over His creation.

I. Creation and the Lordship of God: The Human Condition under God's Lordship

The Bible famously begins with the majestic affirmation, 'In the beginning, God created the heavens and the earth' (Gen. 1:1). After a statement describing the condition of earth at the initial stage of God's handiwork ('without form and void' [= formless and empty], 1:2), the narrative goes on to tell how God gave form to the earth and filled it with living things (1:3-31), culminating with the creation of human beings (1:26-30).

The information provided by this chapter of Genesis (and the next) suggests several implications concerning God's status as Creator and man's status as creature, both for the first humans and for those who would live in later eras of history. In general terms, we may make the following affirmation: *God's creation of the universe and of humanity established God's lordship over every aspect of human life.*

The divine lordship over humans finds expression in three specific ways, encompassing all of human life and activity.

1. God is lord of human existence or being.

God's creation of the universe establishes His absolute superiority over it, and its absolute dependence on Him. 'In the beginning, *God* created the heavens and the earth.' God is self-existent and He is the Creator of all existence outside Himself. He designed the universe, He called it into being, and He sustains it. The universe therefore has no existence independent of God. The created order (including humans) did not originate itself, does not sustain itself, and in the final analysis cannot destroy itself. In technical terms, it could be said that the universe has no 'metaphysical' autonomy ('metaphysics' is that branch of philosophical inquiry concerned with the theory of being or existence[1]).

There are at least two consequences which derive from this reality. The first is that God Himself established the characteristics and parameters of human nature. Humans cannot be anything other than God created them to be. While this requires the recognition of certain limitations, it is also a liberating truth: humans do not have to attempt to be anything other than what God designed them to be as human beings. The second is that God established the proper role of humans under His lordship, that is, under the Creator's right to rule and dispose. As the Creator, God possesses absolute authority over the creation, and the creature has no right to question or protest God's disposal of His creatures according to His own purpose. As Paul put it, 'Will what is molded say to its molder, "Why have you made me like this?" Has the potter no right over the clay, to make out of the same lump one vessel for honorable use and another for dishonorable use?' (Rom. 9:20b-21). The assumed answer to Paul's second rhetorical question is, 'Yes, the potter has absolute rights over his clay and its disposition.' The point of Paul's analogy is clear: God possesses absolute rights over His creation and His creatures by virtue of being their Creator. Old Testament scholar C. John Collins correctly observes concerning the

---

1   Roger Scruton, *Modern Philosophy: An Introduction and Survey* (New York: Penguin, 1994), p. 12.

perspective of Genesis: 'the God who made the world ... is the sovereign owner and ruler of his creation.'[2]

2. God is lord of human knowing

The second sphere in which God's lordship asserts itself over His creation is that of human knowing or knowledge. The philosophical inquiry into human knowing is called 'epistemology'[3] (from the Greek verb *epistamai*, 'to know,' and noun, *episteme*, 'knowledge'); thus, it could be said that humans possess no 'epistemological' autonomy; that is, no knowledge which is independent of God. This is true in two respects: man's knowledge about God, and man's knowledge about himself and the created order.

The epistemological lordship of God is expressed in the simple clause, 'In the beginning, *God* ....' and in the affirmation, '*God created.*' The very facts that God is and that He Himself brought the universe into being are data of God's own self-disclosure to His creatures. He communicates to humans that information about Himself and about their relationship to Himself which He wants them to know. And they have no alternative source of information about such things other than God's self-revelation. God Himself is the most fundamental reality, and it should be observed that in this opening statement of Genesis no effort is made to demonstrate the reality of God's existence; it is simply assumed or presupposed.

And so it is throughout the Bible. God Himself is the only being whose knowledge is autonomous, that is, independent of everything and everyone else. He possesses firsthand knowledge of Himself from the inside and of His creation

---

2   C. John Collins, *Genesis 1-4: A Linguistic, Literary, and Theological Commentary* (Phillipsburg, NJ: Presbyterian and Reformed, 2006), p. 79. On a historical and literary level, Old Testament scholar Jeffrey J. Niehaus, who sees elements of an ancient Near Eastern covenant or treaty form in the narrative of Genesis 1–2, observes: 'by presenting God as the Creator, Gen. 1:1 also implies that he is Suzerain over all, since creator gods in the ancient Near East were understood to be universal suzerains, from whom all other heavenly and earthly authority derived' ('Covenant: An Idea in the Mind of God,' *Journal of the Evangelical Theological Society* 52/2 [June 2009], p. 231.)

3   Scruton, *Modern Philosophy*, p. 12.

from the outside, neither of which humans will ever be able to possess (because they are not God and because they are part of creation). Therefore God Himself must be the source of true information about Himself and about the universe, including His creation of the latter. Humans do not possess an independent, autonomous position from which to judge reliably concerning the ultimate truth relating to God and His universe. As a consequence, the Bible contains no rational argumentation intended to demonstrate God's existence, nor does it call upon humans to argue thus or to draw conclusions from such argumentation (although it does affirm in Romans 1:19-20 that there is an ineradicable awareness of God, based on revelation given in the created order, but which fallen men seek to suppress, 1:18).[4] The Bible simply assumes and declares that God *is* (this reality is closely related to God's name, '*I AM*,' in Exodus 3:14). This is perhaps what we ought to expect, for humans' knowledge of God is dependent upon God's revealing of Himself by His works or His words (for these two forms of revelation, see Psalm 19:1-6 and 7-11, respectively). Thus all humanly-possessed information about God, humans and their surroundings is derived from God's revelation of what He wants humans to know – and ultimately from propositional revelation such as that given to Adam in the beginning or that provided by Holy Scripture.[5] Such information is for humans the opposite of autonomous: it is dependent, secondary, derived, and finite. God is lord in the sphere of human knowing, both about God and ultimately about anything else.

3. God is lord of human ethics

God the Creator possesses lordship (the right to rule or govern) over the ethical life of His human creatures ('ethics and aesthetics' is a third major branch of philosophy, dealing

---

4   For an evaluation of the traditional arguments for the existence of God, see Robert L. Reymond, *A New Systematic Theology of the Christian Faith*, 2nd ed. (Nashville: Thomas Nelson, 1998, 2002), pp. 131-52.

5   See Reymond, *Systematic Theology*, pp. 111-26.

with the theory of value[6]). This lordship or authority is expressed in God's establishing of mandates and obligations and by His giving of commands at the time of the creation of the human race (Gen. 1:28-30; 2:15-17; 2:19; 2:24). Such mandates and commands, which represent God's revealed will for humanity or a portion of it at any given time (and which may be distinguished from His secret will, which is what He has determined shall actually come to pass), establish a binding obligation on humans, an obligation to render what may be termed 'obedience' or 'submission', depending on the circumstances and nature of the obligation. God's lordship in the sphere of ethics thus consists in His right to demand and command certain specific behaviors of His human creatures and in their duty to comply or obey. This divine right and the corresponding human obligation are well expressed by John Calvin (making the matter personal, as Calvin often does):

> For how can the idea of God enter your mind without instantly giving rise to the thought, that since you are his workmanship, you are bound, by the very law of creation, to submit to his authority? – that your life is due to him? – that whatever you do ought to have reference to him? If so, it undoubtedly follows that your life is sadly corrupted, if it is not framed in obedience to him, since his will ought to be the law of our lives.[7]

The same point is made by Collins: God's name *Elohim* 'stresses his relation to the whole of creation as its sole source and owner. Such a deity is in the perfect position to commit himself to caring for everything and to expecting the whole creation to honor and love him.'[8]

This lordship of God – metaphysical, epistemological, and ethical – is inherent in the relationship of God to His human (and other personal) creatures, and ought to be implicitly acknowledged by those creatures. The fact that this has become

---

6   Scruton, *Modern Philosophy,* pp. 12-13.

7   John Calvin, *Institutes of the Christian Religion,* trans. Henry Beveridge (London: James Clarke, 1953), I.ii.2 (1:41).

8   Collins, *Genesis,* p. 75.

difficult for humans willingly to do indicates that something has gone terribly wrong in that relationship. Exactly what it is that has gone wrong and what God has done to provide a remedy for it is the subject of the remainder of this study.

APPLICATORY OBSERVATIONS

1) Human life is not meant to be lived apart from God. This is a fundamental reality which all humans need to recognize in order to occupy their proper place under God's lordship. To refuse to acknowledge this reality is to introduce serious dislocations and distortions into human life, which is the condition of humanity after the Fall described in Genesis 3.

2) Man's dependence on God is found in and to be expressed in every sphere of human existence. Man's being, knowing, and doing constitute the whole of his life, and in none of these is there any true autonomy or independence from God. The failure of fallen humans to acknowledge this truth constitutes their sin and represents a delusional view of reality on their part, while genuine and humble acknowledgment of this truth leads humans to occupy their proper place before their Creator. Denial of this truth does not constitute escape from the truth; it is still God's universe in which all humans must live.

II. Adam and Eve under God's Lordship

The previous section portrayed humans as properly under the lordship of God in three respects: in their being, in their knowing and in their ethics. Now we proceed to consider the specific circumstances of the first humans in their relationship to the lordship of God.

1. Adam under the Government of God

All three general aspects of the lordship of God over humans were established by the circumstances of God's creation of Adam and Eve.

1) God's creation of Adam and Eve placed them under the comprehensive lordship of God, including His right to issue specific directives to them. This lordship of God expressed itself in three aspects of the humans' lives. First, there is *the metaphysical aspect.* The metaphysical aspect of divine lordship is constituted by the reality that God as Creator possesses inherent authority and rights over His creatures – including the first humans – specifically, to command and rule them. Humans as dependent, finite creatures belong to a different order of being than God, the autonomous, infinite creator. God's implicit authority to issue directives that are fitting and appropriate to their nature – as He has designed it – and that are to be obeyed is an expression of that reality.

Second, there is *the epistemological aspect* in which God's lordship is seen in the reality that Adam (and eventually Eve) will be required to accept the truthfulness of what God tells them (in Genesis 2:17 for example) on the basis of God's simple word to them, without any corroborating testimony or evidence. Further, they must trust the goodness of God's commandments as promoting their well-being, again without evidentiary support. God is to be believed simply because He is God.

Third, there is *the ethical aspect* of divine lordship which resides in the humans' obligation to acknowledge God's righteousness in requiring certain behaviors of them and to acknowledge their duty to obey. It is God who possesses the right to define good and appropriate behavior for humans, in accordance with His purpose in creating them and the way He has fashioned the reality they inhabit. The humans therefore fall under God's legitimate ethical authority, and although they have the potential to disregard God's commandments, they do not possess the right to do so.

This comprehensive authority of God, encompassing all three aspects of divine lordship, may be termed the 'government of God'. This term will be used to refer specifically to God's *de jure* (legal) right to rule over His creatures, a right which, in the nature of the case and as reflecting the very structure of the relationship, ought to be acknowledged by humans.[9]

2) God established specific mandates and commands which the first humans were obligated to obey. In examining the mandates

---

9   As noted earlier, God's *de jure* government is to be distinguished from His *de facto* government, which refers to God's sovereign control of all things.

or directives which God issued to the first humans, two assumptions apply for the purposes of this study. First, it is assumed that Genesis 1:1–2:3 provides an overview of God's creative activity, while Genesis 2:4-25 provides a more detailed account of events occurring on the sixth day of creation. Second, it is assumed that God intended humans to reflect, in all they do, the image of God in which they were created. However, since no specific command mentions humans serving as image-bearers, this feature will be considered a reality lying behind and perhaps undergirding the specific directives given to them, but it will not be enumerated among those directives.[10]

The following elements of human life under the government of God may be distinguished and identified. They are presented here in the order in which they appear in the Genesis narrative, with no overall attempt to harmonize the general and detailed accounts. Matters of chronology will be noted as necessary.

Firstly, *humans were to exercise dominion over the earth,* as we can see from Genesis 1:26, 28: 'And let them *have dominion* over the fish of the sea and over the birds of the heavens and over the livestock and over all the earth and over every creeping thing that creeps on the earth.... And God blessed them. And God said to them, "Be fruitful and multiply and *fill the earth* and *subdue it* and *have dominion* over the fish of the sea and over the birds of the heavens and over every living thing that moves on the earth."' This mandate may be understood (as may others) as an expression of humans' reflection of the image of God, involving humanity's lordship over the lesser creatures and inanimate objects of the earth, just as God exercises lordship over all creation. It included populating the earth, subduing it, and mastering it. The intellectual activity of naming its inhabitants (performed by Adam before the creation of Eve) may be included here as well (Gen. 2:19-20).

Secondly, *man* (this obligation and the next were given to the man specifically, before the creation of woman) *was to tend and work the garden*: 'The LORD God took the man and put

---

10 For the first, see Collins, *Genesis*, pp. 109-12, 121-22; for the second, Collins argues that the human exercise of dominion is a consequence of bearing the image of God but does not define the image itself, pp. 66, 85.

him in the garden of Eden to *work it* and *keep it'* (Gen. 2:15). Man was given the task of 'work' before the fall, leading us to conclude that work was not in itself part of the penalty of sin. It may be assumed that this mandate and the next were to be (and indeed were) communicated by Adam to Eve after her creation, thus establishing a pattern of male headship within the marriage relationship.

Thirdly, *man was to love, trust, and respect God to the point of obedience*: 'And the LORD God commanded the man, saying, "You may surely eat of every tree of the garden, but of the tree of the knowledge of good and evil *you shall not eat*, for in the day that you eat of it you shall surely die"' (Gen. 2:16-17). Although the term 'love', either as a verb or a noun, is not used in the first three chapters of Genesis, it may, on the basis of the rest of the Bible, legitimately be regarded as an element in the relationship between the first humans and God. The 'Great Commandment' as stipulated by Jesus (Mark 12:29-30 and parallels, quoting Deuteronomy 6:4-5) requires wholehearted love to God, presumably by all human beings, and thus may be assumed to have applied to Adam and Eve. Thus the nature of the requirement placed on Adam involved esteeming God (= loving Him) more highly than anything else, including man's own potential desire to become more like God (see Gen. 3:5). Trusting God would involve believing that what God told him was in fact true and was for man's own best interest, even if someone else should tell him differently (3:4). Respecting God involved acknowledging God's authority and right to command, even if the man should desire to act in an autonomous way. Obeying God would be the outcome of Adam's acting upon his love for, trust in, and respect for God.

Fourthly, *man was to live in a loving relationship with his wife*: 'Therefore a man shall leave his father and his mother and *hold fast to his wife*, and they shall *become one flesh'* (Gen. 2:24). Although this mandate as presented in the text of Genesis is probably the comment of the narrator, it is quoted by Jesus as the intention of God for human marriage (Matt. 19:4-6).[11]

---

11   See Collins' entire treatment, *Genesis,* pp. 108, 139-45.

C. John Collins and John Murray helpfully refer to these mandates and commandments as 'creation ordinances', and observe how 'they interpenetrate one another'. Collins subsumes them under three headings (family, labor, and religion): 'the family (marriage leading to offspring who will fill the earth and serve as the basis of human society); labor (subduing the earth, exercising dominion, working and keeping the garden); and religion (the Sabbath [which Collins brings in here, although no explicit recorded command was given to the humans concerning this matter], as well as the religious bond with the Creator).' He then offers the alliterated terms 'wedlock,' 'work,' and 'worship' to describe these categories.[12]

APPLICATORY OBSERVATIONS:

1) Humans were to be rulers of the earth under God's lordship. It was thus a royal position that humans were intended to occupy, but as a result of the Fall, many

---

12 Collins, *Genesis*, p. 130; John Murray, *Principles of Conduct* (Grand Rapids: Eerdmans, 1957), 27. These mandates are also helpfully treated in O. Palmer Robertson, *The Christ of the Covenants* (Phillipsburg, NJ: Presbyterian and Reformed, 1980), pp. 68-81. A related theological question is whether the relationship between God and His creation (including the humans) constituted a 'covenant', that is, a formal binding relationship. Although this has been a perennial matter of discussion in Reformed theology, a recent line of historical investigation might prove fruitful. As noted earlier, Jeffrey J. Niehaus has noted common elements in the Genesis narrative and in second-millennium B.C. suzerainty treaties (this approach has been applied to other portions of the Old Testament also, with fruitful results). Niehaus concludes with regard to the creation account: 'Gen 1:1-2:3 (and 2:17) and other data (e.g. Ps. 47:2, Mal. 1:14) display the following facts about God: He is the Creator and Great King over all in heaven and earth; He has provided good things in abundance for those He created; He made the man and woman royalty ('subdue,' 'rule over') and gave them commands; He blessed them; and He pronounced a curse on them should they disobey His commands. These facts are the essence of covenant: a Great King in authority over lesser rulers, with a historical background of doing good to them, with commands and with blessings, but also with a curse in case of disobedience. These facts about the Genesis creation material are the stuff of covenant, and primordially so' (Niehaus, 'Covenant: An Idea in the Mind of God', p. 233). This question will also be addressed further in Chapter 2 below.

distortions have been introduced which serve to degrade man's position on earth.

2) Work is a noble activity. Work is performed by God (Gen. 2:2-3; John 5:17), work was given to Adam to perform before the Fall (Gen. 2:15), and work is commanded of Christians (Eph. 4:28; Col. 3:22-24; 2 Thess. 3:10-12). It is not the activity of work which is demeaning; rather it is the conditions under which human work must be performed after the Fall which render it demanding, frustrating, and wearying (Gen. 3:17-19). With the divine renewal of all things at the consummation, we may expect a change in these conditions, but perhaps not the elimination of all work.

3) The basic reality of the human relationship with God is not a matter of religious ritual but of valuing God so highly as to love, trust and obey Him. The forbidden fruit simply served as an index of these features of the relationship of the first humans with their Creator. The Christian's relationship with God should reflect this reality.

4) Human life is basically relational also on the horizontal human level. Adam was not complete while he was alone (Gen. 2:18), and Adam and Eve were in perfect and harmonious relationship with one another before the Fall. This indicates that human relationships are fundamental to human life as intended by God; such relationships are worth pursuing, even though they are more difficult to develop and sustain since the Fall (Gen. 3:16b; 4:1-12).

2. Adam, the Probation and the Government of God

The text of Genesis informs us that God placed the first humans under certain obligations: (1) to exercise dominion over the earth (Gen. 1:28); (2) to tend and work the garden (2:15); (3) to obey God out of love, trust and respect for Him (2:16-17); and (4) to live in the loving relationship of marriage (2:24). They were to carry out all of these obligations under the lordship and government of God their Creator, with a view to glorifying Him. Of particular significance for the present study is the third mandate mentioned above. The obligation to love, trust and respect God to the point of obedience brought focused emphasis to the matter of man's proper relationship to the government of God.

The arrangement God made with Adam concerning the tree of the knowledge of good and evil required Adam's acknowledgment of the government of God, that is, God's rightful rule over him. This is indicated by the following features of the narrative.

Firstly, *God issued a command to Adam, with a sanction attached.* The command was a prohibition of Adam's eating the fruit of the tree of the knowledge of good and evil; the sanction was the penalty of death (Gen. 2:17). This command with its sanction put the divine–human relationship into the realm of law. Whatever else the relationship of Adam to God involved on the personal level, and whatever motivations should have been operating (such as Adam's love for God), this requirement put the relationship on a legal footing. One may therefore affirm that Adam's relationship to God was certainly *more* than a legal relationship, but it is not faithful to the text to say that is was *less* than a legal relationship.

To put it in other terms, Adam (and later, Eve) was under the government of God, one expression of which was the command of prohibition. The humans were obligated to pursue the mandate God had given them (Gen 1:28) under God's government or rule or dominion, acknowledging His authority and obeying His commands.

Secondly, *the command of prohibition required Adam's submissive obedience to the government of God as expressed in God's mere word.* The command incorporated an arbitrary provision relating to the fruit of a specific tree, while he was permitted to eat the fruit of all the other trees. Thus, Adam's action in this matter carried no inherent moral worth except insofar as it might constitute obedience or disobedience to God. It was precisely at the point of submission to God's government that the issue was located. The arrangement was a test (or 'proving', thus the term 'probation') of whether Adam would acknowledge the government of God, that is, God's sovereign lordship, His right and authority to command. This is apparently the way that biblical theologian Geerhardus Vos understood the arrangement. Vos wrote, 'For the simple practical purpose of this first fundamental lesson it was necessary only to stake everything upon the unreasoned will of God.'[13] Another biblical theologian, Erich Sauer, has understood the command regarding this tree in similar fashion: 'the tree was a sign of the rule of God over man and the subjection of man to God.'[14]

Thirdly, *the command would thus serve to test where Adam's ultimate love, loyalty, and values lay in relation to God.* As Vos further comments: 'it was precisely the purpose of the probation to raise man for a moment from the influence of his own ethical inclination to the point of choosing for the sake of personal attachment to God alone.' Far from being an unworthy motive, Vos suggests, 'the noblest thing of all is the ethical strength, which, when required, will act from personal attachment to God.... The pure delight in obedience adds to the ethical value of a choice.'[15] Significantly, Collins (as noted above) places this creation ordinance under the rubric of 'worship', suggesting the idea of giving God His due, rendering that of which He is worthy. The command of prohibition, according to Sauer, was 'essentially spiritual, inasmuch as it established the absolute authority of God over men, and this as the true good.'[16] O. Palmer Robertson says 'a most radical test of the original man's willingness to submit to the specific word of the Creator is involved.'[17]

The modern Indian writer Vishal Mangalwadi has accurately expressed the significance of the arrangement that God made with the first humans as described in Genesis 2:16-17. 'That command,' writes Mangalwadi, 'defined Adam's position on this planet.'

It meant that every time Adam felt hungry and looked at that tree, he was reminded that he could not say, 'I am the

---

13 Geerhardus Vos, *Biblical Theology: Old and New Testaments* (Edinburgh: Banner of Truth, 1975), p. 32.

14 Erich Sauer, *The Dawn of World Redemption: A Survey of Historical Revelation in the Old Testament* (Grand Rapids: Eerdmans, 1953), pp. 46-47. See also Robertson, *Christ of the Covenants*, pp. 83-84.

15 Vos, *Biblical Theology*, p. 32.

16 Sauer, *Dawn of World Redemption*, p. 46.

17 Robertson, *Christ of the Covenants*, p. 84.

monarch of all I survey.' He was in someone else's creation. Therefore, he was not free to do whatever he wanted. He was a steward, under authority and thus accountable.[18]

This text thus demonstrates that it is certainly possible that a love relationship and a legal obligation may co-exist in the same interpersonal relationship and that they are not antithetical to, or exclusive of, each other. Submission to the requirements of the legal obligation may be an expression of the love relationship (see Jesus' words in John 14:15: 'If you love me, you will keep my commandments'). Underlying the legal relationship, which is explicitly described in the narrative of Genesis 2 and 3, there is the love relationship (Adam's 'personal attachment to God,' as Vos called it). Throughout these chapters the theme of fellowship with God lies just below the surface. It was a fellowship which Adam broke by his disobedience (Gen. 3:8-10) and from which he was shut out, as to its former intimacy, by his expulsion from the garden (3:23-24). It was a fellowship in which was to be found true life for Adam and Eve and which they ought to have valued and prized above all else. Out of a spirit of faith and love Adam was called upon to submit to God's government – in faith trusting that what God commanded was best for him and believing that what God threatened by way of sanction would indeed come to pass, and in love giving himself in obedience to God.

APPLICATORY OBSERVATIONS:

1) A love relationship and a legal relationship to God are not opposed to each other, but are mutually interconnected. In the human act of sinning, humans denigrate the love of God to them and violate both the principle of love to God and the law of God. In God's act of justification His love prompts Him to provide a way to declare humans righteous in His sight on the basis of His law, which was perfectly obeyed by the

---

18 Vishal Mangalwadi, *Missionary Conspiracy: Letters to a Postmodern Hindu* (Carlisle, Cumbria, UK: OM Publishing, 1998), p. 29. See Robertson, *Christ of the Covenants*, pp. 83-84: 'One tree stands in the midst of the garden as symbolic reminder that man is not God.... He is creature; God is Creator.'

Lord Jesus. In Christian sanctification, believers obey God's law (commandments) out of love for Him (1 John 5:3). Love and law are not opposed to each other, and Christians should give no heed to those teachers who would seek to persuade them otherwise.

2) Sometimes humans are called to act on the basis of God's mere word. God's word was all that Adam and Eve possessed in the way of prohibition ('of the tree of the knowledge of good and evil you shall not eat') and in the way of judgment threatened ('in the day that you eat of it you shall surely die'). God's word was what the serpent twisted (3:1) and denied (3:4-5). Eve allowed other considerations to enter her mind (3:6), disobeyed, and Adam followed suit. There will likewise be occasions when Christians are called upon to be faithful to the Lord Jesus and to the gospel in the face of temptation, opposition or persecution, and the only foundation they will have on which to base their actions will be the revelation given directly through the Lord Jesus (e.g., Matt. 10:26-33) or in the rest of the New Testament. They will have to decide whether that word is a sufficient basis on which to stake everything they might hold dear in this world. Generations of Christian martyrs testify that it is, but each believer had best determine the matter for himself or herself before that time arrives.

3) Behind God's word stands God Himself. Christians, like Adam and Eve, are compelled by circumstances and the necessity of responding to them to trust God's love, wisdom and power to work out things for the Christian's best interests and God's own glory. The alternative is for them to refuse or to fail to trust God in His revealed character and thus take things into their own hands (or so they think). We must be assured that it is the faithful God who stands behind His word and that His character is trustworthy.

III. The Fall and the Government of God

As the Genesis narrative continues, it reveals the motives and effects of the event known in Christian theology as the 'Fall'.

1. The actions of Adam and Eve as described in Genesis 3 involved human rejection of the government of God

and thus constituted a grasping for autonomy in every sphere of human life.

Vishal Mangalwadi expresses the meaning of their action: 'Satan tempted Eve to set herself free from God's authority; to become like God, independent, autonomous, and unaccountable.'[19] That this was the case is indicated by the following features of the account.

Firstly, *the point at which Satan pitched the temptation was the potential for the humans to become more like God.* Satan, acting through the serpent,[20] told the woman, 'When you eat of it your eyes will be opened, and *you will be like God*, knowing good and evil' (Gen. 3:5). This proposal played to the creatures' capacity for pride and self-seeking (which may have been Satan's own failing; see Isaiah 14:12-14); the human creature, having been created in the image of God, could by his own action become more like God. This is the first intimation of a theme which carries through the rest of the Bible: the twisted notion that the creature could occupy the place of God. In three texts of the New Testament, the term 'the lie' (with the definite article) is applied to just such a notion, with all three contexts dealing explicitly with either this situation in Genesis (John 8:44) or the idea that the creature may occupy the place of the Creator (Rom. 1:25, involving worship of the creature; 2 Thess. 2:11, involving a man putting himself forth as God, cf. v. 4). For the creature to aspire to occupy the place of God is for him to seek to establish the absolute height of autonomy: not merely independence from God but replacing God as the creature's own ultimate reference point as he becomes a 'law unto himself' (the concept behind the term 'autonomy').[21]

At this point it becomes apparent that the action of the humans (consequent to Satan's suggestion, see below) in

---

19 Mangalwadi, *Missionary Conspiracy*, p. 29.

20 See Collins, *Genesis*, pp. 170-72.

21 Note the comment by Francis A. Schaeffer on John 8:44: Satan stands behind 'the lie back of all lies – that the creature can be equal with God. This was his own point of rebellion against his Creator, God. Every other lie is only an extension of this one. And this is who the devil is – the originator of The Lie' (*Genesis in Space and Time: The Flow of Biblical History*, [Downers Grove, IL: InterVarsity, 1972], p. 78.

seeking to become like God constituted a sort of primal rebellion against divine authority, specifically a challenge to God's metaphysical lordship (God's superiority over humans in the sphere of the nature of their being). The humans sought not merely to be independent of God but *as* God themselves. This seems to have become the primal sin of the human race throughout the ages.

Secondly, *the specific way in which humans could become more like God was in the matter of knowledge: they would 'know good and evil'.* Satan promised the humans independence from God in the sphere of human knowledge, or epistemological autonomy: 'you will be like God, *knowing good and evil*' (3:5). If they came to know good and evil for themselves, they would no longer be dependent on God for such knowledge. They would be independent of God and, in at least some sense, equal to Him (or so Satan's suggestion went).[22]

Thirdly, *the point upon which Eve (and presumably Adam?) acted as she did was the desire for autonomous knowledge.* 'So when the woman saw that the tree was good for food, and that it was a delight to the eyes, and that the tree was to be *desired to make one wise*, she took its fruit and ate, and she also gave some to her husband who was with her, and he ate' (Gen. 3:6). The sole point of distinction of the tree was the knowledge it promised. The narrative has already stated that God placed in Eden '*every* tree that is pleasant to the sight and good for food' (Gen. 2:9). In other respects – beauty and food value – the tree of the knowledge of good and evil was apparently in no way superior to the other trees of the garden. The distinguishing feature of this tree was that its fruit was desirable 'to make one wise'. Thus it was precisely at the point of seeking to gain epistemological independence that Eve took of the fruit and shared it with her husband.

Fourthly, *the humans rejected the ethical lordship of God over them and sought to stake out their own independent ground.* Refusing to love, trust and respect God to the point of obedience,

---

22 For an insightful account of the possible psychology of the temptation and fall, see Reymond, *Systematic Theology*, pp. 442-45.

the humans in effect denied His rightful sovereignty over them in the sphere of human behavior and acted contrary to His command. As Collins points out, God's question to Adam in Genesis 3:11, 'Have you eaten of the tree of which I commanded you not to eat?' (see also 3:17, which contains similar language) provides a veritable description of 'disobedience'. Later biblical texts use terms such as 'sin', 'transgression', and 'trespass' as well as 'disobedience' (Rom. 5:12-19; 1 Tim. 2:14) to refer to this event, surely reflecting a more perceptive understanding of the Genesis narrative than some modern interpreters who deny that any such elements are present.[23]

It may be observed then that all three aspects of divine lordship are challenged by the transgression of Adam. The situation has been admirably summarized by Robert Reymond:

> It was at its core the creature's deliberate rejection of God's authority and an act of willful rebellion against the Creator. It was man claiming the stance of autonomy and freedom from God. It was man believing he had the right to determine for himself what he would be *metaphysically* ('You will be like God'), what he would know *epistemologically* ('like God, knowing good and evil'), and how he would behave *ethically* ('she took and ate ... her husband ate'). It was man heeding Satan's call to worship the creature rather than the Creator. Authority was the issue at stake, and man decided against God and in his own favor.[24]

Adam and his wife had rejected the government of God. In taking and eating the fruit which represented the acknowledged authority of God over them, Adam and Eve were rejecting that authority, rebelling against God's rule. As Sauer puts it, 'Adam through his disobedience had denied the lordship of his Creator over himself.'[25]

2. The result of the human revolt against God's rule was that all aspects of human life came under the influence of the Fall.

---

23 Collins, *Genesis*, p. 155.

24 Reymond, *Systematic Theology*, p. 446.

25 Sauer, *Dawn of World Redemption*, p. 57.

Although the humans subjectively rejected the government of God, their action did not alter the objective reality of their being under His rule. They were still accountable to God, and God called Adam to account (Gen. 3:8-11). They were still responsible before God for their actions and had to bear His judgment upon them (Gen. 3:16-19, 22-24). They were still under the sovereignty of God and began immediately to experience the death (both spiritual and physical) that God had promised as the penalty of disobedience of that command which most pointedly expressed His government (Gen. 2:17; 3:19, 22-24).

The consequences of the Fall were thus disastrous for human life in this world. The image of God in humans was defaced. Man's dominion activities came to be carried out by humans while in a state of rebellion against God. Humans were expelled from the garden, and the tending of the earth (and man's work in general) became more difficult and less fruitful. Man's fellowship with God was disrupted and alienation was introduced. And the human relationship with one's spouse, and by extension with other humans as well, was distorted and corrupted. Indeed, all of human life, all human activities, and all human relationships became distorted and corrupted.[26]

APPLICATORY OBSERVATIONS

1) Human sin still has the same basic nature that it had at its origin. It is an expression of the desire to be and to act as independent from God, to live according to one's own laws, to be autonomous. The difference is that now this disposition is ingrained into fallen human nature whereas it was only a potential course of action for Adam and Eve. The consequence is that even Christians cannot fully escape this inclination, even while in the process of experiencing redemption from sin through God's grace in Jesus Christ. Thus the Christian must still struggle against this inclination in order to overcome it – but the Christian now possesses the hope of some measure of success in this struggle against sin, through God's grace.

---

26 Reymond, *Systematic Theology*, lists 'Seven Effects of the Fall,' largely in accord with the above two paragraphs, but in greater detail, pp. 446-49.

This is the aspect of redemption known as sanctification, and it requires the Christian's full effort.

2) Sin has corrupted and distorted every aspect of human life, making it more difficult and less satisfying than it otherwise would be. This is the futility spoken of in Ecclesiastes and in Romans 8:20-25. Such futility is actually an expression of God's goodness, for He thereby keeps humans from feeling too comfortable in a fallen world. It makes humans long for something more than anything this present world can offer, something that only God Himself can provide by means of a positive personal relationship with Him through the Mediator, Jesus Christ. Such a relationship is entered through the doorway of abandoning one's claim to autonomy ('repentance') and receiving God's forgiveness of one's rebellion through the person and work of Jesus Christ ('faith').

2

Redemption and God's Lordship:

The Old Testament Anticipation

PART 1 – THE COVENANTS OF PROMISE

I. Redemption and the Government of God

Barely had the alienation of the human race from God and His rule occurred when God began to reveal a purpose and a plan. The *purpose* was to deliver humans from that alienation, and the *plan* was to accomplish that deliverance by means of a specific human agent.[1]

1. God purposed to provide a remedy for mankind's rebellion against the government of God.

Almost immediately upon their rebellion against God's rule the first humans began to experience God's gracious provision of a remedy to deal with that rebellion. An analysis of their situation might suggest that their need (and that of future humans, their descendants) was at least threefold.

First, they needed someone to *instruct* them of the necessity of coming back under God's acknowledged rule, where their true well-being and the fullness of divine blessing could be experienced, and to announce to them an available opportunity to do so.

Second, they needed *forgiveness* of their rebellion and reinstatement to right standing before God so that they might not have to experience the fullness of the divine judgment which their action merited (final spiritual death, or permanent separation from God). This might also clear the way for the

---

1   For a treatment of the purpose of God in allowing the entrance of evil into the universe, see Reymond, *Systematic Theology,* pp. 376-78.

eventual restoration of (or even an advancement upon) the conditions which prevailed before their rebellion

Third, they needed a means, a *concrete mechanism*, for being brought back under the acknowledged government of God. This could consist of a specific act which would indicate a change of attitude toward God's rightful rule over human life.

The humans needed to be informed of the truth about their situation as it related to the government of God and of their need to abandon their rebellion. They needed somehow to be made right before the justice of God – an expression of His government – through the expiation (removal of the guilt) of their sin, the penalty of which was death (Gen. 2:17). And they needed a concrete representation of God's rule to which they could in principle render submission and thus express the abandonment of their rebellion (just as their taking of the fruit of the tree had been a concrete symbol and means of their revolt), an instrument that allowed for the genuine acknowledgment of God's rightful rule over humans. In short, they needed the intervention and work of a prophet, of a priest and of a king: a prophet, to speak to them on behalf of God and in the interests of His government; a priest, to represent them before their rightful Sovereign and to secure for them a favorable standing; and a king, to rule over them as the agent of God.

2. God planned to provide the remedy for mankind's rebellion through a specific human agent.

God began to express His provision for these needs even before the pronouncement of judgment upon the man and woman, for it is found in the judgment pronounced upon the serpent, which came first (Gen. 3:14-15). After the initial declaration of physical judgment on the serpent (3:14) God moved on to the spiritual and historical realm (3:15). God declared that He would put enmity (a condition of hostility) between the serpent and the woman and between the serpent's spiritual offspring among humans and her offspring.

He will be a single individual. The woman's offspring is singularized and personalized in verse 15c: '*he* shall bruise your head, and you shall bruise *his* heel.' Collins argues that the features of this text warrant the conclusion that 'the text envisions an individual who will engage the serpent (really, the Dark Power that used the serpent as its mouthpiece) in combat and defeat him, thus bringing benefits to mankind.'[2] He will be a *human* (as the seed of the woman). And He will achieve *victory*: the offspring will possess sufficient resources and power to achieve success (bruising the serpent's head).

That is, God here promised a powerful human Champion who, representing humanity, would reverse the effects of the human rebellion against the government of God and overturn the consequent human captivity to forces hostile to God and His purposes. Collins maintains that the rest of the book of Genesis 'will unfold the idea of this offspring and lay the foundation for the developed messianic teaching of the prophets'; as a result, one may conclude that 'Genesis fosters a messianic expectation, of which this verse is the headwaters.'[3]

The singular and personal offspring of the woman as mentioned in Genesis 3:15 is commonly recognized among evangelical interpreters as Jesus Christ and the 'bruising of his heel' as a reference to His death. This phrase, according to biblical theologian Gerard Van Groningen, 'is a euphemistic statement which, in the process of time and history, was demonstrated to refer to the suffering, condemnation, death, and burial of Christ Jesus who suffered the wrath of God and had humanity's curse placed on Him (Rom. 5:9; 1 Thess. 1:10; Gal. 3:10-13).'[4] Through the death of Jesus Christ God established the means (or mechanism) for granting forgiveness of their rebellion for those humans who would seek it. This relates to the second need mentioned above.

The 'bruising of the head' of the serpent is commonly recognized as a reference to the victory over Satan that was achieved by Jesus Christ in His incarnation, ministry, death and resurrection, through which He brought the kingdom of

---

2   Collins, *Genesis*, p. 157.

3   Ibid.

4   Gerard Van Groningen, *From Creation to Consummation* (Sioux Center, IA: Dordt College P, 1996), p. 116.

God into reality in human history during this present age, with the consummation of the victory yet to come (see Rom. 16:20; Heb. 2:14-15). By this means humans would be released from the dominion of Satan and brought under the acknowledged government of God. This relates to the third human need mentioned above, an instrument for bringing fallen humans under God's rightful and acknowledged lordship over them.

Both these accomplishments are mentioned in such a New Testament passage as Colossians 1:13-14: 'He [God the Father] has delivered us from the domain of darkness and transferred us to the kingdom of his beloved Son, in whom we have redemption, the forgiveness of sins.' The 'kingdom' involves acknowledgment in principle of the rule of God through Jesus Christ, and 'forgiveness' involves removal of the penalty which human rebellion deserves. In such a fashion the New Testament portrays the culmination of the 'messianic expectation' which is fostered in Genesis, and it is directly connected to the government of God ('the kingdom of his beloved Son'). The first human need mentioned above (for instruction about this kingdom of God) will be seen to have been met in similar fashion, as Jesus during His earthly ministry delivered a message whose central burden was the near arrival of God's kingdom (Mark 1:14-15).

The purpose and the plan of God which were thus announced immediately upon the occurrence of the human rebellion indicate that the event did not catch God by surprise. He had already purposed to deal with that rebellion in a way which would begin to overturn the effects of the Fall in this present age and completely defeat the 'domain of darkness' in the age to come.

APPLICATORY OBSERVATIONS:

1) Christians may have confidence in God's sovereign purpose because it is an 'eternal purpose' (Eph. 3:11). The rebellion of the human race did not catch God off guard or cause Him to switch to 'plan B'. It was all part of His eternal purpose to redeem a people for His own possession through His Son, incarnate as Jesus of Nazareth, who would Himself be glorified alongside God the Father and God the Holy Spirit. The glory of God is the ultimate aim of this purpose and plan

(Rom. 11:36; Eph. 1:6, 12, 14; 2:7). Christians can be gratified when they serve this purpose, even through their own hardships and difficulties, as they show through their faithfulness that knowing and glorifying God is worth the loss of everything it may cost them.

2) Christians may observe the perfect fitness of the Lord Jesus to meet their every need in relation to God. It was not accidental that the New Testament (and the Old as well) and the later Christian tradition identified the offices in which the Lord Jesus functioned as those of prophet, priest, and king. It is in these respects that fallen humans need just the kind of intervention that He supplies.

II. The Continuing Human Revolt against the Government of God

Much of the rest of the biblical account of primeval history in Genesis 1–11 is devoted to showing that the rebellion against God's rule was perpetuated by the human race (Adam and Eve's descendants), that the effects of the rebellion and God's judgment on it were experienced by humans generally and that it manifested itself in specific historical circumstances. There were also displays of God's grace, but this study must necessarily focus on the human revolt.

1. The disposition (and penalty) of rebellion against God's rule was passed on from Adam to his descendants so that it came to characterize the entire human race.

Willem VanGemeren suggests that 'in biblical language, sin involves 'rebellion ..., an act of opposition to God's rule. From the first days in the Garden of Eden to the dispersion over God's earth, the history of mankind shows a persistent tendency toward revolution against God's rule.'[5]

The transmission of this rebellion against God's rule from Adam to his offspring requires us to understand some kind of mechanism by which this took place. The mechanism is likely to be found expressed in the phrase 'in Adam', used by the Apostle Paul in 1 Corinthians 15:22: 'in Adam all die'.

---

5   Willem VanGemeren, *The Progress of Redemption: The Story of Salvation from Creation to the New Jerusalem* (Grand Rapids: Baker, 1988), p. 85.

That phrase seems to represent a conception of 'corporate solidarity' by which all succeeding human generations are regarded as being united to Adam in his transgression and fall, resulting in death for all. Such corporate solidarity involves the transmission to later generations of both the guilt of Adam's transgression and the corruption of nature which he immediately began to experience. The latter, the corruption of human nature, is perhaps less problematic, for whatever the mechanism involved, it seems patently clear from our own experience and observation that all humans are born with a proclivity toward rebellion against the God of the Bible and a tendency toward evil which does not need to be taught but is passed along through the process of natural generation. However, the former, the passing on of the guilt of Adam's sin, may need a fuller elaboration.

Paul's discussion of the matter in Romans 5:12-19 suggests that the specific mechanism for the transmission of guilt was an arrangement established by God between Adam and the human race according to which Adam represented the race, much in the way that Jesus Christ represents those who are justified in Him. Paul here points out that 'death spread to all men' after Adam's sin, that 'death reigned from Adam to Moses' although the Mosaic Law had not yet been given, and that death reigned over those 'whose sinning was not like the transgression of Adam', that is, those who had not transgressed a specific revealed command. What accounts for this reign of death? It is because 'all sinned', plausibly meaning that they sinned in their representative Adam, 'who was a type of the one who was to come,' that is, Jesus Christ, 'the last Adam' (1 Cor. 15:45). Paul makes it clear that there was a relationship of solidarity between Adam and his sin on the one hand and the rest of the human race on the other:

'many died through *one man's trespass*' (Rom. 5:15);
'the judgment following *one trespass* brought condemnation' (5:16);
'because of *one man's trespass*, death reigned through that one man' (5:17);
'*one trespass* led to condemnation for all men' (5:18);
'by the *one man's disobedience* the many were made sinners' (5:19).

Paul does not say that death, judgment, and condemnation came to all men because *they personally* sinned but rather because of the *one* sin of the *one* man, Adam. This reality parallels that by which justification is brought to all those in Christ as a result of His 'one act of righteousness' (5:18), 'the one man's obedience' (5:19). It should be noted that both 'condemnation' and 'justification' are legal terms, indicating that they are ultimately related to God's law, that is, to His government.[6]

Granting that such a relationship did indeed exist, both its precise nature and the proper terminology to be used in describing it have been a matter of some debate in Reformed literature. John Murray refused to call it a covenant, preferring instead 'the Adamic Administration'. Reymond defends the traditional 'covenant of works' concept and terminology. Collins defends the notion that a covenant is to be discerned in Genesis 2:16-17, and he suggests that the idea of representation is central to such a covenant. (A term deriving from Collins's discussion, but not actually used or proposed by him, is one that may prove serviceable albeit narrow 'covenant of representation.') Robertson notes some of the problems connected with the traditional term 'covenant of works' and suggests as an alternative 'covenant of creation'. Niehaus summarizes several arguments (including the later appearing of Christ as the Second Adam) on behalf of seeing a covenant relationship between God and Adam at creation (Gen. 1:1-2:3; 2:17), and calls it the 'Adamic covenant' or 'creation covenant'.[7] At any rate, one can hardly understand

---

6   Wayne Grudem, in his *Systematic Theology: An Introduction to Biblical Doctrine* (Grand Rapids: Zondervan, 1994, 2000), presents clear, accessible, and biblical rationale for what he calls 'inherited guilt' and 'inherited corruption' pp. 494-98.

7   John Murray, *Collected Writings of John Murray* (Edinburgh: Banner of Truth, 1977), 2:47-59; Reymond, *Systematic Theology*, pp. 430-40; Collins, *Genesis*, pp. 112-14 (the term 'covenant of representation' is mine, not that of Collins, but was derived from his discussion; it may obviate some of the common objections to 'covenant of works'); Robertson, *Christ of the Covenants*, pp. 54-57, 67-87; Niehaus, 'Covenant: An Idea in the Mind of God', pp. 231-33 (his grounding of the idea of covenant in the ancient Near Eastern understanding of 'covenant', deriving ultimately from God Himself, may eliminate Murray's [perhaps artificially-imposed] requirement/objection, that a covenant must be redemptive in nature).

the rest of the Old Testament story (including the immediately following events), the condition of the human race generally and the necessity for and the nature of the work of Jesus Christ apart from some notion of a legal as well as organic connection of the human race to Adam.

2. **The practical outworking of opposition to God's rule and its effects on the history of the human race are seen in the degeneracy and pride of humanity, leading to two catastrophic judgments.**

The effects of the Fall are evident immediately in the biblical account of primeval history, as the moral degeneracy of the human race led to the flood (Gen. 4–9), and as the humanistic pridefulness of the race led to its dispersion and the confusion of languages (Gen 10–11).

1) The degeneracy of humanity as exemplified in the godless Cainite culture led to the divine judgment of the great flood. Cain killed his brother Abel in response to the differing reactions of God to their respective acts of worship (Gen. 4:1-8). God placed a curse upon Cain (4:11-12), and Cain went away to lead a life apart from God (4:16). In the activities of Cain (Gen. 4:1-16) VanGemeren sees the birth of the 'spirit of secularism' in that Cain disobeys God (4:6-7) 'in order to pursue his own interests' and departs from the presence of God (4:16) to pursue 'life without God', which is the essence of secularism.[8]

Erich Sauer outlines the characteristics of 'Cainite civilization' as follows:

(1) Rapid advance of all mechanical arts (Gen. 4:17-22);
(2) Great increase of population (Gen. 6:1);
(3) Disregard of the divine law of marriage (Gen. 4:19);
(4) Rejection of the call to penitence and faith (Gen. 4:26; 5:21-24, 28-29; 2 Pet. 2:5);
(5) Union of the professing people of God with the world (Gen. 6:1-4, though some interpret this as the commingling of fallen angels with human women; 6:5-8);
(6) Self-glorification of mankind (Gen. 4:23-24).[9]

---

8   VanGemeren, *Progress of Redemption*, p. 89.

9   Sauer, *Dawn of World Redemption*, pp. 66-69.

The practical outworking of this culture led to the conditions described in Genesis 6:5: 'The LORD saw that the wickedness of man was great in the earth, and that every intention of the thoughts of his heart was only evil continually.' The flood of Genesis 6–8 represented the judgment of God upon this degenerate culture; the covenant God made with Noah (Gen. 6:17-22; 8:20-22; 9:1-7; 9:8-17) represents God's preserving relationship with surviving and subsequent humanity at large, and as such (as Niehaus points out) constitutes a renewal after the flood of the original Adamic covenant and provides a foundation on which to establish the later redemptive covenants.[10]

2) The pride of humanity as exemplified in the Tower of Babel resulted in the divine judgment of the confusion of languages and the scattering of humans over the earth. Chapters 10 and 11 of Genesis belong together and follow upon the events of the great flood. Chapter 10 details the dispersion of the human race in its national (ethnic) entities through the descendants of the three sons of Noah, moving toward the fulfillment of Noah's prophecy of Genesis 9:25-27. Chapter 11 describes the reason for this dispersion.

The tower of Babel (Gen. 11:1-4) represents another attempt at the self-glorification of humanity independently of God. In the tower of Babel, humans sought to 'develop a civilization without God': the tower was 'a symbol of man's revolutionary spirit against God, who is Creator, Ruler, and Sustainer.' They were planning to 'usurp God's authority on earth and in heaven'. Babel was nothing less than an attempt to achieve human autonomy. 'The spirit of secularism,' VanGemeren continues, 'can coexist with religions and deities, but not with the absolutism of the Creator–God. Humanism and secularism are bound to run counter to theism.'[11]

Sauer similarly analyzes the sins of Babel as those of pride (a tower with its top reaching to the heavens, Gen. 11:4a);

---

10 See Robertson, *Christ of the Covenants*, pp. 109-25; Jeffrey J. Niehaus, 'Covenant and Narrative, God and Time,' *Journal of the Evangelical Theological Society* 53/3 (September 2010), pp. 541-42; and Niehaus, 'An Argument against Theologically Constructed Covenants,' *Journal of the Evangelical Theological Society* 50/2 (June 2007), pp. 261-62.

11 VanGemeren, *Progress of Redemption*, pp. 89-90.

a determination to hold together (11:4c; VanGemeren: to control their destiny apart from God); and vainglory (desire to make a name for themselves, 11:4b). God's judgment corresponded to these: His 'coming down' to assert Himself (11:5, 7); His scattering and dividing of humanity (11:8, 9); and placing on them the 'name of shame' ('Babel'=confusion, 11:9a).[12]

As a result of these events, as VanGemeren points out, 'Babel/Babylon becomes in the Bible a symbol of a self-reliant, imperialistic secularism: control without accountability to the Creator.'[13] That is, 'Babylon' becomes a code-word for the human attempt to attain autonomy – independence from God – an attempted autonomy which manifests itself in hostility toward the God of the Bible and His purposes.

APPLICATORY OBSERVATIONS:

1) All humans are sinful because of their connection with Adam. The organic and legal connection of Adam's descendants with their forebear renders them sinful by nature (Eph. 2:3) and guilty from conception (Ps. 51:5). There is no escaping the penalty of this reality except by renouncing one's identification with the 'first Adam' and choosing the 'last Adam' (1 Cor. 15:45) – Jesus Christ – to be one's new representative.

2) The degeneration of human culture which followed the Fall is always a consequence of human rejection of the God of the Bible and His laws. The result is the attempt to 'live by one's own laws', the very definition of autonomy. Such degeneracy is evident in Western culture in our own day as the leaders and people of the culture increasingly reject the biblical God and His ways.

3) The entire civilization of the West is, since the 'Enlightenment' of the eighteenth century, increasingly devoted to the glorification of humanity and the pursuit of its goals independently of God. Such an outlook is not hostile to all religion, only that which acknowledges and submits to the

---

12   Sauer, *Dawn of World Redemption*, p. 81.

13   VanGemeren, *Progress of Redemption*, p. 90.

holy and sovereign God of the Bible. Christians should seek to ensure that they are far removed from such a human-centered approach.

III. Establishing the Covenant Purposes of God: Part 1

The Abrahamic Covenant

The account of Babel brings the story to the juncture at which Abraham is introduced. There occurs here a narrowing of the focus of revelation and redemption to one man and his family, but only so that both might later reach to all the nations of the earth. The rest of the Old Testament, both as history and as document, prepares the way for the accomplishment of God's redemptive purposes in the person of Jesus of Nazareth. This preparation is achieved by God by means of a series of covenants (binding commitments sovereignly administered by God) made with the Hebrew patriarchs (made with Abraham, renewed with Isaac and Jacob), with Moses and the Hebrew nation (made at Sinai, renewed at Moab [Deuteronomy]), and with David and the Davidic line of kings. The culmination of this process is found in the institution of the New Covenant announced by Jeremiah (Jer. 31:31-34) and established by Jesus through His death (Luke 22:20). The kingdom or government of God is the goal; the covenants are the means for reaching that goal.

The tangible outworking of God's purpose of redemption found early historical expression in God's covenant with the patriarch Abraham.[14]

1. Institution of the Abrahamic Covenant

Several passages in Genesis describe the history of God's relationship with Abraham, while the formal institution of God's covenant with Abraham is described in Genesis 15.

---

14 The following treatment is intended as a survey of the historical–theological elements and features of the Old Testament redemptive covenants, and does not address technical aspects of the literary form and structuring of the covenants; for the latter, and for a helpful analysis more generally, see Niehaus, 'Covenant and Narrative', pp. 542-56; for the Abrahamic covenant specifically, pp. 542-50.

1) Genesis 12:1-3, 7: In pursuance of fulfilling the promise of a Deliverer expressed in Genesis 3:15, God purposed to bring this blessing to all the nations of earth through the instrumentality of the Hebrew patriarch Abraham. The initial divine call and promises to Abram (his original name) are recorded in Genesis 12:1-3. God called Abram to leave his native land and his family to go to a land God would show him (12:1). At the same time, God promised to make him a great nation (12:2a); to bless him and make his name great (12:2b); to protect him, (12:3a); and to make him a blessing to all the peoples of the earth (12:2c, 3b). In the latter promise is to be seen God's purpose to bring a blessing to all nations through Abram, namely the redemption from sin accomplished through Messiah Jesus (see Gal. 3:13-14). This salvation is one of the primary blessings of God's kingdom as proclaimed in the New Testament. This purpose to bless all nations through Abraham was one that was repeated often, as recorded throughout these chapters (Gen. 18:18; 22:18; 26:4). It is cited by the Apostle Paul in Galatians 3:8 as being fulfilled in the good news about Jesus Christ (see Gal. 3:14).

Abram was 75 years old when he left Haran (in northern Mesopotamia) to enter Canaan (12:4). It was after Abram's removal to Canaan in obedience to God's command that God promised to give that land to Abram's offspring (12:7). In accord with the principle of progressive revelation, additional features of God's purpose for Abram would be disclosed at critical junctures in God's dealings with him.

2) Genesis 13:14-17. Elements of the earlier promises are repeated in Genesis 13:14-17. God promised to give Abram and his offspring the land of Canaan (13:15); and to make his offspring as numerous as the dust of the earth (13:16), both of which were remarkable promises in view of the fact that Abram at the time possessed no offspring.

3) Genesis 15:1-21: As a means of advancing His purpose to bring a Deliverer into the world in order to bless all nations, God made a covenant with Abram (Abraham) which granted to him the covenant gifts of justification, posterity, and the land of Canaan. Strictly speaking, the establishment of the Abrahamic

Covenant did not occur until the events of Genesis 15, where the word 'covenant' is used for the first time of God's arrangement with Abram (15:18). In the events of this chapter, God promised to protect Abram (v. 1c); to reward him greatly (v. 1d); to give him an heir from his own body (v. 4); and to make his offspring numerous (v. 5). Abram's response to these promises was to believe what Jehovah had told him, whereupon God pronounced him righteous in his sight (15:6), the first mention of God's justification of sinners in the Bible. Then God mentioned giving the land of Canaan to Abram as a possession (v. 7), to which Abram responded by asking how he could know that he would possess it (v. 8). There follows an account of an elaborate and impressive ceremony of sacrifice in which God, by means of a covenant (v. 18), committed Himself to give to Abram's offspring the land of Canaan (vv. 7-21).

The essential elements of the Abrahamic Covenant are thus (a) justification through faith, (b) the promise of posterity and (c) the promise of land:

> *(a) Justification through faith* (Gen. 15:6). The covenant involved the personal and individual response of trust in God's revelation on the part of the human participant in the covenant (at this time, only Abram), resulting in the status of his being accounted righteous before God.[15] It is worthy of note that this individual and personal response of trust (faith) in God's word was accorded the role of the instrumental means of justification while Abram was still a solitary figure, that is, before he was actually constituted the forebear of a nation. This intimates that faith would continue to play this role among his descendants, both physical and spiritual (see Rom. 4:11-12). Thus Erich Sauer argues that the New Covenant is, with regard to the crucial role played by faith, 'the continuation and glorious perfection of the covenant

---

15 In his analysis of the covenantal elements found in the narrative of Genesis 15, Niehaus lists 15:6 as among the 'blessings' of the covenant (a verse which mentions only Abraham's being justified as a result of believing God's revelation), but he does not give justification specific mention ('Covenant and Narrative', p. 543).

with Abraham (Gal. 3:9, 14; Rom. 4).'[16] This feature should be understood to set the pattern for and to regulate all later covenants that God made in pursuance of the provisions of the Abrahamic Covenant. That is, nothing that occurs later in redemptive history should be seen as overturning the principle of justification through faith.

(b) Posterity (Gen 15:5). God promised Abram that his offspring would be as numerous as the stars of heaven. This affirmation of a numerous posterity as a result of the covenant promise would be physically fulfilled in the birth of Isaac (Gen. 21:1-7) and Isaac's offspring Esau (forebear of the Edomites) and Jacob (heir of the covenant and forebear of the nation of Israel, derived from his twelve sons) and their descendants. The provision of offspring would also be accomplished through the births of Ishmael (Gen. 16:10; 17:20; 21:13, 18; 25:12-18) and the sons of Abraham's second wife Keturah (Gen. 25:1-4). Thus would be fulfilled also the word of Genesis 17:4, that Abraham would be the 'father of a multitude of nations'. However, the point of interest in Genesis 15 is that specific descendant who would become the heir of God's covenant with Abraham, namely Isaac (Gen. 15:4).

(c) Land (Gen. 15:7-20). God promised to give Abram the land of Canaan (15:7); however, Abram did not himself receive the land personally (except for a burial place which he purchased from the locals, Genesis 23; see Acts 7:5) but only through the persons of his descendants (15:13-20).

4) Genesis 17:1-27. In the meantime a son was born to Abram by fleshly means (Ishmael, by Sarah's handmaid Hagar; Gen. 16), when Abram was 86 years old (16:16). In the events of Genesis 17, when Abram was 99 years old, God appeared to Abram and took the following actions:

(a) God summarized His intentions regarding the covenant made with Abram and the offspring promised to him (vv. 1-2).

(b) God affirmed the covenant with Abram (vv. 3-8). This included reasserting the establishment of the covenant (v. 4a);

---

16   Sauer, *Dawn of World Redemption*, p. 97.

declaring that Abram would become the father of many nations, and changing his name to Abraham (vv. 4b-6); and promising 'to be God to' him and his offspring and to give them the land of Canaan (vv. 7-8). The words of God's promise, 'to be God to you and to your offspring after you' (17:7b), according to Baptist theologian John L. Dagg, 'were not designed to be a promise of spiritual grace, or eternal life, to all the descendants of Abraham.... As contained in this covenant, the promise engaged a special divine care over Abraham and his descendants; and particularly over the nation of Israel....' Such care was indeed exercised by God throughout Israel's history, and thus, 'In this sense, the promise was literally fulfilled.' That is, it was a promise of God's temporal care and spiritual guidance for Israel as a national entity, not a promise of saving grace to all its individual members.[17]

(c) God instituted the covenant sign of circumcision, to be applied to all the males of Abraham's household (vv. 9-14).

(d) God promised a son to Abraham by his wife Sarai, whose name was changed to Sarah (vv. 15-16). God also promised that she would be the mother of nations and kings (v. 16), which was fulfilled through Isaac's descendants Jacob and Esau, progenitors of the Israelite and Edomite nations respectively, and the rulers descending from them.

(e) He asserted the covenant succession through Isaac, the son to be born of Sarah (vv. 19, 21).

5) Genesis 18:18-19. God's intentions with regard to Abraham were described in the third person.

6) Genesis 22:15-18. After Abraham showed his faith in God by his willingness to sacrifice his son Isaac, God swore that He would bless Abraham (vv. 16-17a); that He would make Abraham's offspring numerous (v. 17b); that He would make Abraham's offspring victorious over their enemies (v. 17c); and

---

17 J. L. Dagg, *Manual of Theology. Second Part: A Treatise on Church Order* (Harrisonburg VA: Gano, 1990), pp. 168-69. Dagg goes on to describe the ways in which God acted as God toward the nation, p. 169.

that He would bless all nations through Abraham's offspring (v. 18). This is the first instance in which God promised to bless all nations through Abraham's *offspring* rather than through Abraham himself (see Gen. 12:3; 18:18). The Apostle Peter quoted this promise as being fulfilled in God's sending of Jesus (Acts 3:25-26).

2. Features of the Abrahamic Covenant

The following broader observations may be drawn from the Genesis narratives.

1) The Abrahamic Covenant brought Abraham under the government of God. Abraham was expected to submit himself to God's rule as expressed in the command to leave his homeland and family (Gen. 12:1), and additional features of the arrangement were not disclosed until he had obeyed (12:4-7). In addition, God told Abram before the institution of circumcision, 'Walk before me, and be blameless, that I may make my covenant between me and you and may multiply you greatly' (Gen. 17:1-2). Also, Abraham was to instruct his own family in the ways of God: 'I have chosen him, that he may command his children and his household after him to keep the way of the LORD by doing righteousness and justice, so that the LORD may bring to Abraham what he has promised him' (Gen. 18:19). The family of Abraham was to be a human community in which the government of God was acknowledged (though some branches of that family eventually moved outside the sphere of special revelation). Furthermore, perpetuation of the covenant promises to succeeding generations was secured, God said, 'because Abraham obeyed my voice and kept my charge, my commandments, and my laws' (Gen. 26:5). While the covenant was initiated and maintained by God's sovereign action and thus was unconditional, yet its continuation was in some way contingent on (a result of) Abraham's obedience to God and submission to His rule.

2) The Abrahamic Covenant was preparatory to the extension of the government of God through Abraham's remote offspring, Jesus the Messiah. When the message about Jesus was first being proclaimed by His disciples, it was set forth in such terms. Matthew 1:1 refers to Jesus as son of David and son of Abraham, that is, a Davidic king who was descended from Abraham. In Acts 3:13, Peter spoke of the God of Abraham glorifying His servant Jesus, meaning exalting Him to a position of lordship. Later in the same message, he referred to the covenant God made with Abraham and the blessing it promised (3:25). The fulfillment of that promise of blessing was to be found, Peter said, in God's raising up of Jesus (perhaps a reference to the incarnation) and sending Him to 'you first' (the Jewish people) 'to bless you by turning every one of you from your wickedness' (3:26), a reference to repentance (see 3:19) and personal acknowledgment of the government of God exercised through the exalted Jesus.

3) *The covenant succession ran through Abraham's descendants Isaac and Jacob.* Isaac was indicated as the heir of the covenant in preference to Ishmael (Gen. 17:19, 21; 21:12; 26:3-5) and Jacob was chosen in preference to Esau (Gen. 25:3; 28:13-14). From Jacob sprang the Hebrew nation through his twelve sons (Gen. 29:1-30:24; 35:16-21), and the covenant succession incorporated that entire nation.

4) *The Abrahamic Covenant provided a people, a promise, a place and a pattern for the outworking of the divine purpose.* The *people* were the Israelites, through whom God would bring the Deliverer mentioned in Genesis 3:15. The *promise* was that of blessing to all nations of the earth through the Deliverer. The *place* was the land of Canaan, where the Israelites would live, where most of God's dealings with them were centered, and where the promised redemption would be accomplished. The *pattern* was that of justification through faith, granted to Abraham and proclaimed to the nations as a result of the mission of Jesus the Messiah (Gal. 3:8).

5) *The Abrahamic Covenant envisioned, and Abraham had, three kinds of offspring.* The *first* kind was the purely physical offspring (his natural descendants who did not follow in his faith, typically those outside the line of Isaac and Jacob [Mal. 1:2-3] and unbelieving Israelites [Matt. 3:9]). A *second* type was those who were both physical and spiritual offspring (natural descendants who did follow in his pattern of faith, Rom. 4:12, that is, believing Israelites). A *third* was the purely spiritual offspring (metaphorically of Gentiles who followed in

his pattern of faith by trusting in Jesus the Messiah, Rom. 4:11; Gal. 3:7, 9, 29).

APPLICATORY OBSERVATIONS:

1) Abraham was the object of divine grace just as much as later believers are. He possessed nothing to commend himself to God, but was an idolater (Josh. 24:2) who was commanded to separate himself from his country and family. There was no principle of merit operating in God's choice of Abram just as there was none in his choice of a people in the Lord Jesus (1 Cor. 1:26-31; Eph. 1:4-5). No basis for pride exists among God's people of any era. All is of grace.

2) The fact that Jesus the Messiah was descended from Abraham constitutes the ultimate fulfillment of the promise of a blessing for all nations through Abraham. That blessing involves entry into the benefits of the kingdom of God through faith in Jesus, and includes forgiveness of sin, fellowship with God, and willing acknowledgment of God's rightful rule through King Jesus. These benefits are to be spread to all peoples through the making of disciples of Jesus among all nations (Matt. 28:18-20).

3) Every believer in Jesus Christ is regarded as Abraham's spiritual offspring (Gal. 3:7, 9, 29; Rom. 4:11) since Abraham was the prototype of justification through faith apart from works (Rom. 4:3-8). This puts believers into the company of 'the Israel of God' (Gal. 6:16) and in a position to receive the benefits promised to Abraham's (spiritual) descendants.

IV. Establishing the Covenant Purposes of God: Part 2

The Mosaic Covenant

After the enactment of the Abrahamic Covenant (about 2080 B.C.) and its confirmation to Isaac and to Jacob, the descendants of Jacob entered Egypt under the administration of Joseph (about 1875 B.C.) and spent 400 years there, as God had prophesied to Abraham (Gen. 15:13; chs. 37–50). At the end of the 400 years, as also God had told Abraham (Gen. 15:14), God, remembering His covenant with Abraham, Isaac and Jacob (Exod. 2:24), brought the Israelites out of

Egypt under the leadership of Moses in the event known as the Exodus (Exod. 1:1–15:21; 1446 B.C.). A few months after leaving Egypt the Israelites arrived at Mount Sinai in the Sinai Peninsula, and there God made a covenant with them, of which Moses was the mediator. The institution of the Mosaic Covenant is described in the middle chapters of the Book of Exodus.[18]

1. Institution of the Mosaic Covenant (Exod. 19:1–24:11)

By means of the Mosaic Covenant God constituted Israel a nation, expressed His absolute moral law in external form and regulated the civil and religious life of Israel in order that He might make Israel a channel of revelation and redemption for the world. The account of the institution of the Mosaic Covenant may be analyzed as follows:

1) Arrival at Sinai (19:1-2). The Israelites arrived at Sinai three months after leaving Egypt.

2) God proposed a covenant relationship between Himself and the Israelites (19:3-6), and the people agreed (19:7-8). God called Moses to Himself (19:3) and proposed a covenant relationship with the Israelites. A covenant was a binding formal commitment to a personal relationship, with stipulations, obligations, and penalties attached. The divine covenants of the Bible were enacted by sovereign action of God, as in this case. This covenant would be based on God's deliverance of the Israelites from Egypt (19:3-4). It would impose certain obligations on the Israelites (19:5a). And it would grant to the Israelites the privileged position of being a people for God's own possession, a kingdom of priests, and His holy nation (19:5b-6). Moses reported God's proposal to the Israelites, and they agreed to enter into the covenant relationship (19:7-8).

3) The Israelites prepared themselves for the covenant ceremony as God had instructed them (19:9-25). The preparation of the Israelites involved maintaining ceremonial cleanliness and strict instruction concerning avoidance of physical contact with the mountain by man and beast.

---

18 For a brief overview of the Mosaic Covenant from the perspective of ancient Near Eastern covenants, see Niehaus, 'Covenant and Narrative', pp. 550-53.

4) God delivered the Ten Commandments to Moses with a great display of majesty, to which the Israelites responded with fearfulness (20:1-26). These Ten Commandments formed the heart of the covenant relationship; they were presented separately from the rest of the stipulations, and they are referred to later as the 'ten words' of the covenant (Exod. 34:28; Deut. 4:13). The covenant relationship was based in Jehovah's (or 'Yahweh's'; it is God's personal and covenant name) identity as their God who had redeemed them from slavery in Egypt (20:2). The primary obligations of the covenant thus related to the Israelites' honoring of Jehovah as their God, solely and supremely and properly (20:3-11). Significantly, and at the heart of all else, this section mentions love for God as the basis for keeping His commandments (v. 6). The secondary (but no less obligatory) requirements related to their behavior and attitudes toward other human beings (20:12-17).

The display of thunder, lightning, trumpet sound and smoke frightened the people, for apparently they had been hearing God's voice directly, prompting them to ask for Moses' mediation in dealing with God (20:18-21). The instructions of 20:23-26 may relate especially to the ratification ceremony of 24:1-8.

5) God delivered to Moses additional laws and ordinances (21:1–23:19). This lengthy section contains further laws and ordinances relating to treatment of slaves, personal injury, theft, crop protection, personal property, sexual irregularities, protection of the vulnerable, respect for God, matters of honesty and justice, and mandatory Sabbaths and festivals. They were intended to regulate Israel's religious, legal, social and economic life.

6) Promises of blessing and punishment (23:20-33). God promised the presence of the Angel of the LORD to guide and protect the Israelites on their way to the land of Canaan, but He also promised retribution for disobedience (23:20-21). But most of the section is devoted to promises of blessings which God will bring on the Israelites if they obey Him (22-33).

7) Ceremony of Covenant Ratification (24:1-11). God commanded Moses to gather the leaders of the people for a ceremony of covenant ratification (24:1-2). The people of the nation heard the terms and commandments of the covenant, and responded, 'All the words that the LORD has spoken we will do' (24:3b). Moses conducted a ceremony involving burnt offerings (slain animals burned on an altar) and the reading of the covenant scroll, to which the people responded again, 'All that the LORD has spoken we will do, and we will be obedient' (24:4-7). Moses sprinkled the people with the blood of one of the animals, the 'blood of the covenant' (v. 8), and the public portion of the ceremony was concluded. The people of Israel had entered into a formal covenant commitment with God. At the conclusion of the ceremony the leaders of Israel were granted a theophany (an appearance of God) and participated in a covenant meal (24:9-11).

2. Features of the Mosaic Covenant

1) The Mosaic Covenant served to constitute Israel as a nation. Before the events at Sinai, the Israelites were just a group of descendants from a common ancestor, Jacob. As a result of the events at Sinai they became a nation with leadership, laws and regulations to govern their corporate life. Biblical theologian O. Palmer Robertson has observed, 'To this point, God's dealing had been with a family. Now he covenants with a nation.'[19]

2) The Mosaic Covenant brought the nation of Israel under God's acknowledged government. As Robertson goes on to say, 'Such a national covenant would be impossible without externally codified law.'[20] The most characteristic feature of the Mosaic Covenant was its comprehensive statement of God's will in the form of the Law given to Israel. Robertson argues that 'the Mosaic covenant manifests its distinctiveness as an externalized summation of the will of God.... This external-to-man, formally ordered summation of God's will constitutes the distinctiveness of the Mosaic covenant', and later states that this feature is 'the very heart and core' of its 'distinctive element'.[21] In particular it is the Ten Commandments which

---

19 O. Palmer Robertson, *The Christ of the Covenants*, p. 187.

20 Robertson, *Christ of the Covenants*, p. 187.

21 Robertson, *Christ of the Covenants*, pp. 172, 186. Robertson's emphasis on the external nature of the Mosaic Law is intended to contrast it with that provision of the New Covenant according to which God's law will be 'placed within' His people and 'written on their hearts' (Jer. 31:33; Heb. 8:10) by God Himself. See p. 190.

'contain a complete summation of the will of God', for these embody the entire will of God for humans as they relate to God and to one another. The Ten Commandments are such an integral feature of the Mosaic Covenant that they are in fact identified with the covenant in Exodus 34:28 ('the words of the covenant, the ten commandments') and Deuteronomy 4:13 ('he declared to you his covenant, which he commanded you to perform, that is, the Ten Commandments'). Thus, 'These words ["ten words"=Ten Commandments] summarize the essence of the Mosaic covenant.'[22]

This reality reflects the element of authoritative ownership which is inherent in God's lordship over the Israelites. According to a major theological dictionary, 'In ancient Israel the first laws are rooted in the doctrine of the covenant. The basic principle is that the whole life of the people belongs to God.... They are the requirements of the God to whom Israel belongs in virtue of the exodus and they come directly from God at Sinai.' The features of the law given at Sinai manifest this character: they are unconditional; they are negative, prohibiting that which would destroy the covenant relationship; they appeal to the will; they are comprehensive; and they are addressed to all Israel.[23] Even though usage of the term 'torah' ('teaching', 'law') is broad enough to include ritual instructions for priests as well as moral instruction, yet, 'The essential point ... is always divine authority.' When the term is broadened to refer in a general way to divine revelation (Ps.1:2), it is still done 'always with a strong sense of authoritativeness.'[24]

3) The Mosaic Covenant regulated Israel's civil and religious life. As noted above, much of the law given at Sinai addressed matters of civil justice and equity. Much detailed instruction that was later given to Moses (Exod. 25–31) served to order

---

22 Robertson, *Christ of the Covenants*, p. 173.

23 Geoffrey W. Bromiley, *Theological Dictionary of the New Testament*. Ed. Gerhard Kittel and Gerhard Friedrich. Trans. Geoffrey W. Bromiley. Abridged in one volume. (Grand Rapids: Eerdmans, 1985), p. 648. Thus it must be observed in the most pointed terms possible that the element of God's authority is in the forefront in the giving of the law to Israel.

24 Bromiley, *Theological Dictionary*, p. 649.

the nation's worship of Jehovah, provided ritual instructions for the Israelites and their priests (Lev. 1–7), established standards of diet, ceremonial cleanness and hygiene (Lev. 11–15), and addressed many other moral, ceremonial and civil matters (Lev. 16–27). The entire life of the nation was to be governed by God's commandments. His lordship was to be manifested in every area of Israel's life.

4) The Mosaic Covenant foreshadowed the work of Jesus the Messiah. By means of its place of worship at the tabernacle, its priesthood, its offerings, precepts and practices relating to the worship of God, and its appointed Sabbaths, festivals and special years, the Mosaic Covenant included as one of its essential components a provisional means of dealing with human sin. These elements indicated the necessity of, the nature of, the divine provision of and the restored fellowship resulting from atonement offered as a covering for the guilt of sin. Forgiveness of sin was thus real for believing Israelites (Lev. 4:26, 31, 35, etc.), but since 'it is impossible for the blood of bulls and goats to take away sins' (Heb. 10:4), such forgiveness was actually effected by the later sacrifice of Jesus Christ, which these earlier forms foreshadowed and which were abolished by Christ's sacrifice (Heb. 10:8-10).[25]

APPLICATORY OBSERVATIONS:

1) The Mosaic Law was never intended to be a means of justification of sinners before God. It was rather a revelation of the holiness of God, of the moral inability of fallen humans to do what God requires and of the need for a substitutionary sacrifice.

2) The Law also served to order and direct Israel's life so the nation could function as a channel of further revelation and of the promised Deliverer's entrance into the world.

3) The Law reveals God's holiness and exposes human sin as a 'missing of the mark' of God's ideal standard for human behavior, as disobedience of God, as transgression of a given command, as lawlessness and as rebellion against God (these are terms the New Testament uses to describe human sin). That is, the Law exposes sin as the human attempt to be

---

25　See Sauer, *Dawn of World Redemption*, pp. 131-40.

autonomous – 'to live by one's own laws' – while rejecting God's rule as exercised through His laws.

4) The Law of Moses was intended to lead the Israelites to place their trust in God's provision of forgiveness of sins through the later effective sacrifice of a substitute, which the New Testament reveals to be the death of Jesus the Messiah. The Law should lead us to exercise the same trust.

V. Establishing the Covenant Purposes of God: Part 3

The Davidic Covenant

After the institution of the Mosaic Covenant God led the Israelites to the southern border of the land of Canaan, but they refused to enter, so He condemned that generation to a further thirty-eight years of wandering in the wilderness (Num. 10–14). After their passing, Moses led the nation to the eastern border of Canaan at the Jordan River, there led the nation in renewal of the Sinai covenant for a new generation, and delivered his last exhortation to the Israelite community (Deut. 1–33) before his death. The nation entered the land of Canaan under Joshua's leadership (Josh. 1–6; about 1405 B.C.), proceeded to partially conquer the land (Josh. 7–12), and allotted the land among the various Israelite tribes (Josh. 13–22). Joshua's last charge to Israel to obey the Mosaic Law (Josh. 23, especially vv. 6-8) was followed by a covenant renewal ceremony (Josh. 24:1-28) and Joshua's death and burial (Josh. 24:29-33; about 1390–1380 B.C.). Joshua's demise led to the period of the judges, an era of temporary local rulers who led the Israelites in opposition to neighboring hostile nations, which lasted over 300 years (Book of Judges). A monarchy was established in Israel in response to popular demand under the last judge and prophet Samuel (1 Sam. 1–12), but the first king, Saul (reigned 1043–1011 B.C.), of the tribe of Benjamin, was an unspiritual man, disobedient to God, and paranoid about his potential rival David, who had already been anointed as future king by Samuel (1 Sam. 13–31; David's anointing is described in ch. 16).

After Saul's and his son Jonathan's deaths in battle, David was anointed king of Judah by the men of that tribe (2 Sam. 2:4).

Saul's royal line continued briefly under his son Ish-bosheth but both he and Saul's military leader Abner were murdered treacherously, leaving only Jonathan's son Mephibosheth, who was crippled in both feet (2 Sam. 2:8–4:12). The northern tribes then joined with Judah in acknowledging and anointing David as king over all Israel (2 Sam. 5:1-3; 1004 B.C.). David then conquered the Jebusite city of Jerusalem and made it his capital, taking up residence there, fortifying the city, and living in a cedar palace built for him by Hiram, King of Tyre (2 Sam. 5:6-12). David had the ark of the covenant (where God manifested His presence to Israel; it was constructed during Moses' day) moved to Jerusalem and placed in a tent, as it had been housed since the time of the Exodus. This move made Jerusalem the religious as well as the political capital of Israel. At this juncture the events transpired which resulted in the Davidic Covenant.

1. Institution of the Davidic Covenant (2 Sam. 7:1-29)

By means of the Davidic Covenant, God established a perpetual royal dynasty in the Davidic line. The account of the institution of the Davidic Covenant may be broken down as follows.[26]

1) David expressed his desire to build a permanent structure to house the ark of the covenant (7:1-3). During a period of relative peace, David noted the incongruity of his dwelling in a fine palace of cedar while the ark of God was housed in a tent. Nathan the prophet approved of David's plan to build a permanent edifice to house the ark, that is, a temple. Apparently the original tabernacle of the Exodus era had been destroyed by this time. The entire passage turns on a play on the word 'house'. The Hebrew word *beth* exhibits three meanings in this context: it refers to the king's palace in 7:2; to a temple in 7:5; and to a royal dynasty in 7:11.

2) God sent a message to David that He would establish an everlasting Davidic dynasty (7:4-17). The message God sent through Nathan contained the following elements:

---

26 For an analysis of the Davidic Covenant from a Near Eastern perspective, including elements of the covenant form which appear in this passage, see Niehaus, 'Covenant and Narrative', pp. 553-55.

(a) God had not requested a permanent earthly dwelling-place (vv. 4-7). Jehovah reminded David that He had traveled with Israel since the Exodus with only a tent as His dwelling-place, and that He had never demanded anything more.

(b) God described His care and His purpose for David and for Israel (vv. 8-11a). The LORD recalled His previous care and provision for King David and for the nation of Israel, and described His purpose to grant them security in the future.

(c) God expressed His purpose to establish the dynasty of David (vv. 11b-17). God's message to David had begun with the question, 'Would you build me a house?' (7:5), meaning a temple; now He declares, 'The LORD will make you a house' (7:11), meaning a royal dynasty. In detail, this promise included at least six aspects: (1) God declared that He would raise up David's descendant in his place and establish his kingdom, 7:12; (2) this son would build a temple for Jehovah, 7:13a; (3) God would establish the throne of David's son forever, 7:13b; (4) David's offspring would be a son to God, and God a father to him, 7:14a; (5) God will discipline David's descendant if he does wrong, 7:14b; (6) God's faithful love would never be removed from David's descendant, 7:15. Thus, in summary, David's dynasty, kingdom and throne would be established forever, 7:16.

This was the content of Jehovah's message to David as delivered by Nathan (7:17).

3) David responded with a prayer of thanksgiving and petition that Jehovah would make good His word (7:18-29). David first expressed his unworthiness to be the object of so great favor as God was showing to him (vv. 18-21) for God had already established him as king (v. 18), but not being content with this (v. 19a) God had also guaranteed David's dynasty for the distant future (v. 19b). Significantly, David observed that this constituted instruction (torah) for mankind (v. 19c), indicating perhaps the broader significance of this promise for the human race.

Next, David affirmed that God's greatness was confirmed by his unique actions on behalf of Israel (vv. 22-24), the only nation He has so treated. Finally, David called upon Jehovah to perform His promise (vv. 25-29), mentioning it twice in verse 25 and again in verse 29. Between these petitions, David affirmed the general truthfulness of God's words (v. 28a), mentioned the specific promise made to him, and made these the basis of his prayer (v. 27).

2. Features of the Davidic Covenant
The following features may be observed to pertain to the Davidic Covenant.

1) While the term 'covenant' is not used in this context, later Scripture uses that term to describe this arrangement with the Davidic dynasty. Elements of the covenant form are evident (see the reference to Niehaus above), and the term is used, for example, in Psalm 89, an extensive psalm which makes explicit reference to God's promise to David. This psalm refers to the arrangement as a 'covenant' in verses 3, 28, and 34, using the imagery and language of 2 Samuel 7. The psalm concludes with a long passage arguing that God has 'renounced the covenant' (vv. 38-51, see below, on the historical outworking of the Davidic Covenant). The nature of the relationship as a covenant suggests a binding relationship to which God has irrevocably committed Himself.

2) The relationship between God and the Davidic king would be that of a father to a son. Robertson notes the unique role occupied by the king in Israel, mediating the divine covenant to the people, and representing the people to God (see 2 Sam. 5:3). This dual role expresses itself especially in 'the king's position as son to God. As son he shares the throne with God his Father. As son he possesses the privileges of perpetual access to the father.'[27]

This feature would find ultimate fulfillment in Messiah Jesus, who is presented as son of David and Son of God in an even higher sense than any of David's other sons, as several Old Testament and New Testament passages bear witness (Ps. 2:7 with Acts 13:33; Ps. 45:6; Isa. 9:6-7; Matt. 22:41-46; Rom. 1:3-4; Heb. 1:5). This feature also suggests that the

---

27 Robertson, *Christ of the Covenants,* pp. 235-36, citation from p. 236.

covenant relationship included not only the benefits relating to the authority and inheritance passed on from father to son, but also the exercise of fatherly discipline when that should be needed, as would be the case with David's merely human sons.

3) The element of discipline indicates that the Davidic king himself was brought under the government of God. David's son would not be a law unto himself (autonomous) but would be under divine law and under divine discipline if he should 'commit iniquity' (7:14b). David, before his death, reminded Solomon of his obligation to obey Jehovah 'as it is written in the Law of Moses' (1 Kings 2:1-4).

4) The Davidic dynasty provided for the regular administration of divine law. As Robertson observes, 'the permanent establishment of a representative king over Israel indicates an advancement in law-administration.' There was no means of succession and enforcement following Moses, but 'with the anointing of David, law began to be administered in Israel by the "man after God's own heart."'[28] Later kings would seek to enforce the law after periods of decline.[29]

5) The location of Jerusalem became the place where God's kingship and rule would be represented and expressed. Robertson again points out that 'the localization of God's throne in the Zion/Jerusalem complex also represents an advancement beyond preceding revelations of God's law in Israel.... Under David, God's rule of righteousness was established in permanency.'[30] The throne of God on earth would henceforth be connected with the Davidic throne at Jerusalem, as the rest of the Old Testament bears witness.

3. The Historical Outworking of the Davidic Covenant

God Himself saw to the preservation of the Davidic dynasty through His providential oversight of Israel's history. The

---

28 Robertson, *Christ of the Covenants*, p. 189.

29 Robertson, *Christ of the Covenants*, p. 235.

30 Robertson, *Christ of the Covenants* p. 189; see also pp. 232-33: 'The net effect of this close interchange on the basis of the "house" figure is to bind David's rule to God's rule, and *vice versa*. God shall maintain His permanent dwelling-place as king in Israel through the kingship of the Davidic line' (p. 233.)

story of the Books of Kings is the story of God's maintenance of the Davidic line on the throne of Judah, in fulfillment of His promise to David.

1) The Davidic dynasty was perpetuated through Solomon. David's son Solomon became the chosen heir of the promise of the Davidic Covenant (1 Kings 1:28-31; 2:1-4).

2) Although God removed most of the nation from under the Davidic rule after Solomon, yet He did not remove all of it, so as to continue the Davidic throne. Because Solomon allowed his foreign wives to lead him astray into idolatry, the majority of the kingdom of Israel was taken from him (1 Kings 11:9-11). However, (1) this was not done during Solomon's lifetime, 'for the sake of David your father' (11:12); and (2) the kingdom would not be entirely taken from Solomon's son 'for the sake of David my servant and for the sake of Jerusalem that I have chosen' (11:13). God's covenant with David causes him to preserve the Davidic line and throne. In contrast, the northern kingdom of Israel, after its separation from Judah, experienced a long series of different ruling families.

3) Although the Davidic rule was interrupted at the time of the Babylonian exile and afterward, yet the Davidic line was continued intact in preparation for resumption of its rule later. After preserving the Davidic line of kings on the throne of Judah for four hundred years, God finally sent Judah into exile at the hand of the Babylonians because of their idolatry (2 Kings 25:1-21). Nevertheless, the royal line of David was preserved (2 Kings 25:27-30), so that its rule could be resumed at a later day (Matt. 1:1-14).

APPLICATORY OBSERVATIONS:

1) God is true to His word. He maintained the Davidic line, first on its own throne, and then even after the collapse of that earthly monarchy. He is still true to His word and can likewise be trusted today to do what He has said.

2) God intends to exercise His authority through a *king*. This indicates that He purposes to bring humans into submission to His rule and to secure their obedience. Redeemed humanity cannot then rightly deny Him that obedience and submission in the present.

3

Redemption and God's Lordship:

The Messiah of Promise

The Old Testament anticipates a human who is to be appointed by God to serve as the agent of divine revelation, redemption and rule. This human agent came to be known as 'Messiah'.

I. The Meaning of the Term 'Messiah'

The Book of Genesis, in the words of C. John Collins already quoted, 'fosters a messianic expectation'.[1] The Abrahamic, Mosaic and Davidic covenants together constitute a single-minded movement toward both fostering and fulfilling that expectation. And that expectation, as it manifests itself in the rest of the Old Testament, must now be considered. While of necessity the present treatment must be only a cursory summary, yet it will be sufficient to demonstrate both (1) that the nature of the office of Messiah as predicted in the Old Testament included the exercise of kingship on God's behalf and (2) that the redemption which the Messiah was to bring included the element of willing submission to the government of God.

1. In Old Testament history the concept or act of *anointing* was used in connection with the setting apart of individuals to God for a specific office or function.

The term 'messiah' derives from the Hebrew verb 'masah', meaning 'to smear' or 'anoint' (usually by the pouring of oil on the head) resulting in the verbal noun 'one who is anointed', or *mashiach*. This term is used only sparingly in the Old Testament to refer to the primary figure of expectation and

---

1   Collins, *Genesis*, p. 157.

hope, or (in Reymond's words) 'the future Davidic Deliverer of the people of God'.[2] While in Psalm 2:2 it refers to a kingly figure, that figure must in the first instance be understood to be David. In Daniel 9:25-26 it designates a 'prince' who in some fashion deals with sin and establishes righteousness, probably the only strictly 'Messianic' uses of the word in the Old Testament.

Scholars distinguish between narrower and wider uses of the concept of messiah in the Old Testament. The narrower usage refers to the royal personage of a king himself as an anointed one (such as a reigning or promised king). The wider usage may refer to aspects of the work of such a king, such as the promises of and the carrying out of the work of salvation, and the qualifications, goals, means, realm or results of the reign of messiah. Gerard Van Groningen's study of Old Testament usage reveals four nuances or functions of the act of anointing: (1) to designate, appoint, or elect; (2) to set apart or consecrate; (3) to ordain or bestow authority to act; and (4) to qualify or equip for office and the fulfilling of its tasks.[3] Thus the ultimate meaning of the term as it came to center on one specific individual is that of God's chosen man, appointed, set apart, equipped, and authorized to accomplish God's purpose.

J. A. Motyer illustrates, from a 'secular' usage of *mashiach*, how the term functions. In Isaiah 45:1 Cyrus, the Persian king, is referred to as Jehovah's 'anointed'. Five features are evident.

> Cyrus is a man of God's choice (Is. 41:25 [45:4]), appointed to accomplish a redemptive purpose towards God's people (45:11-13), and a judgment on his foes (47). He is given dominion over the nations (45:1-3); and in all his activities the real agent is Yahweh himself (45:1-7).[4]

---

2   Robert L. Reymond, *Jesus, Divine Messiah: The New Testament Witness* (Phillipsburg, NJ: Presbyterian and Reformed, 1990), p. 45.

3   The above two paragraphs summarized from Gerard Van Groningen, *Messianic Revelation in the Old Testament* (Eugene, OR: Wipf and Stock, 1997), 1:17-28; and Reymond, *Jesus, Divine Messiah*, p. 45. See also J. A. Motyer, 'Messiah', in *New Bible Dictionary*, 3rd ed. (Leicester, Eng.: Inter-Varsity Press, 1996), pp. 753-60.

4   Motyer, 'Messiah,' p. 753.

Motyer observes that these five features, 'in the light of the rest of Scripture, are clearly definitive of certain main lines of OT Messianism.... There could be no better summary of the OT view of the anointed person....'[5]

2. In ancient Israel there were three anointed offices: those of priest, prophet, and king.

The rite of anointing could be – and at various times was – used in ancient Israel to designate the occupants of three offices. These were priest (Exod. 29:7; 40:13-15), prophet (1 Kings 19:16), and king (1 Sam. 10:1; 16:3; 1 Kings 19:16). Van Groningen emphasizes that the various functions of these offices were mediatorial; that is, they involved representation of the people before God or of God before the people.

Van Groningen identifies the functions of the office of priest as eight: making atonement through offering sacrifices; sanctifying and maintaining the sanctity of the covenant people; hearing worshippers' confessions of faith and receiving their sacrifices of thanksgiving; supervision of the tabernacle; representing the work of mercy; teaching or supervising the instruction of God's people; keeping the written Book of the Covenant; and hearing cases of disagreement and disposing of them.[6]

The primary function of the office of prophet, narrowly considered, was serving as God's spokesman. More broadly considered, the prophet repeated, explained and applied the words of the Lord; led the people in proper response to the spoken and explicated Word; and served as an anointing agent.[7]

Of particular interest here is the threefold function of the anointed king: (1) to deliver the covenant people; (2) to rule over the covenant community; and (3) to shepherd the people of God, which included more nurturing aspects than merely ruling.[8]

---

5   Motyer, 'Messiah', p. 753.

6   Van Groningen, *Messianic Revelation*, 1:35-36 (the terms are taken verbatim from Van Groningen but not placed in quotations marks here in order to avoid excessive repetition of that punctuation; likewise for the next two paragraphs).

7   Van Groningen, *Messianic Revelation*, 1:36.

8   Van Groningen, *Messianic Revelation*, 1:36-37.

3. **Initially, the term *mashiach* was used of anointed persons generally, but toward the end of the Old Testament period it was applied to a specific expected Deliverer.**

The specific term *mashiach*, 'one who is anointed', occurs 38 times in the Old Testament. As Van Groningen observes, 'it was not used in the initial stages of the revelation of the messianic concept', that is, in reference to the ultimate deliverer of God's people.[9] In its initial occurrences it refers to the anointed priest in the context of instructions concerning Israel's system of sacrificial worship (Lev. 4:3, 5, 16; 6:22; about 1445 B.C.). It next appears early in 1 Samuel (2:10, 35; these events occurred about 1105 B.C.), apparently referring in prospect to the Davidic line of kings. Nearly two dozen occurrences follow in the books of Samuel, all in reference to Israel's king (Saul or David; about 1043–1011 B.C.). It occurs in 1 Chronicles 16:22 in a prayer of David in reference to the Israelites (1004 B.C.), and in 2 Chronicles 6:42 in a prayer of Solomon, most likely referring to David or Solomon. Most uses in the Psalms (about a dozen times; variously dated) refer to Israel's king. Isaiah 45:1, as already noted, speaks of the Persian emperor Cyrus as the LORD's anointed (about 700 B.C.). Habakkuk 3:13 (about 600 B.C.) uses the word either of the nation of Israel or of her king. Lamentations 4:20 (about 586 B.C.) applies the term to Judah's King Zedekiah, who was captured by the Babylonians.

Chronologically (according to the date of the events recorded), the last two occurrences of the word – Daniel 9:25, 26 – are the only ones in which it used as 'the official title of the central figure of expectation',[10] that is, of 'the Messiah'. Here it is translated 'Messiah' by some English versions (KJV; HCSB). Thus, 'as God's revelation progresses in the OT, *mashiach* takes the added nuance of an eschatological "Anointed One", who will appear in the last days. This person is clearly evident in Dan. 9:25-26....'[11]

---

9   Van Groningen, *Messianic Revelation*, 1:22.

10 Motyer, 'Messiah', p. 753.

11 William D. Mounce, gen. ed., *Mounce's Complete Expository Dictionary of Old & New Testament Words* (Grand Rapids: Zondervan, 2006), p. 25.

This analysis fits well with the resultant messianic expectation as described by Reymond: '"Messiah" or "Anointed One" came to be the most popular designation of the future Davidic Ruler who would usher in the promised eschatological Kingdom of God [the function of king] and represent the people before God [the function of priest] and God before the people [the function of prophet] in that Kingdom.'[12] It should be noted that while all three functions (and thus the corresponding offices) would be exercised by the expected Messiah, in ancient Israel the same person was not permitted to serve as king and as priest (these functions and offices were exercised by different tribes and thus different persons).

4. Features of the Messianic Office

1) God established in Israel the three anointed offices which Messiah would occupy. It was God who established the offices of prophet, priest and king. In God's providence, this set the stage for and prefigured the fullness of the work to be accomplished by the ultimate historical Messiah, Jesus of Nazareth. Van Groningen observes, 'As this revelation progressed and unfolded the various human messiahs [prophets, priests, and kings] who, along with events and phenomena, portrayed, prefigured, or foreshadowed the great coming Messiah and his work, increasingly gave clarity to the messianic concept; in time, the term *mashiach* came to designate him and his work.'[13]

2) The functions of Messiah would correspond to human need. The threefold office of the historical Messiah (prophet, priest and king) along with His dual nature (divine and human) would allow Him to serve as a singular and complete mediator between a holy God and sinful humans (1 Tim. 2:5). This corresponds to the threefold need all humans would experience as a result of the fall into rebellion against God's government. These included the need for infallible instruction in God's truth, forgiveness before God's law and a concrete representation of and means of submitting to God's rule. All are provided in Jesus the Messiah.

---

12 Reymond, *Jesus, Divine Messiah*, p. 45 n2.

13 Van Groningen, *Messianic Revelation*, 1:22-23.

APPLICATORY OBSERVATIONS:

1) Jesus the Messiah can perfectly meet the need of every human before a holy and just God. And He is the means that God Himself has provided, with the result that we may be assured of our complete acceptance before God as we put our trust in this Messiah.

2) The long period of promise and expectation served to demonstrate both the universal human need of a Deliverer and the natural inability of humans to meet that need on their own. Thus it was that 'when the time came to completion, God sent His Son, born of a woman, born under the law, to redeem those under the law, so that we might receive adoption as sons' (Gal. 4:4-5, HCSB).

II. Messiah and the Government of God

A multitude of Old Testament passages represent the future messianic figure as a ruling king and often more specifically portray Him as the agent of God or of God's own rule or government. A sampling of Old Testament passages relating to the reign of Messiah may be noted.

1. Genesis 49:10: 'The *scepter* shall not depart from Judah, nor the *ruler's staff* from between his feet, until tribute comes to him; and to him shall be the obedience of the peoples.' Here Jacob addresses his sons in view of his impending death. Passing over the three older sons with negative comments, he assigns preeminence to Judah. Apart from the various difficulties of interpreting this entire passage (49:8-12), its central idea, according to Van Groningen, seems to be that of 'royalty and the exercise of it by Judah', specifically 'the duration of Judah's royal preeminence, power, and authority, and his exercise of it.' Van Groningen believes that the passage refers to royal authority to be exercised by the tribe of Judah and eventually by a single 'personal Messiah', 'a ruler to whom people, at home and abroad, would surrender and offer homage.'[14] The emphasis here is upon the ruling function of this figure; it is natural to observe that King David, and later Jesus, arose from the tribe of Judah.

---

14   Van Groningen, *Messianic Revelation*, 1:167-85; citations from pp. 173, 183.

2. 2 Samuel 7:11-13, 16: '... the LORD will make you a house. When your days are fulfilled and you lie down with your fathers, I will raise up your offspring after you, who shall come from your body, and I will establish his kingdom. He shall build a house for my name, and I will establish the *throne* of his *kingdom* forever.... And your house and your *kingdom* shall be made sure forever before me. Your *throne* shall be established forever.'

In this passage, God promises to David to build for him a house (royal dynasty) which will continue in perpetuity. Van Groningen sees the 'messianic reference' here to be 'first of all to Solomon and to the sons to be born to David's and Solomon's descendants', a family, house and dynasty 'to be established firmly and for perpetuity'. Then 'from and through this dynasty, Yahweh would accomplish his purposes on behalf of his people. He would do this through the Messiah, the Christ, the Lord who would come forth from the dynasty Yahweh established with David and his seed.'[15] Thus, the emphasis of this passage is on the identity and function of messiah as royal descendant and ruling king.

3. Psalm 2:6-9: 'As for me, I have set my *King* on Zion, my holy hill.' Van Groningen regards this psalm as 'definitely messianic'. It portrays Jehovah as setting His 'anointed' (v. 2) King (who in the immediate historical context is David) on Mount Zion (v. 6) in opposition to the nations (v. 1), whose rulers 'exhort one another to rebellion against Yahweh and his *mashiach*.' The King represents Jehovah ('my King,' v. 6), He receives a kingdom which includes not only Israel but 'the nations' (v. 8), and His rule is absolute (v. 9). The Messiah (the term is used in verse 2) is here set forth in no uncertain terms as a reigning king.[16]

4. Psalm 110:1-2: 'The LORD says to my Lord: Sit at my right hand, until I make your enemies your footstool. The LORD sends forth from Zion your mighty *scepter*. *Rule* in the

---

15 Van Groningen, *Messianic Revelation*, 1:316-17.

16 Van Groningen, *Messianic Revelation*, 1:338, 337. In the symbolism of this psalm, Van Groningen seems to see an intimation of the divine nature of the future King (p. 338).

midst of your enemies!' This psalm is also messianic, and is one of the Old Testament passages most frequently quoted in the New Testament. David speaks of Jehovah as appointing David's Sovereign LORD ('my Lord' [*adoni*], v. 1, whom we should understand to be Messiah) to the position at His right hand. According to Van Groningen 'the right hand is the place of honor, power, and privilege. The command to sit gives the right and authority to occupy that position and the ruling function that accompanies it.' (Van Groningen emphasizes that this position and its privilege are not merely royal but divine: 'it is the reign of Yahweh that is transferred to "my Lord,"' thus intimating the divine nature of the person who occupies that position.) The language in verse 2 of 'rule' and the 'exercising of the scepter (carrying out the Law of Yahweh) ... is the means' by which the Messiah achieves His victory. While there is much else of interest in this psalm (especially the ascription of priesthood to the King [v. 4], contrary to the practice of historical Israel), sufficient has been noted to indicate the reigning function of Messiah.[17]

5. *Isaiah 9:6-7*: 'For to us a child is born, to us a son is given; and the *government* shall be upon his shoulder, and his name shall be called Wonderful Counselor, Mighty God, Everlasting Father, Prince of Peace. Of the increase of his *government* and of peace there will be no end, on the *throne* of David and over his *kingdom*, to establish it and to uphold it with justice and with righteousness from this time forth and forevermore. The zeal of the LORD of hosts will do this.'

The term translated 'government' in verse 6 is an unusual one, as pointed out by Van Groningen, and 'refers to princedom or royalty which is to be known by its exercise of the full authority of the highest ruling official in the land (world). This child or son will carry the complete responsibility of the royal house.'[18] The figure in view here is none other than a future Davidic king.

---

17 Van Groningen, *Messianic Revelation*, 1:390-97; citations from p. 392, 393. For comments on the priesthood of the King, see pp. 393-95.

18 Van Groningen, *Messianic Revelation*, 2:544.

6. Isaiah 11:1, 3b-4a, 10: 'There shall come forth a shoot from the stump of Jesse, and a branch from his roots shall bear fruit.... He shall not *judge* by what his eyes see, or *decide disputes* by what his ears hear, but with righteousness he shall *judge* the poor, and *decide* with equity for the meek of the earth; and he shall strike the earth with the rod of his mouth, and with the breath of his lips he shall kill the wicked.... In that day the root of Jesse, who shall stand as a signal for the peoples – of him shall the nations inquire, and his resting place shall be glorious.'

Van Groningen asserts that the theme of this entire chapter is 'the universal King'. The King in view here is of Davidic origin (11:1, 10a); possesses divine qualification (11:2-3a) and virtuous character (11:3b-5); will reign over the cosmos (11:6-9), over the nations (11:10), and over the exiles of Israel (11:11-16).[19] The verbs of 3b-4 indicate the activities of a ruler who exercises authority and judges evil in a righteous fashion. Verse 10 indicates that His reign 'will have universal impact', as He serves as a rallying point for the nations, who will seek him, and that His reigning place (implied: Zion) will be one of glory.

APPLICATORY OBSERVATIONS:

1) While it is true that Israel's Messiah would be more than a reigning king (He would also occupy the offices and perform the functions of a prophet and a priest), it is also certainly the case that He would be *no less than* a king. This suggests that a proper relationship to Messiah Jesus must be one which acknowledges His kingship as well as taking advantage of the benefits of His priesthood. He cannot be divided, and no one can partake of merely a portion of His work while rejecting the rest of it.

2) As is the case with many messianic prophecies, the prophecies noted here have both begun to be fulfilled in that historical work of Jesus of Nazareth already accomplished, and are yet to be fulfilled in their completeness in the future, at the consummation of this age upon His return. Christians today are

---

19   Van Groningen, *Messianic Revelation*, pp. 556-57; for the historical and literary context of this prophecy, see pp. 554-55.

those who live 'between the times', resting in His work already accomplished, and also looking forward to that which is yet to come. Thus we partake of the 'already' but 'not yet' nature of the divine work of salvation. We have entered into the enjoyment of that salvation during this present age but still await its future completion (see Phil. 1:6). This calls for understanding, patience, diligence and faithfulness in the present.

7. *Isaiah 42:1-4*: 'Behold my servant, whom I uphold, my chosen, in whom my soul delights; I have put my Spirit upon him; he will *bring forth justice* to the nations.... he will faithfully *bring forth justice*.... He will not grow faint or be discouraged till he has *established justice* in the earth; and the coastlands wait for *his law*.'

This passage is found in the first of the so-called 'Servant Songs' of Isaiah (42:1-7; 49:1-6; 50:4-9; 52:13–53:12). Here Jehovah introduces His individual Servant for the first time (national Israel had earlier been called His servant, 41:8-10). The Servant is the chosen one of God in whom God's soul delights and on whom God's Spirit has been placed (v. 1); this call and enablement will equip Him to bring justice to the nations, the first of three times here in which the Servant is said to establish justice, the function of a ruler. Concerning this first instance, Van Groningen says: 'The nations, considered here as national, politically organized entities, will continually receive this justice in a wide range of governmental activities ... because the Servant will cause this virtue to go out constantly.'[20]

The second instance, in verse 3b, reveals that the Servant will faithfully 'administer justice as king, judge, counselor, leader of hosts, and law maker.' The third instance of the use of the term is in verse 4, where it is connected with 'his law' or 'His instruction' (HCSB). Van Groningen prefers the latter, 'more inclusive meaning' of the term *torah*, because 'the Servant's ministry is reflected as having a wider range than just the judicial aspect.' The entire fourth verse affirms that 'with strength, stamina, courage, and steadfastness he will minister in all his royal capacities, continually, until he has accomplished what he has been given to do.'[21]

---

20 Van Groningen, *Messianic Revelation*, 2:584.

21 Van Groningen, *Messianic Revelation*, 2:585.

This passage envisions the Servant of the LORD exercising supreme governing authority, and doing so over all the earth. The entire passage is quoted in Matthew 12:18-21 to indicate the quiet, gentle authority with which Jesus conducted His earthly ministry.

8. Jeremiah 23:5: 'Behold, the days are coming, declares the LORD, when I will raise up for David a righteous Branch, and he shall *reign as king* and deal wisely, and shall *execute justice and righteousness* in the land.'

This verse follows upon a paragraph (23:1-4) in which the LORD denounces the rulers (shepherds) who destroy and scatter His people of Israel (sheep, flock), 1-2. He promises to re-gather a remnant of the flock (from exile) and bring them back to the land (v. 3), and to put faithful shepherds over them (v. 4). Whoever those faithful shepherds might have been (there were several during the post-exilic period), they were not the ultimate shepherd that God intended to provide for His people. In 23:5 God promised to (1) raise up a Davidic ruler (2) who would reign as king and (3) who would act prudently and (4) administer justice and righteousness. This will result in the salvation and security of His people (23:6a). The king who would accomplish all this shall be called 'Jehovah Our Righteousness' (v. 6b, ASV; there is no verb in the term, although some translations insert 'is' between 'Jehovah' and 'our').

The broader context of this prophecy (Jer. 21–22) involves the pronouncement of judgment on the last four kings of Judah by name (21:1; 22:11, 18, 24) and calls upon the house of David (21:11–22:9) to administer justice and righteousness (22:3), which these kings failed to do, but which is precisely what the promised Davidic king is said to accomplish (23:5b). Thus the ruler to come stands in stark contrast to the contemporary members of the Davidic dynasty. The name given to Him, 'Jehovah Our Righteousness', implies the divine nature (as well as human) of the Messiah, who becomes, according to the New Testament, 'the source, means, and guarantee of righteousness reckoned to those who by faith accept the

Messiah and his work as presented in the Scriptures'[22] (see Rom. 3:22; 5:17-19; 1 Cor. 1:30; 2 Cor. 5:21; Phil 3:9).

9. *Ezekiel 37:24, 25b*: 'My servant David shall be *king* over them, and they shall all have one shepherd. They shall walk in my rules and be careful to obey my statutes.... David my servant shall be their *prince* forever.' This prophecy occurs in the midst of a passage in which Jehovah promises to restore Israel after the exile, to reunite the nation, to cleanse them of their idolatries and apostasies, and to dwell with them forever (37:15-28). Among God's commitments is one to place a Davidic king over His people as a shepherd, one who will serve as their prince forever. With respect to these two terms 'king' and 'prince', Van Groningen says: 'Both nouns emphasize the royal character and status of David. The term *king* (which does specifically refer to one reigning on a throne) is used in this prophecy to emphasize the certainty of David's true and unique descendant being enthroned and actively functioning as such.'[23] The passage thus speaks of Messiah as a reigning king.

10. *Daniel 7:13-14*: 'I saw in the night visions, and behold, with the clouds of heaven there came one like a son of man, and he came to the Ancient of Days and was presented before him. And to him was given *dominion* and glory and a *kingdom*, that all peoples, nations, and languages should *serve him*; his *dominion* is an *everlasting dominion*, which shall not pass away, and his *kingdom* one that shall not be destroyed.'

In this highly controverted passage only a few bare features may be mentioned. Daniel, after describing a vision of four successive beasts representing four kingdoms (7:1-8), sees One on a throne who is called 'Ancient of Days', representing God presiding over a court of judgment (vv. 9-10). After the four beasts are disposed of (vv. 11-12), Daniel saw one 'like a son of man' brought before God; to this 'son of man' were given dominion, glory, and a kingdom which was to be universal and everlasting (v. 14). It is worthy of note that verse 14 multiplies

---

22 Van Groningen, *Messianic Revelation*, 2:706. He concurs with this understanding of the messianic name.

23 Van Groningen, *Messianic Revelation*, 2:780-81.

90

terms and phrases in describing the rule of this 'son of man', indicating that He was to be a reigning king. Van Groningen considers the passage to be messianic in its original intent.[24]

It may also be observed that the term 'son of man' was the favorite self-designation of Jesus, probably because it was *not* used as a messianic title in contemporary Judaism, and thus He could fill it with content appropriate to His ministry, which included suffering and dying as well as reigning. Jesus applied the passage directly to Himself in Matthew 26:64 (and parallels).

11. Micah 5:2: 'But you, O Bethlehem Ephrathah, who are too little to be among the clans of Judah, from you shall come forth for me one who is to be *ruler* in Israel, whose origin is from of old, from ancient days.' This verse, part of a larger passage describing the rule of Jehovah's king (5:1-6), was recognized in later Judaism as having messianic import (Matt. 2:1-6). The one 'coming forth' is said to be a 'ruler' in Israel as God's agent ('for me'), and the following verses describe His coming, His reign and its effects (vv. 3-6). Van Groningen argues that the language of the phrase 'to be a ruler over Israel' emphasizes the authority and activity of reigning.[25]

12. Zechariah 9:9: 'Rejoice greatly, O daughter of Zion! Shout aloud, O daughter of Jerusalem! Behold, your *king* is coming to you; righteous and having salvation is he, humble and mounted on a donkey, on a colt, the foal of a donkey.' This verse announces the coming to Jerusalem of its king. The following verses (vv. 10-17) describe some of the benefits of His reign, with verse 10 suggesting that it is not an ordinary king who is in view, for His reign will be one of universal dominion and peace. The passage thus must be considered messianic. Verse 9 is quoted in Matthew 21:5 and John 12:15 as fulfilled in Jesus' entry into Jerusalem. 'In this proclamation by Zechariah ... various elements of the Messiah's person, presence, and power ... are brought together.'[26]

---

24 Van Groningen, *Messianic Revelation*, 2:818.

25 Van Groningen, *Messianic Revelation*, 2:502.

26 Van Groningen, *Messianic Revelation*, 2:901; he discusses these aspects, pp. 899-902.

The passages collected here are sufficient to demonstrate that the Old Testament contained, prior to Jesus' coming, an expectation of a king who would rule as the agent of Jehovah. The various and sundry images used by the Old Testament prophets to portray God's coming kingdom and its king depict a reality which is both historical and trans-historical. That is, it will have its locus in human history, but its origin is from beyond human history. This dual reality is aptly described by New Testament scholar Martin Franzmann. 'One motif unites all the figures and is common to all the imagery, whether the Coming One is explicitly linked with the kingdom of God or not: God will in the latter days establish His reign, and that *in and through One whom He raises up in history* for a mission and a ministry in history.' 'Always,' Franzmann asserts, the hope of God's future kingdom 'is linked with the person and the work of the One who is to come in history.' And yet, though God's kingdom and God's King will be manifested on the stage of human history, it cannot be accounted for by mere human history.

> The kingdom which God is to establish in and through the Coming One breaks the limits of the merely historical. It transcends anything which men might expect from the normal course of historical development. The kingdom of God is not the development of forces latent in mankind and mankind's history. It comes by way of a radical break with the merely historical, by a direct intervention of God in history....

Franzmann's observations highlight the features of the Old Testament anticipation of Messiah: God will exercise His rule through One who will serve as His agent and who will be both a truly human figure appearing in real human history and at the same time One who will transcend the merely human and merely historical, One who is a divine figure as well. Thus it will be with His kingdom also: it will be manifest in history, but both its origin and its culmination are ultimately beyond the merely human historical sphere.[27]

---

27 Martin H. Franzmann, *Follow Me: Discipleship According to Saint Matthew* (St. Louis: Concordia, 1961), p. 21, italics added.

APPLICATORY OBSERVATIONS:

1) Some of these passages indicate the dual nature of Messiah's ministry. Psalm 110 portrays God's king as also a priest (v. 4), and Jeremiah 23:5 represents the Davidic king as serving also as His people's righteousness, a priestly function. This compound nature of Messiah's office and work indicates that He will redeem a people before He rules over them. This in turn is an expression of God's grand purpose of mercy: the great Messianic King will first die on behalf of rebels against His rule in order to make them the willing subjects of His reign when He assumes His throne. How grateful those subjects should be that they are the objects of such mercy!

2) Such passages also indicate the agency of the messianic rule in Jehovah's behalf. God has never relinquished His determination and purpose to re-establish His acknowledged rule among humans. What was perhaps unexpected was that God would exercise that rule through One who is Himself fully man while simultaneously exercising divine prerogatives, because He is the divine–human Messiah. As Paul says in Romans 11:33-36, how wondrous is the plan of God – and how worthy He is of our worship and praise – and submission!

III. Messiah as Agent of Divine Redemption

As well as the agent of divine rule, the Old Testament represents Messiah as the agent of divine redemption.

The Nature of the Redemption Accomplished by Messiah

There are Old Testament passages which describe the salvation which God shall bring about during the days of the Messiah. The most notable of these for the purposes of this study are those found in Jeremiah 31:31-34 and in Ezekiel 36:24-27 and 37:24.[28] The Jeremiah passage identifies the arrangement which God will institute as a 'new covenant' (Jer. 31:31), while the Ezekiel passages seem to describe a situation that

---

28 While only the last of these passages (Ezek.37:24) contains explicit mention of the messianic king, yet Van Groningen recognizes such passages generally as messianic in the wider sense, for they refer to the work which will be accomplished by the Messiah; see *Messianic Revelation*, 2:724.

is very much the same while identifying the effective agent as 'My servant David' (Ezek. 37:24) who 'shall be king over them', an apparent reference to the expected Davidic Messiah. In both cases a new relationship to God's law is envisioned.

Jeremiah 31:31 contains the first and only explicit mention in the Old Testament of a 'new covenant', language which was utilized by Jesus as He claimed to be instituting the 'new covenant' through His death, as recorded in Luke 22:20 and Matthew 26:28 (some Greek manuscripts). The Jeremiah passage was later taken up by the author of the Epistle to the Hebrews, who argued that Jesus was the guarantor and mediator of a new and better covenant (Heb. 7:22–10:18), and emphasized some features of the new covenant.

First, it is necessary to examine the Old Testament passages themselves.

1. The redemption or salvation wrought by God through the work of the Messiah is such that it brings about the willing submission of God's people to God's rule or government.

The central point to be observed in both the Jeremiah and Ezekiel passages is that the new situation that will be brought to pass by God's action through Messiah involves the genuine and heartfelt submission of God's people to His government as expressed in His law.

1) Jeremiah 31:31-34: 'Behold, the days are coming, declares the LORD, when *I will make a new covenant* with the house of Israel and the house of Judah, not like the covenant that I made with their fathers on the day when I took them by the hand to bring them out of the land of Egypt, my covenant that they broke, though I was their husband, declares the LORD. But *this is the covenant* that I will make with the house of Israel after those days, declares the LORD: *I will put my law within them*, and I will write it on their hearts. And *I will be their God, and they shall be my people*. And no longer shall each one teach his neighbor and each his brother, saying, "Know the LORD," for *they shall all know me*, from the least of them to the greatest, declares the LORD. For *I will forgive their iniquity*, and I will remember their sin no more.'

This passage occurs within a context of encouragement and hope for the people of Israel (Jer. 30–31). As the culmination of God's promise to restore the fortunes of His people, the LORD declared that He would establish a new covenant with His people Israel (31:31-40). This new covenant would present a sharp contrast with that one which He made with them when He brought them from the land of Egypt, namely, the Mosaic Covenant, which they broke or nullified.[29]

Arguably there are four specific elements contained in this description of the features of the new covenant.

(a) *God's law written on the heart (v. 33b)*. In contrast to the Mosaic Covenant, in which the law of God was disclosed externally on graven tablets of stone (it was only the Ten Commandments which were thus revealed), the New Covenant will involve the writing of God's law on the human heart. This involves an internal expression and validation of the law ('I will put my law within them'), suggesting personal regeneration and a heart inclined toward submission to God's law rather than hostility to it.

(b) *Personal commitment in a binding relationship (v. 33c)*. Jehovah had earlier promised to take national Israel as His people if they would obey Him (Exod. 19:5), and He required them to acknowledge Him alone as their God (Exod. 20:2-3). This involved a binding covenant relationship for both parties, but national Israel had violated the terms of the covenant by their idolatry and was about to suffer (in Jeremiah's time) the penalties of disobedience. The New Covenant, involving as it would an individual relationship of personal commitment (as the writing of the

---

29 For the argument that Israel 'nullified' the Mosaic Covenant rather than merely 'broke' it, see Robertson, *Christ of the Covenants*, pp. 284-85. It may be observed that some scholars minimize the feature of 'newness' in the New Covenant; see Van Groningen, *Messianic Revelation*, 2:721-24, where he prefers the idea of 'renewal'. Others emphasize the element of 'newness': Fred A. Malone, *The Baptism of Disciples Alone: A Covenantal Argument For Credobaptism Versus Paedobaptism*, 2nd ed. (Cape Coral, FL: Founders Press, 2007), pp. 82-83; Robertson, *Christ of the Covenants*, p. 281. The agreement of the latter two authors indicates it is not merely a matter of paedobaptist vs. Baptist views.

law on the heart implies), must necessarily take this binding relationship to a deeper level, no longer one of merely national and corporate relationship, but one binding the individual human soul to God. Such a binding relationship is inherent in the covenant concept.

(c) *Personal knowledge of God (v. 34a, b)*. It will not be necessary for members of the New Covenant community to exhort one another to 'know the LORD' for they shall each one know Him – 'they shall all know Me' – in personal relationship. This feature stands in contrast to the Mosaic Covenant in which the majority of those in the covenant community did *not* know God, as demonstrated by their actions (see, e.g., the parable of Ezekiel 16). Rather, among the new people of God, the personal knowledge of God shall be a universal characteristic of the covenant community. External rank will be no factor or hindrance ('from the least of them to the greatest') in a person's relationship to God. This feature, taken as a whole, also implies the grace of regeneration for all the participants in the New Covenant.

(d) *Forgiveness of sin (v. 34c)*. The basis for each member of the New Covenant community possessing a personal knowledge of God ('for') is that they shall all be forgiven. Forgiveness of sins removes the barrier to a personal relationship with God, and all members of the New Covenant community will enjoy this benefit (as implied in the previous qualification that 'all' shall know Jehovah) because He will forgive their sins.

It appears that a distinctive feature of the New Covenant, as pointed out by Fred Malone, is that the blessings of the New Covenant shall be realized for each member of the New Covenant community. There shall be no one in this community who does not have the law written on his heart, who does not take Jehovah as his God, who does not possess the knowledge of God, who does not enjoy forgiveness of sin. This is the emphasis expressed in Jeremiah's use of the term 'all' in 31:34. These were potential benefits to the individual Israelite under the Old Covenant; they shall be the realized possession of each and every member of the New Covenant people of God.[30] This implies a stance for each member of the New Covenant community (that is, each person who is truly under the New Covenant by virtue of regeneration) of *substantial submission to the government of God*. It cannot be otherwise.

2) Ezekiel 36:24-27; 37:24: 'I will take you from the nations and gather you from all the countries and bring you into your own land. I will sprinkle clean water on you, and *you shall be clean from all your uncleannesses*, and from all your idols I will cleanse you. And *I will give you a new heart*, and a new spirit I will put within you. And I will remove the heart of stone from your flesh and give you a heart of flesh. And *I will put my Spirit within you*, and *cause you to walk in my statutes and be careful to obey my rules.*'

'*My servant David shall be king over them*, and they shall have one shepherd. *They shall walk in my rules* and be careful to *obey my statutes.*'

These passages also occur in a context of the promise of restoration from the Babylonian exile. They look, however, to a period and a condition far beyond the physical return from exile which the Israelites experienced upon being released by Cyrus the Persian to return to their homeland, for they describe a situation very much like that of the New Covenant passage of Jeremiah. Again it seems that four features are evident.

(a) *Cleansing from sin (36:25)*. The sprinkling of clean water (25a) seems to symbolize the cleansing, or forgiveness, spoken of in 25b and 25c. It is from uncleannesses and idolatries into which Israel had fallen that she would need cleansing, and Jehovah will provide such cleansing.

(b) *A new heart (36:26)*. The provision as well of a new heart is expressed not only in that exact phrase but also as the installation of a new spirit and the replacing of a heart of stone with a heart of flesh. Such language seems to imply regeneration (in New Testament terms).

(c) *Indwelling of the Holy Spirit (36:27a)*. Jehovah says that He will put His Spirit within them, apparently to remain as

---

30 Malone, *Baptism of Disciples Alone*, 84-86.

an indwelling presence. It is the Spirit who is responsible for the renewal spoken of in the previous verse. This is explicitly a benefit of the New Covenant of Messiah (Acts 2:16-21, quoting Joel 2:28-32; Acts 2:33, 38).

(d) *Obedience to God's law (36:27b, 37:24).* Most germane to the topic of current concern, those who are the objects of this work of God are said to be caused to walk (live) in His statutes and be careful to obey His rules. This represents a heart willingness to submit to God's government as expressed in His law as an integral feature of the new situation that God shall bring about.

The same thought is expressed in Ezekiel 37:24, which is a more explicitly messianic passage. The rule of the Davidic king shall bring about the condition that God's people will walk in His rules and obey His statutes. Again this implies submission to God's rule as exercised through His king. Both these passages represent a parallel to and advance upon the statement of the Jeremiah passage that God would put His law in the heart of His people; now it is explicitly said that they will obey it. Again there is present here the feature of substantial submission to the government of God.

2. The fulfillment of these messianic promises is to be found in the new conditions which God has brought to pass through the person and work of Messiah Jesus, as expounded by the entire New Testament.

The references to Israel in the Old Testament texts should probably be understood to find their fulfillment in an 'expanded' Israel under the New Covenant, a body which includes Gentiles who place their faith in Messiah (Christ) Jesus. The imagery of the New Testament suggests a broadened concept of 'Israel' which involves Gentile believers who enjoy, along with ethnic Israelite believers, the benefits of the New Covenant (see Rom. 11:17-24; Eph. 2:11–3:12). Likewise, it is probably in such a fashion that Paul's reference to 'the Israel of God' in Galatians 6:16 is to be understood, that is, as including Gentile believers in Jesus the Messiah (see Paul's argument in Galatians 4:21-31, where Gentile believers are said to belong to 'the Jerusalem above', v. 26, and where Paul finds the fulfillment of the promises of blessing upon Zion in Isaiah 54:1 as including converted Gentiles, vv. 27-28).[31]

APPLICATORY OBSERVATIONS:

1) The contrast established between the provisions of the Mosaic Covenant (an external administration of God's law) and the New Covenant (an internal administration) may encourage Christian believers to be grateful that they live under the new arrangement. Greater benefits accrue to believers under the New Covenant than under the Old.

2) Gentile believers in Messiah Jesus may be thankful that God has expanded the boundaries of His people to include those who were formerly excluded. It is surely a great mercy that God has shown such grace to undeserving Gentiles.

3) The Jeremiah and Ezekiel passages show that God intended His New Covenant people to exhibit the reality of a substantial degree of submission to His government – His rule over their lives – in contrast to their former way of life and in contrast to the surrounding world (Eph. 2:1-3). The exhibition of this reality is one basis of their assurance that they indeed are under the New Covenant (see Chapter 10 below); the lack of it raises the question of whether they truly possess the salvation which the New Covenant brings.

---

31 For a treatment of the phrase 'the Israel of God' in Galatians 6:16 which supports this interpretation, see O. Palmer Robertson, *The Israel of God: Yesterday, Today, and Tomorrow* (Phillipsburg, NJ: P&R, 2000), 38-46.

PART TWO

THE HISTORICAL ESTABLISHMENT OF JESUS' LORDSHIP

4

The Prophetic Function of Jesus the Messiah:

Proclaiming God's Lordship through the Kingdom of God

INTRODUCTION: MESSIAH'S PROPHETIC FUNCTION AND THE GOVERNMENT OF GOD

As the New Testament opens it presents Jesus as the Messiah of Old Testament expectation. Matthew 1:1 applies the term *christos* ('anointed,' the Greek equivalent of the Hebrew *mashiach*) to Jesus, and the term is used again in 1:16, 1:17, and 1:18. The occurrence in 1:17 is accompanied by the definite article, indicating that it is the office of Messiah which is in view here and suggesting that the term is used as a title, not merely as a proper name.

Not only is Jesus introduced immediately as Messiah, He is portrayed as fulfilling the three anointed functions of king, priest and prophet. These official functions all relate to the government of God: the prophetic, in announcing its presence in a new way; the priestly, in interceding with respect to its judgment against sin; and the kingly, in exercising its ruling authority, all of which Jesus is presented in Matthew's Gospel as accomplishing.

The kingly function is foremost in Matthew's emphasis early on, with Jesus being identified as a descendant of David in 1:1 (David 'the king' in 1:6). The legal descent of Jesus from Abraham and David through the reigning line of Davidic descendants is demonstrated through the genealogy of His adoptive father Joseph, provided in 1:2-17.

The priestly function of Jesus is intimated in the angel's assertion in 1:21 that 'he will save his people from their sins', for it was part of the Old Testament priests' office to deal with the people's sins through their ritual ministrations (though no true and final atonement could be provided by the Old Testament sacrifices). A hint of the priestly function is also seen (by hindsight, perhaps) in Jesus' assertion that John the Baptist should proceed to baptize Him in order 'to fulfill all righteousness' (3:15; see the treatment of Jesus' baptism later in this study).

But it is the prophetic function that is brought to the forefront in Matthew's account of Jesus' active ministry. Its description of the beginning of the public ministry of Jesus finds His initial activity to be that of preaching (Matt. 4:17), that is, functioning as a prophet who proclaims God's message. Further, the central element in His preaching is the proclamation of the government of God and its arrival in His own person (although the latter element is often present in a veiled fashion). This emphasis is particularly to be seen in the centrality of the concept of the 'kingdom of God' in the public ministry of both Jesus and His forerunner, John the Baptist.

I. Jesus' Initial Preaching: The Arrival of God's Kingdom

As the New Testament era opens with the public ministry of its two initial heralds (approximately A.D. 26–27), the burden of the proclamation of both was the arrival of God's kingdom. The rough figure of John the Baptist appeared first, Elijah-like in his visage, manner and message. John called for repentance in light of the near approach of God's kingdom: 'Repent, for the kingdom of heaven is at hand' (Matt. 3:2). The same was true of Jesus.

1. Jesus proclaimed the approach of the kingdom of God and the need for the appropriate human response to it.

After His baptism and temptation, and after the arrest of John, Jesus appeared in Galilee, preaching the same message that John had proclaimed: 'From that time Jesus began to preach, saying, "Repent, for the kingdom of heaven is at hand"' (Matt. 4:17; the message of Jesus is verbally identical to that of John).[1] The difference between the two was that John was merely the appointed herald of the kingdom while Jesus was the Anointed Bringer of the kingdom. Matthew introduces John by citing Isaiah 40:3, describing a herald who prepares for the coming of the LORD God (Matt. 3:1-3). He introduces Jesus' preaching in Galilee by citing Isaiah 9:1-2, which speaks of a great light dawning upon that region (Matt. 4:12-16). But the passage in Isaiah 9 goes on to say:

> For to us a child is born, to us a son is given;
> and the *government* shall be upon his shoulder,
> and his name shall be called Wonderful Counselor, Mighty God,
> Everlasting Father, Prince of Peace.
> Of the increase of his *government* and of peace there will be no end,
> on the *throne* of David and over his *kingdom*, to establish it and to uphold it
> with justice and with righteousness from this time forth and forevermore.
> The zeal of the LORD of hosts will do this (Isa. 9:6-7, italics added).

The intervening verses (9:3-5, English) speak of the overcoming of Israel's enemies. Matthew's implication seems to be that Jesus Himself is the one on whose shoulder the government shall rest, the one of whom it could be said that 'of the increase of his government there shall be no end'.

Thus the New Testament in its opening pages draws attention to the government of God under the terminology of 'the kingdom of heaven' (conceptually identical to 'the kingdom of God') and to the role of Jesus as the agent of the bringing of that kingdom to men. Biblical theologians such as Geerhardus Vos and George Eldon Ladd and other

---

1   The significance of this proclamation by Jesus is emphasized by I. Howard Marshall, who observes that the parallel account in Mark 1:14-15 presents Jesus' proclamation of the coming of the kingdom as Jesus' *only* message to the general public in Mark's Gospel, thus pointing up the crucial importance of this element of Jesus' ministry (*New Testament Theology: Many Witnesses, One Gospel* [Downers Grove, IL: InterVarsity, 2004], p. 60.

modern scholars have expended considerable effort toward determining and elucidating the nature of the kingdom of God and its coming, and the relationship of Jesus to that kingdom. Ladd summarizes his findings in the following way:

> Our central thesis is that the Kingdom of God is the redemptive reign of God dynamically active to establish his rule among men, and that this Kingdom, which will appear as an apocalyptic act at the end of the age, has already come into human history in the person and mission of Jesus to overcome evil, to deliver men from its power, and to bring them into the blessings of God's reign. The Kingdom of God involves two great moments: fulfillment within history, and consummation at the end of history.[2]

Several elements are evident in Ladd's summary:

1) The kingdom of God is redemptive. That is, the kingdom is intended to overturn in some fashion the effects of the human rebellion against God and bring humans into a right relationship with God.

2) The kingdom is God's reign, dynamically active among humans. The kingdom is primarily *God reigning*, His activity of exercising kingly authority, and only secondarily the domain over which He reigns.[3]

3) Its purpose is to establish God's rule among humans. That is, the kingdom involves God's active presence in human history to bless and to judge, and to be acknowledged and received by human beings. It is this reception which Jesus (and John) indicated by His exhortation, '*Repent*, for the kingdom of heaven is at hand.' The appropriate human response to the arrival of God's kingdom is to adopt a different, receptive attitude toward God's rule and to live accordingly (Matt. 3:7-10; 4:17; Mark 1:14-15; Luke 3:7-14).

4) The kingdom has appeared in the person and mission of Jesus. The kingdom of God has entered into human history through Jesus' own person and ministry to bring its blessings and benefits in advance of the final consummation of all things.

---

2 George Eldon Ladd, *A Theology of the New Testament* (Grand Rapids: Eerdmans, 1974), p. 91.

3 Ladd, *Theology*, p. 63.

Several sayings of Jesus indicate that the kingdom of God was a present reality in the context of His ministry (Matt. 11:11-13; 12:28; 21:31; 23:13; Luke 17:20-21).

5) The kingdom will be consummated at the end of the present age. In a climactic way, God will bring the kingdom to its full manifestation and consummation at the end of this age (Matt. 7:21-23; 8:11; 13:41; 25:34). Vos is in substantial agreement with Ladd's portrayal of a two-stage coming of the kingdom: 'our Lord's conception was that of one kingdom coming in two successive stages.'[4]

2. The new order is designated 'the kingdom of God' because it is an expression of God's supremacy, power, righteousness and sovereign graciousness.

The question might be asked: Why is this new order of things called 'the kingdom of God'? What is the significance of the term 'kingdom' as applied to this new arrangement which both John and Jesus heralded as near at hand? Vos addresses this question and suggests that Jesus' parabolic and other teaching emphasizes four recurring aspects of this new order which explain why the term 'kingdom of God' is applied to it.

1) 'Kingdom of God' expresses God's supremacy. The term 'kingdom of God' is used 'because in it as a whole and in every part of it *God is supreme.*' That is, 'everything is in its ultimate analysis intended for the glory of God.' This is indicated by the pattern of prayer which Jesus provided for His disciples: 'Our Father in heaven, hallowed be *your* name. *Your* kingdom come, *your* will be done, on earth as it is in heaven (Matt. 6:9b-10). As Vos observes: 'because the kingdom is thus centered in God Himself and in His glory, it can be represented by our Lord as the highest object after which men are to strive.' The centrality of the honoring of God's name, the advancing of His kingdom and the doing of His will all witness to the supremacy of God in His kingdom.[5]

---

4   Geerhardus Vos, 'The Kingdom of God,' in *Redemptive History and Biblical Interpretation: The Shorter Writings of Geerhardus Vos*, ed. Richard B. Gaffin, Jr. (Phillipsburg, NJ: Presbyterian and Reformed, 1980), pp. 304-16, citation from p. 309.

5   Vos, 'Kingdom of God,' p. 311, italics added.

2) *'Kingdom of God' expresses God's power.* This new order is called God's kingdom because 'it is the sphere in which God manifests his supreme, royal *power.*' It is, says Vos, 'a kingdom of conquest', conquering, in its present manifestation, Satan, sin and death. 'If it is by the Spirit of God that I cast out demons,' Jesus said, 'then the kingdom of God has come upon you' (Matt. 12:28). And Vos observes: 'All the miracles, not merely the casting out of demons, find their interpretation in this feature. The powers which will revolutionize heaven and earth are already in motion.'[6]

3) *'Kingdom of God' expresses God's righteousness.* The kingdom 'is the sphere in which *God as the Supreme Ruler and Judge* carries out His holy will in righteousness and judgment.' Vos points out that the verb 'to judge' as used in the Bible often carries the meaning of 'to reign or rule' (as in Matthew 19:28), and that 'the kingdom is represented by our Lord not merely as involving the judging activity of God, but likewise as identical with righteousness' (Matt. 6:33), meaning here that 'the standard, the norm of righteousness, in the kingdom of God lies in God himself.' God's reign is exercised in accord with His own holy character, which becomes the standard or norm of righteousness in His kingdom, and to which all its citizens are to aspire.[7]

4) *'Kingdom of God' expresses God's sovereign graciousness.* This order is called the kingdom of God because 'all its blessings are gifts *sovereignly and graciously bestowed* by God'. Whether under the image of a royal banquet (Matt. 8:10-11; 22:1-14) or that of a gracious father (Matt. 25:34), the teaching of Jesus presents God as the beneficent bestower of all good things to citizens of His kingdom. 'To the kingdom belong all the gifts of grace – the forgiveness of sins, the reception into sonship, the enjoyment of the love of God, the bestowal of life – in short, the entire content of the idea of salvation in its widest range.'[8]

---

6   Vos, 'Kingdom of God', p. 312, italics added.

7   Vos, 'Kingdom of God', pp. 313-14, citations from p. 313, italics added.

8   Vos, 'Kingdom of God', pp. 314-15, italics added.

In sum, adds Vos, 'In all the four aspects enumerated the designation "kingdom of God" rests upon the abstract conception of the *divine rule* exercised and carried through in the work of salvation.' This new spiritual (in this age) order is the expression and manifestation of God's kingly rule exercised in the creation of a new people of God who willingly see themselves as rightly under the government of God, enjoy its benefits, and seek for its extension in the world. The idea of an authoritative divine rule could hardly be more emphatically underlined by Jesus than through the use of this concept.[9]

APPLICATORY OBSERVATIONS:

1) If the kingdom of God is the overriding burden of Jesus' message, then this concept is crucially central to a proper understanding of the significance of His person and work and of the rest of the New Testament. Christians must apply themselves to gaining a grasp of this concept if the message of the New Testament is to be properly understood.

2) If God expresses the heart of His relationship to humans by means of the concept of His kingdom, then those who profess to know Him can best demonstrate that reality by their submission and obedience to His rule. Any other stance belies what they claim.

II. The Sermon on the Mount: The Standards of God's Kingdom

Not only did Jesus' initial preaching center upon the kingdom of God but so also did His instruction of His disciples as to the nature of discipleship. Matthew's account of Jesus' teaching in this regard is found in chapters 5 through 7 of his Gospel, a section commonly known as the 'Sermon on the Mount'. It is instructive to note the centrality of the idea of the kingdom of God in this discourse. The first and last beatitudes (encompassing all the rest, in the rhetorical technique called

---

9   Vos, 'Kingdom of God', p. 315, italics added. It must be recognized that these four aspects by no means exhaust or even adequately explain the full significance of the biblical idea of the kingdom of God.

inclusio or inclusion[10]) promise the blessing of the possession of the kingdom (Matt. 5:3, 10). The relation of the disciple to the teaching and doing of the Law has a role in determining his standing in the kingdom (5:19). Entrance into the kingdom requires possessing a righteousness exceeding that of the scribes and Pharisees (5:20). The disciple is to pray daily for the coming of the kingdom (6:10) and is to give priority in his life to seeking that kingdom (6:33). Entrance into the kingdom is dependent on knowing Jesus and doing the will of God (7:21-23). In short, the entire teaching of the Sermon on the Mount seems to be circumscribed by and suffused with the idea of the kingdom of God.

The theme of the Sermon on the Mount thus seems to be that of 'discipleship and the kingdom of God'. It constitutes Jesus' instruction to His disciples ('his disciples came to him. ... he ... taught them,' 5:1-2) about the privileges and demands placed upon them by virtue of their repentance in light of the approach of God's kingdom (4:17) and their following of Jesus (4:18-22). Jesus' further preaching of the good news about the kingdom of God and His healing activity (4:23) had attracted great crowds (4:24-25). Apparently He sought at this point to explain the obligations placed on His disciples by their commitment to Him and their newfound association with the kingdom of God (it is instructive that the two are linked together).

In the Sermon on the Mount, Jesus called for a complete reorientation of His disciples' lives toward the claims of the kingdom of God. The resulting instruction may be analyzed as follows.

1. Discipleship means exhibiting the values of the kingdom (5:3-12).

As the first and last beatitudes specifically mention the kingdom of God, all the beatitudes may be understood as describing the

---

10 D. A. Carson, *The Sermon on the Mount: An Evangelical Exposition of Matthew 5–7* (Grand Rapids: Baker, 1978), p. 16; Grant R. Osborne, *The Hermeneutical Spiral: A Comprehensive Introduction to Biblical Interpretation* (Downers Grove, IL: InterVarsity, 1991), p. 39.

attitudes or mentality of one who has by God's mercy come to enjoy the blessings of His kingdom – His redemptive reign. The result is that a new set of attitudes and values comes to prevail in the disciple's life, attitudes and values which are countercultural, standing in sharp contrast to those of the surrounding world. The mentality of the kingdom places high value on an awareness of one's personal sinfulness, with the resultant sorrow and humility and sense of need (5:3-6), and consequently a spirit of gentleness and compassion toward others (5:7-10). Verses 11-12 are an expansion upon the last blessing, pronounced upon those who suffer persecution for the sake of righteousness (v. 10; tellingly, Jesus makes it 'on my account' in verse 11). New Testament scholar R. T. France suggests understanding the pronouncement of blessing found in each beatitude in the sense of 'to be congratulated' or 'good for you!'; such a person has developed that set of values and attitudes which God most prizes in people.[11]

2. Discipleship means manifesting the works of the kingdom (5:13-16).

Jesus compared His disciples to salt and light in the world of corruption and darkness. Their transformed lifestyle is to be evident to those around them so that God may be praised on account of them.

3. Discipleship means exercising a heightened degree of submission to the law of God (5:17-48).

Jesus made it clear that the kingdom of God and discipleship to Himself do not involve any lesser degree of conformity to the express will of God, but rather a higher degree (5:17-20). He went on to explain that the law of God is to rule in the heart and mind, in contrast to merely external observance or humanly-devised distortions of the law. Jesus provided examples of this principle with respect to murder and anger (5:21-26); adultery and lust (5:27-30) and the related matter of divorce (5:31-32); oaths (5:33-37); retaliation (5:38-42); and love for

---

11 R. T. France, *Matthew*, TNTC (Grand Rapids: Eerdmans, 1985), pp. 108-109; *Gospel of Matthew*, NICNT (Grand Rapids: Eerdmans, 2007), pp. 160-61.

others (5:43-48). God's law, of course, is an expression of His government, and Jesus' standards simply apply the demand for submission to the inner recesses of the human heart and not just to external actions. His disciples are to reflect the reality of the law placed 'within them' and 'written on the heart' as promised in the New Covenant (Jer. 31:33).

4. Discipleship means developing a concern for God's approval rather than man's (6:1-18).

Another expression of the disciple seeing himself as under God's rule is to be found in how he approaches traditional acts of piety. Jesus laid down the principle that such actions of 'righteousness' are not to be performed for the observation and praise of people but of God alone (6:1). The issue here is that of motive and the intended audience of one's actions, not necessarily whether other people see them. Jesus applied the principle to such activities as charitable giving (6:2-4), praying (6:5-13, with an expansion, 14-15) and fasting (6:16-18).

5. Discipleship means pursuing God's kingdom as one's first priority and avoiding anxiety over one's material needs (6:19-34).

Living under God's rule requires a reorientation toward laying up heavenly treasures rather than earthly ones (6:19-21) and living with singlemindedness toward God in contrast to slavery to money (6:22-24). The common human material needs of food and drink, clothing and shelter, are not to be the consuming passion of the disciple, as they are for much of the world; rather, the disciple is to seek God's kingdom and righteousness as his first priority, and God will in turn provide for his needs (6:25-34).

6. Discipleship means avoiding self-righteous judgment of fellow disciples while at the same time exercising due discernment (7:1-6).

The admonition here is not to exercise no judgment at all but to avoid judgment which is self-righteous, ignoring one's own failings (7:3-5) and to be aware that the standard that one applies to others will be applied to oneself (7:2). The language of 'brother', used in verses 3-5, indicates that it is specifically this type of unworthy judging within the community of disciples that Jesus has in view (passages such as Matthew 18:15-20; and 1 Corinthians 5:12 in context, indicate that the disciple community is indeed to exercise discerning judgment and remedial discipline upon its own members). At the same time, due discernment is to be exercised (7:6) in determining that some people may manifest such an unappreciative attitude and hostile opposition to the kingdom message that further attention to them is unprofitable at the present time.

7. Discipleship means approaching God with kingdom or personal concerns while maintaining a generous spirit toward others (7:7-12).

The disciple living under God's rule and care, is to approach his heavenly Father with his needs and concerns, confident that God will give that which is good (7:7-11). In turn, disciples are to relate to all people (not just other disciples) in the same way, seeking their good (as measured by that treatment which the disciple would prefer for himself). Significantly, Jesus remarks that this latter principle is the sum of Old Testament teaching (7:12).

8. Discipleship involves entering the kingdom of God by the narrow way, being alert for false teachers and doing the will of God (7:13-23).

Entering 'life' (=eternal life, 7:14) is coordinate with entering the kingdom (in its consummation, 7:21), for eternal life is one of the blessings of the kingdom of God. Jesus warns His disciples that the way of entry to the kingdom and its eternal life is narrow and difficult (but of course worth it; 7:13-14). And there will be false teachers ('prophets' who claim to speak for God but do not) who will seek to deflect people from the true path. They can be recognized by their unrighteous fruit (personal lifestyle, result of ministry; 7:15-20). The mere claim to be a disciple of Jesus (and even performing acts of ministry) is not sufficient to secure one's entry into the consummated kingdom, for only the doing of God's will genuinely reflects the reality of the inward reorientation of the professed disciple to the reign of God. All other claims will come to nothing and will bring rejection by the King and Judge (who happens to be Jesus Himself; 7:21-23).

9. Discipleship means acting positively and decisively in response to Jesus' teaching (7:24-27).

Jesus concluded with a call to action in response to His teaching. To build one's life on Jesus' message would be wise, like building a house on a rock foundation (7:24-25). To refuse His message would be foolish, like building a house on sand (7:26-27). Like the other demands of the kingdom of God, there is no middle ground here; one's stance is either one of wholehearted commitment or complete rejection of the claims of Jesus and the kingdom of God. And the issues are those of life and death.

Summary: Jesus' prophetic ministry as Messiah involved not merely His calling people to repentance and discipleship to Himself, but also His setting forth of the claims of the government of God upon them. The disciple of Jesus is to live a life that is radically reoriented to the claims of God's redemptive reign.

APPLICATORY OBSERVATION

The overwhelming impression created when one is confronted with the entire Sermon on the Mount at one time is the sense of uncompromising stringency in the claims of God's kingdom on the life of the disciple. It is a call that can be received or rejected, but it is not one that can be moderated or conformed to human desires. It becomes a personal decision of all or nothing for God's kingdom. That seems to be the way Jesus intended it. Its demands implicitly involve the practical renunciation of personal autonomy and the recognition of God's right to rule one's life.

III. The Parables of the Kingdom: The Manifestation of God's Kingdom

The nature of the kingdom of God, and of Jesus' own role in the advent of the kingdom, is also expressed in the parables of the kingdom found in Matthew 13 and Mark 4. In Matthew's account, there are seven parables, interspersed with three interludes of comment about Jesus' practice of teaching in parables. Several features of the passage are significant for the present discussion.

1. All of this parabolic teaching is explicitly related to the kingdom of God.

The parable of the sower (Matt. 13:3-9; the terminology is that of Jesus, 13:18) is explained by Jesus (13:18-23) as involving the varying reception afforded the 'word of the kingdom' (13:19). The other six parables are introduced by Jesus as providing a simile to the kingdom. The parables of the weeds (13:24-30; its interpretation, 13:36-43, mentions the kingdom three times, 13:38, 41, 43), of the mustard seed (13:31-32), of the leaven (13:33), of the hidden treasure (13:44), of the pearl of great value (13:45-46), and of the net (13:47-50) are all introduced by the formula 'the kingdom of heaven may be compared to' or 'is like' (13:24, 31, 33, 44, 45, 47). There can be little doubt that Jesus' instruction in these parables relates to the kingdom of God.

2. Jesus' explanation of His purpose in utilizing parabolic teaching emphasizes His disciples' privileged stance in witnessing and understanding the coming of the kingdom of God (13:10-17).

When Jesus' disciples asked, after His telling of the parable of the sower, why He used parables to speak to the crowd, He replied, 'To you [the disciples] it has been given to know the secrets of the kingdom of heaven, but to them [the crowd; 'those outside,' Mark 4:11] it has not been given' (13:11). The term 'secrets' translates the Greek *mysterion* (in the plural, though Mark has it in the singular, 4:11), meaning 'the secret thoughts, plans, and dispensations of God which are hidden from human reason, as well as from all other comprehension below the divine level, and await either fulfillment or revelation [as in this case] to those to whom they were intended.'[12] Thus

---

12 Frederick William Danker, *A Greek–English Lexicon of the New Testament and other Early Christian Literature*, 3rd ed. (Chicago: University of Chicago Press, 2000), p. 662. Hereinafter this work will be abbreviated BDAG (for Bauer–Danker–Arndt–Gingrich), as recommended on the title page.

the positive purpose of these parables is to disclose the mystery of the kingdom to Jesus' disciples. George Ladd argues with a good deal of persuasiveness that the 'mystery of the kingdom' is 'the coming of the Kingdom into history in advance of its apocalyptic manifestation. It is, in short, "fulfillment without consummation."' The role of Jesus in this newly-given revelation is central. Ladd again:

> The mystery is a new disclosure of God's purpose for the establishment of his Kingdom. The new truth, now given to men by revelation in the person and mission of Jesus, is that the Kingdom that is to come finally in apocalyptic power, as foreseen in Daniel, has in fact entered the world in advance in a hidden form to work secretly within and among men.

Ladd maintains that the purpose of Jesus' parables of the kingdom is to state this single truth (or aspects of it).[13] Jesus' disciples occupy the uniquely privileged position of being able to witness the arrival of God's kingdom, an event that earlier generations of God's people could only long for (13:16-17). Thus also, as Ladd points out, the appropriate context for the proper understanding of Jesus' kingdom parables was Jesus' own earthly ministry.[14]

The negative purpose of the kingdom parables (Matt. 13:12b-15) was to conceal the truth of the kingdom from those who were not receptive to the kingdom. Matthew's account states the reason as 'because' (*hoti*) and Mark's as 'so that' (*hina*) they do not understand, but the reality includes both: continued failure to understand is a judgment upon their unbelief. As Franzmann puts it, 'the revelation which enriches the believing disciple becomes an instrument of judgment on those who disbelieve and contradict. That which clears the vision of faith blinds the eyes of unbelief.'[15]

3. Jesus' role as Bringer of the kingdom is explicit or implied in the message of some of the parables themselves.

The most explicit statement is found in the explanation Jesus gives of the parable of the weeds (Matt. 13:36-43). There

---

13 Ladd, *Theology of the New Testament*, pp. 93-94.

14 Ladd, *Theology of the New Testament*, p. 92.

15 Franzmann, *Follow Me*, p. 122.

He said that 'the *one who sows* the good seed is the Son of Man' (13:37). This seems to have immediate reference to His own proclamation of the urgency of repentance in view of the arrival of the kingdom (Matt. 4:17) and the resulting creation of disciples which His preaching produces ('the good seed is the children of the kingdom', Matt. 13:38). Most significantly, the same parable also speaks of Jesus' role in the consummation of the kingdom. 'The harvest is the close of the age' (13:39). 'The Son of Man will send his angels, and they will gather out of *his* kingdom all causes of sin and all law-breakers, and throw them into the fiery furnace' (13:41-42). These statements taken together indicate Jesus' role both in the inauguration of the kingdom through his person and mission during the first century and in the consummation of the kingdom at the end of the age (thus incidentally supporting Ladd's and Vos' view of a two-stage coming of the kingdom). Jesus' explicitly-mentioned role as the inaugurator of the kingdom (13:37) is seen by Herman Ridderbos as also implied in the parable of the sower: it was Jesus himself who sowed the 'word of the kingdom' (13:19) and garnered the varying responses described in the parable.[16]

It may rightly be maintained, therefore, that Jesus served a prophetic function in proclaiming and explaining the coming of the kingdom of God – the acknowledged reign, dominion, or government of God for those who would receive it – at its inauguration, brought about through Jesus' own Messianic person and mission. But further, it may be argued that this parabolic teaching either implies or explicitly affirms the central role of Jesus Himself in every aspect of the advent of the kingdom of God, and that the central role of Jesus involves every aspect of the messianic mission, the prophetic, the priestly, and the kingly. It may be helpful to summarize as follows.

1) Jesus is the announcer of the kingdom of God. The concept of sowing of seed as the propagation of the 'word of the kingdom' was introduced in Matthew 13:19, and the

---

16 Herman Ridderbos, *The Coming of the Kingdom*, trans. H.de Jongste, ed. Raymond O. Zorn (Philadelphia: Presbyterian and Reformed, 1962), pp. 130-32, 136-37.

continuation of similar imagery in the 'parable of the weeds' is therefore natural. Since Jesus identified Himself as the 'sower' in the latter parable (13:37), it is natural also to identify Jesus as the 'sower' in the earlier parable as well (as argued by Ridderbos, as mentioned above). This corresponds well with the central burden of Jesus' public prophetic preaching as the arrival of God's kingdom (4:17).

2) *Jesus is the inaugurator of the kingdom of God.* Jesus not only sows the 'word of the kingdom', but He also makes that proclamation effective in producing disciples and introducing them into the surrounding world; such is the implication of the parable of the weeds, for there the good seed are 'the children of the kingdom' (13:38) and the one who sowed them is the Son of Man (13:39). In some way that was not yet fully explained, Jesus' ministry was responsible for the inauguration or beginning of the kingdom of God in human history. Its historical origin was in Jesus' public proclamation of the kingdom; it had yet to be revealed that such an inauguration of the kingdom was not to be effectuated apart from His own death and resurrection, involving Jesus' priestly work.

3) *Jesus is the consummator of the kingdom of God.* The parable of the weeds also explicitly states that 'at the close of the age' it will come about that 'the Son of Man will send *his* angels' to bring the kingdom to its consummation. The angels will 'gather out of *his* kingdom [not just "the" kingdom] all causes of sin and all law-breakers,' and then 'the righteous will shine like the sun in the kingdom of their Father' (13:40b-43). The Son of Man will exercise the divine prerogatives of command of *His* angels and rule over *His* kingdom (which is identical with the kingdom of the Father). Thus appears the kingly function of Jesus in His messianic work.

APPLICATORY OBSERVATIONS:

1) Something momentous was happening in Jesus' own historical ministry. The long-awaited kingdom of God had begun to arrive. It was that for which God's faithful people had watched and waited, and which Jesus' disciples were privileged to observe (Matt. 13:16-17). Christians today may be thankful that they are likewise highly privileged to live in the era of fulfillment.

2) The kingdom of God, though present and manifest in Jesus and His messianic mission, was easy to miss because it was small and inconspicuous (Matt. 13:31-32, 33). It required faith for anyone to see it and grasp its significance. God's way of doing things may not at present be spectacular in the world's terms and estimate, but it is not therefore to be despised. God's word will bear its fruit (Matt. 13:23) and His work will proceed; Christians may be confident of that and may pursue their daily tasks of ministry in that confidence.

3) Jesus insisted that the kingdom of God is so valuable that it must control or rule a person's present values and choices. This is the point of the parables of the hidden treasure (Matt. 13:44) and of the pearl of great value (13:45-46). The kingdom of God is so valuable that it is worth giving up all else in this life in order to attain to it. Thus even for a person who is merely considering or approaching the kingdom of God the demands of the kingdom are absolute. The government of God and its benefits are worth the loss of everything less, which is *everything else.*

IV. Jesus' Assertion of the Absolute Claims of Discipleship:

The Demands of God's Kingdom

Later in His ministry, Jesus asserted in other language the point made by these latter two parables (the hidden treasure; the pearl of great price), namely, that the would-be disciple must be prepared to give up all else in preference to Jesus, His gospel and His kingdom. This assertion is recorded in Matthew 16:24-28 (Mark 8:34–9:1; Luke 9:23-27). While other passages which include Jesus' teaching on the demands of discipleship could just as easily be utilized, this one may serve as characteristic of His teaching on the subject.

It is significant that this paragraph follows upon the confession of Jesus' messiahship by Peter and Jesus' exchange with Peter about what that messiahship meant for Jesus personally (Matt. 16:13-23). The office of messiah was one that would lead to Jesus' death and resurrection (v. 21) – He was not at this point a conquering kind of messiah but a dying and rising kind of messiah. Of the necessity for Jesus' death Peter was uncomprehending and merited Jesus' rebuke, for to die was God's purpose for His Christ (16:22-23). To be identified with such a messiah would likewise implicate the disciples in suffering; thus Jesus responded by laying out in stark terms the demands of discipleship to Himself. In short, the disciple is called upon to give up his claimed autonomy over his own life: he must in principle turn over control of his life to another, in this case, God acting through Jesus. The outcome is eternal life and eventual vindication by the Son of Man.

1. Following Jesus requires abandonment of claims to personal autonomy (v. 24).

Jesus is said to have 'told his disciples', indicating that what He says here has particular reference to them in their identity as disciples. Mark's account has Jesus speaking also to the crowd (8:34), suggesting that Jesus was warning against lightly-considered conversion, and thus was not at all separating discipleship from conversion but emphasizing rather that the two go together. And what He said was quite stringent.

1) The disciple must deny himself. The language 'come after me' at the beginning of Matthew 16:24 (represented by different but roughly equivalent Greek terminology [verbs] in Mark and Luke), 'is used,' according to R. T. France, 'as a term for discipleship.'[17] Thus it is the requirements of discipleship to Jesus which are in view in this paragraph. The next verb, stating one of those requirements, 'let him deny himself', here suggests to 'deny/renounce utterly', with denying oneself meaning to 'be without regard for one's own advantage or convenience.'[18] France observes: 'In the light of what follows it must mean here to dissociate oneself from one's own interests, which in this case means the willingness to risk one's own life. It means putting loyalty to Jesus before self-preservation.'[19]

2) The disciple must take up his cross. Three observations may be made. (a) The cross was a well-known *instrument of*

---

17 France, *Matthew*, NIC, p. 635, n. 1.

18 Max Zerwick and Mary Grosvener, *A Grammatical Analysis of the Greek New Testament.* 5th ed. (Rome: Editrice Pontificio Istituto Biblico, 1996), p. 54.

19 France, *Matthew*, NIC, p. 638

death in first-century Palestine. France argues vigorously that the language of 'taking up one's cross' must be understood primarily literally, of physical death to be suffered by Jesus' disciples.[20] And certainly it must be recognized that Jesus is not referring to minor inconveniences or discomforts, as the term 'bearing one's cross' has often been used to include in popular language; there is a 'death' involved. However, though the possibility of literal martyrdom is certainly included within the purview of Jesus' demands, yet the possibility of a figurative meaning must also be allowed. Luke's account (Luke 9:23) inserts the term 'daily' ('take up his cross daily') and this calls for a figurative sense, as it requires a repeated action (and a person could die literally only once; although admittedly being continually prepared for martyrdom could be in view). (b) As I. H. Marshall has pointed out in commenting on the Lukan text, carrying one's cross is the posture of a person who is *already condemned to death*. Jesus' teaching does not envision some far-off future possibility (potential martyrdom), but rather a present reality. 'Hence the saying refers not so much to literal martyrdom as to the attitude of self-denial which regards its life in this world as *already finished*; it is the attitude of dying to self and sin which Paul demands.'[21] (c) Jesus' teaching calls for a *continuing attitude* of the death of self-will. Marshall again observes, 'Whereas Mark [by omitting 'daily'] has in mind the initial act of self-renunciation, Luke stresses the need for daily renewal of such an attitude. For the thought see also 1 Corinthians 15:31; Romans 8:36.'[22]

3) The disciple must follow Jesus. The language 'follow me' here is the same in all three Synoptics. To follow Jesus would be to emulate the pathway of self-denial that He Himself trod; or, alternatively, the construction could indicate the outcome of the previous two imperatives, i.e. the disciple would then by

---

20 France, *Matthew*, NIC, pp. 636, 638.

21 I. Howard Marshall, *The Gospel of Luke: A Commentary on the Greek Text*, The New International Greek Testament Commentary (Grand Rapids: Eerdmans, 1978), p. 373.

22 Marshall, *Luke*, p. 374.

this means be following Jesus.[23] 'The point is,' Marshall says, 'that the disciple who takes up his cross is doing what Jesus does; he is following in the same way as his Master.'[24] J. P. Lange comments, summarizing the entire verse: 'To follow Jesus requires both inward self-renunciation and an outward manifestation of it, in willing submission to whatever sufferings may befall us as disciples. The renunciation must amount to self-denial, that is, it must become complete abnegation and surrender of our selfish nature and of our self-will.'[25] The basic principle involved seems to be what could be called the 'death of self-will' (which in practical terms might look different for different disciples), or, in the language being used in this study, the 'renunciation of personal autonomy': the willingness to give oneself entirely to the interests of Jesus and His kingdom, with the outcome potentially involving suffering or martyrdom.

2. Following Jesus involves reckoning according to the calculus of the kingdom (vv. 25-26).

In the calculus of the kingdom, self-preservation results in self-loss (perdition, condemnation in the final judgment) but self-abandonment for Jesus' sake leads to self-preservation (understood as true life, eternal life; 25). And that self-loss is not something that anyone should be willing to deal for. The gaining of the whole world is not worth the final loss of one's true self (26).[26]

3. Following Jesus involves considering the prospect of recompense by the glorified Son of Man (vv. 27-28).

The reason that the follower of Jesus can afford to give up his own self in the present is that he will eventually be vindicated by Jesus acting as the exalted Son of Man.

1) The Son of Man shall eventually serve as judge (v. 27). The language of this verse speaks of Jesus functioning in the role

---

23 Zerwick, p. 54. Marshall seems to prefer the latter interpretation: 'the force must be "and (in this way) follow me,"' *Luke*, p. 374.

24 Marshall, *Luke*, p. 374.

25 Lange, 'Matthew', p. 303.

26 Thus both France (*Matthew*, NIC, pp. 638-39) and Marshall (*Luke*, pp. 374-75).

of Judge at the final judgment, for 'he will repay each person according to what he has done', which France understands as 'whether or not they have maintained their commitment to Jesus in the face of hostility.' The point is clear: 'it is worth remaining faithful even to the loss of earthly life *because* there is an ultimate judgment to come, and on the outcome of that judgment the enjoyment of *true* life will depend.'[27]

2) The Son of Man will soon enter His kingly power (v. 28). Jesus' statement here is a highly controverted one, for its interpretation is most difficult. Suffice it to say that the solution probably lies in the direction of understanding Jesus to be referring to His own resurrection and ascension, constituting His exaltation to His active messianic reign and supreme lordship (under God) over the universe (Matt. 28:18; Acts 2:36), and His subsequent pouring out of the Holy Spirit (Acts 2:33), which activated the worldwide extension of His kingdom, to be consummated in His *parousia* (second advent at the end of the age). The transfiguration (Matt. 17:1-8) likely provides a preview of His kingly glory, meant to be an encouragement to the leading disciples.[28] All the disciples present (excluding Judas Iscariot) would observe Jesus entering His kingly reign, and three of them would glimpse the preview of it, thus being fortified for the persecution and suffering that was later to come. Vindication shall come for them as surely as it shall for their Master.

APPLICATORY OBSERVATION

The demands placed upon the disciple by Jesus are stringent and uncompromising: they involve the renunciation of personal autonomy in the death of self-will. What the 'death of self-will' looks like will be different for each disciple, for each one has his or her own purposes, plans, ambitions and desires, any of which may have to be surrendered to the interests of God's kingdom and God's purposes for one's life. Such surrender may be painful in the present (crucifixion is never

---

27 France, *Matthew*, pp. 640, 639.

28 See the discussions in France, *Matthew*, NIC, pp. 640-41; Marshall, *Luke*, pp. 377-79.

fun), but there will be an eternal payoff which will make it all worthwhile; as Paul says: 'I consider that the sufferings of this present time are not worth comparing with the glory that is to be revealed to us' (Rom. 8:18).

5

The Priestly Function of Jesus the Messiah:

Providing Atonement for Human Rebellion against God's Lordship

INTRODUCTION: MESSIAH'S PRIESTLY FUNCTION AND THE GOVERNMENT OF GOD

Not only Jesus' prophetic function but also His priestly function served the interests of the government of God. There were at least two ways in which Jesus the Messiah's priestly function related to it. First, He refused to assert His own autonomy as the human race had done ever since the Garden of Eden but instead explicitly placed Himself under the government of God. The positive commitment of Himself to God's will occurred at His baptism; the testing of that commitment occurred in His temptation immediately following His baptism, and His complete obedience to the will of His Father followed throughout His ministry. Second, He offered Himself in His death as an atoning sacrifice on behalf of those who had rebelled against God's government, thus securing their forgiveness.

I. Personal Refusal of Autonomy and Perfect Submission to God's Lordship

The first aspect of Jesus' priestly work involves His refusal to assert His autonomy.

1. The Baptism of Jesus

The first public act of Jesus in His messianic ministry was His baptism at the hands of John the Baptist (Matt. 3:13-17). Geerhardus Vos argues persuasively that Jesus' baptism should be considered a messianic act, that is, it was related to Jesus' entrance upon His ministry as God's Anointed, God's

Messiah, and thus was preparatory to all that followed. In sum, Vos maintains, on the basis of the conversation between John the Baptist and Jesus recorded in Matthew 3:14-15, (1) that both John and Jesus recognized that there was no subjective reason for Jesus to receive John's baptism (for He had no sin to repent of); (2) that there was, however, an objective reason that constituted the 'fulfilling of all righteousness' which Jesus urged upon John, namely that submission to John's baptism was that action which God at that moment required of Israelites; (3) and that Jesus, as an Israelite, received baptism at the hands of John as a means of identifying Himself with the people of Israel and their sins (while He Himself had none). Thus Jesus' baptism was 'an expression of the vicarious relation of Jesus to the people of God'; 'Jesus' identification with the people in their baptism had the proximate end of securing for them vicariously what the sacrament aimed at, the forgiveness of sin.' Vos goes so far as to say that 'there can be no objection on principle to saying that He repented for the people vicariously'. As Everett Harrison has put it, Jesus' baptism was 'a deliberate identification of himself with the nation', 'the first public step taken in the direction of bearing the sins of the people', 'a consecration to the death that awaited him'. The voice from heaven expressed the Father's approval of Jesus' life to that point and His commitment to this course of action, while the descent of the dove symbolized the empowering of Jesus by the Holy Spirit for the pursuance of this aim (Matt. 3:16-17).[1]

Vos's suggestion that Jesus 'repented for the people vicariously' may bear further consideration. While it might at first seem rather shocking to say that Jesus repented for others, the concept does fit well with His role as Mediator. Jesus had no sin of His own of which to repent; however, as a priestly representative of humans, He was required to face and deal with the primal sin of the human race: the assertion of human autonomy over against God, humanity's rightful ruler. Stated negatively, that to which Jesus committed Himself in His baptism was the refusal to

---

1   Geerhardus Vos, *Biblical Theology* pp. 319-20; Everett F. Harrison, *A Short Life of Christ* (Grand Rapids: Eerdmans, 1968), pp. 74-75.

assert that personal autonomy which all humans since Adam and Eve had asserted; He would not participate in that primal sin. Stated positively, Jesus renounced in principle any assertion of human autonomy; He determined to assume the proper human stance before God, that of loving submission and obedience, both personally and officially. Thus while He had no sin of His own requiring repentance, as a representative of humanity He still needed to repudiate that primal sin of the human race – the assertion of autonomy – and in His own person to abandon the stance which humanity had occupied ever since the Fall. And He was the *only* human being, both because of His unique sinless nature and because of His unique messianic office, who *could* accomplish this. The future of the human race in its relationship with God depended uniquely on Him.

Thus the British Christian author C. S. Lewis has probably exhibited a valid spiritual insight when he entitled his chapter on the death of Jesus 'The Perfect Penitent'. Lewis claims not to know how the atonement works for the divine forgiveness of human sin. Nevertheless, after describing the human position as that of 'a rebel who must lay down his arms', Lewis observes, 'Only a bad person needs to repent: only a good person can repent perfectly. The worse you are the more you need it and the less you can do it. The only person who could do it perfectly would be a perfect person – and he would not need it.' What is the solution? 'But supposing God became a man.... He could surrender His will, and suffer and die, because He was man; and He could do it perfectly because He was God.' Lewis seems to understand Jesus as engaging in vicarious repentance – as Vos has suggested – as well as a vicarious death on behalf of humans.[2] In the earthly career of Jesus the question then became: if Jesus had renounced human autonomy in principle (at His baptism), could He renounce it in practice? That is what the temptation was designed to demonstrate.[3]

---

2   C. S. Lewis, *Mere Christianity, An Anniversary Edition of Three Books: The Case for Christianity, Christian Behavior, and Beyond Personality*. Edited and with an Introduction by Walter Hooper (New York: Macmillan, 1981), Book II, Chapter 4, 'The Perfect Penitent', pp. 49, 50.

3   Jesus' death as an atoning sacrifice is treated later in this chapter of the present study. For further elucidation of the nature of repentance, see the relevant section in Chapter 9.

2. The Temptation of Jesus

The priestly function of Messiah was also deeply involved in the probation that He underwent, a probation that in some ways cast Him into the role of another 'Adam', just as the first Adam had faced a probation or testing.

1) INTRODUCTION

It is not without significance that the temptation of Jesus (Matt. 4:1-11; Mark 1:12-13; Luke 4:1-13) occurred immediately after His commitment of Himself, through His baptism, to the mission divinely established for Him. The two may thus be assumed to be closely related. The nature of the temptations Jesus faced seems to confirm that assumption. If Jesus at His baptism had vicariously repented on behalf of His people (as Vos suggests), then the question presents itself as to whether He would be willing and able to devote Himself in practice to His divinely-ordained mission, denying Himself the claim to autonomy in preference for the will of God. Thus the divine purpose in the temptation of Jesus may be said to be the overturning of the established stance or pattern (since the fall) of human autonomy over against God. Jesus in His baptism had committed Himself to the purpose of God for His life and ministry and had identified Himself with a sinful people in need of repentance (though He Himself needed none). But could he, and would he, follow through with that commitment? That question was what the temptation was decisively to answer.

The temptation of Jesus was essentially messianic in nature. The suggestion of Geerhardus Vos is almost certainly to be taken as correct that the temptation of Jesus as described in varying detail by the synoptic gospels should be understood as messianic in character. That is, the temptation that Jesus faced before the beginning of His public ministry related to Him not merely on the personal level as a private individual but rather on the official level of one who in His identity and function was Messiah, God's anointed agent of revelation, redemption and rule.[4]

---

4   Vos, *Biblical Theology*, pp. 332-35.

Several general features of Jesus' temptation are noted by Vos.

First, the temptation involved the procuring of a positive gain. Jesus in His messianic office was seeking to regain what had formerly been lost to the human race in the Adamic fall. If Jesus should be successful in resisting the temptations then He could reverse the effects of the Adamic fall for those who are redeemed by Him (see Rom. 5:19).

Second, the true analogy of Jesus' temptation is Adam's probation as described in Genesis 2 and 3. Luke may hint at this when he traces Jesus' genealogy back to Adam, whom he identifies as the 'son of God' (Luke 3:38), then immediately relates Jesus' experience of temptation (Luke 4:1-13) where in the first and third temptations Jesus is referred to as the Son of God (Luke 4:3, 9). Paul also draws a parallel in 1 Corinthians 15:45, where he refers to Jesus as the 'last Adam', and in Romans 5:12, 18-19, where he seems to emphasize the representative character of both Adam and Jesus.

Third, there is a divine purpose in the temptation of Jesus. This is indicated by the activity of the Holy Spirit in leading Jesus into the temptation (Matt. 4:1; Mark. 1:12; Luke 4:1). The divine movement took the initiative in engaging the enemy. From God's standpoint, this event constituted a probation, a testing, a proving of Jesus and His commitment to His messianic mission. From Satan's perspective, it was a temptation to abandon that mission (or perhaps more correctly, to achieve that mission by less stringent means), an enticement to sin by asserting His independence from God.

Fourth, the subsequent ministry and work of Jesus are founded upon His successful endurance of this probation. Jesus Himself seems to allude to this in Matthew 12:29. Because He had 'bound' Satan in His own successful resistance of these temptations, He was able to invade Satan's domain and reclaim its victims for God.

Fifth, the general tone of the temptations was framed so as to attempt to induce Jesus to move from the proper stance (at this point in His messianic career) of humiliation, dependence on God and submission to God.

Sixth, the temptations, abstractly considered, involved no inherently sinful desires but rather actions which were not commensurate with Jesus' messianic office in His current state of humiliation and suffering in human conditions. As Vos observes, 'the animus of the temptation, from Satan's point of view, consisted in the attempt to move him out of this spirit and attitude of service and humiliation, so as to yield to the natural desire for His Messianic glory without an interval of suffering.'[5] Harrison concurs: 'It will be Satan's effort to persuade [Jesus] to such action as will be contrary to complete dependence on [God], by asserting a measure of independence based on self-interest.'[6]

Given the messianic nature of Jesus' probation considered as a whole, it is possible to determine something of the precise nature of each of the three specific temptations. To summarize in advance the findings stated later: Jesus was tempted, by all of Satan's suggestions, to act autonomously – that is, independently of God – in order to gain for himself provision (the first phase, following Matthew's order), protection (the second phase) and power (the third phase). In addition, each successive temptation raised the level of autonomy that Jesus was encouraged by Satan to exercise. In approaching the specific temptations, it seems wise methodologically to adopt the two assumptions set forth by Vos: first, that Jesus answered Satan with regard to the point at issue in each temptation; and second, that Jesus' handling of the Old Testament scripture passages He quoted suggests the proper interpretation of those passages.[7]

APPLICATORY OBSERVATIONS:

1) If it is indeed the case that Jesus' temptations were messianic in character, then He was engaging in a work that no one else could do. He was God's appointed Representative Man, a New Adam who would, as a true man, have the

---

5 The above points are from Vos, *Biblical Theology*, 330-35; citation from p. 335.

6 Harrison, *Short Life of Christ*, p. 85.

7 Vos, *Biblical Theology*, p. 336.

opportunity to overcome the effects of the human fall into rebellion against God. If He were to be successful, He would become the 'last Adam' (1 Cor. 15:45), for no other would be needed. And by being successful, He could Himself provide a suitable atonement for the sins of His people. Of course He was successful. In this event, therefore, we may see the uniqueness and magnificence of Jesus: He went where no one else could go, and He accomplished what no one else could do.

2) People should not minimize the reality of the temptations in Jesus' case. That they were genuine temptations (enticements to sin) is indicated by the following features: (a) An opportunity was placed before Jesus to meet a legitimate need or desire in an illegitimate way. (b) There was a certain attractiveness to the proposals, i.e. they would allow Him to achieve His ends without suffering. (c) There was no external impediment to taking the proposed course of action, i.e. He could have acted so if He had wanted to. (d) Jesus had to decide whether He would take the proposed course of action. Thus it is not subjective inclination that constitutes a temptation but opportunity and cause to take a given course of action. These Jesus faced, and thus He 'in every respect has been tempted as we are, yet without sin' (Heb. 4:15b). This becomes the basis in Hebrews for encouragement that, as High Priest, Jesus is able 'to sympathize with our weaknesses' (4:15a) and that 'with confidence' we may 'draw near to the throne of grace' that we might 'receive mercy and find grace to help in' our 'time of need' (4:16), that is, in the face of our temptations.

2) THE THREE SPECIFIC PHASES

It has been argued that Jesus' temptation was essentially messianic in nature, that is, it related to His office of Messiah. Now the specific phases of Jesus' temptation may be considered. The accounts of Jesus' temptation or probation in Matthew and Luke divide it into three distinct phases.

(1) *Phase One: Provision.* The first phase (Matt. 4:2-4) involved Jesus' hunger after forty days of fasting. Satan proposed that Jesus make provision for Himself by turning stones into bread, that is, by creating His own food. Jesus refused, citing Deuteronomy 8:3, a passage in which Moses

reminded the Israelites that God's purpose in the wilderness was to humble and test them, and that God provided manna to show them that man lives by God's provision, in this case a supernatural provision (Deut. 8:2-4). In Jesus' reply there is no suggestion of a contrast between spiritual food over against physical food (which is the way His words are often interpreted), which would not, in this case, be appropriate, for it was precisely physical sustenance that Jesus needed, nor does such an interpretation fit the Deuteronomy context. The point is rather one of conscious dependence upon God for one's material provision. Such was the attitude the Israelites were to exhibit (but often failed to do so); such was the attitude that Jesus was determined to exhibit. This is the stance of faith or trust in God. As Vos points out,

> God expected him to hunger.... The probation consisted in placing before [Jesus] the necessity of exercising implicit trust in God as the One able to sustain His life notwithstanding the protracted fast. The 'word proceeding from the mouth of God' refers to the miracle-working word of omnipotence, the mere word requiring no natural means.[8]

Indeed, the term 'word' does not appear in the Hebrew text of Deuteronomy 8:3; man is to live 'by everything [Heb. 'all'] that proceedeth out of the mouth of Jehovah' (ASV), trusting God (while pursuing His explicit will) to provide that which he needs. In reality, the divine provision need not be miraculous or supernatural (as Vos interprets God's provision for Jesus, and as it was in fact for the ancient Hebrews), but could be merely providential. The issue is simply the maintaining of a stance of conscious trust in God for one's material provision.

Thus Satan was suggesting that Jesus, in order to meet His own need for physical sustenance (which would not be evil in itself), act autonomously from God (which would be evil). Satan, according to Vos, 'was endeavoring to move Jesus out of this faith with reference to His humiliation into an attitude of independent sovereignty, such as properly belonged to

---

8   Vos, *Biblical Theology*, p. 337.

His exalted state only.'[9] Vos's term 'independent sovereignty' refers precisely to that autonomous human action which constitutes a declaration of independence from God. Jesus' response indicated that He would not so act but would trust His heavenly Father to provide for Him as He saw fit.

(2) *Phase Two: Protection.* The second phase of the probation was prompted by Satan's suggestion that Jesus prove God's protection of Him by casting Himself from the height of the temple (Matt. 4:5-7). Such an act on Jesus' part would involve acting autonomously because God had authorized no such action and it would put God in the position of being compelled to preserve Jesus from harm (if indeed He were to be preserved). That Jesus so interpreted the matter is indicated by His citation of Deuteronomy 6:16 in response: 'You shall not put the LORD your God to the test.' The context in Deuteronomy refers to the Israelites' behavior at Massah (as described in Exodus 17:1-17). On that occasion they demanded water and complained against their circumstances, seeking proof of God's presence among them, as indicated by 17:7: 'they tested the LORD by saying, "Is the LORD among us or not?"' The sense seems to be, 'if he is among us, we demand that he show himself and deliver us – immediately!' As Vos observes, 'It was a proving springing from doubt or outright unbelief.' For Jesus, as for the Israelites, 'the venture would have been inspired by the shrinking from a protracted life of faith.... It would have involved an impious experimenting with the dependability of God.' For Jesus to have acted on Satan's suggestion would thus have constituted the very opposite of a life of genuine faith, for faith trusts God to provide protection and deliverance when and where they are needed. This action would amount to an effort to force God's hand, in short, an effort to control God. Vos correctly perceives the spirit of the proposed action: on Jesus' part it would have been a 'demonstration solicited *by Himself*', not something authorized by God or prompted by trust in God. Hence Jesus rejected it.[10]

---

9 Vos, *Biblical Theology*, p. 337.
10 Vos, *Biblical Theology*, p. 338 (emphasis added).

(3) *Phase Three: Power.* The third phase of the probation involved Satan's offer to Jesus of the kingdoms of the world in exchange for Jesus' act of worshipping Satan (Matt. 4:8-10). For Jesus to have worshipped Satan would have been the ultimate act of autonomy from God; it would have rendered Jesus the agent of Satan rather than the agent of God in governing the world and would have made Jesus beholden to Satan. Satan dropped the language referring to Jesus as the 'Son of God' used in the first two temptations (Matt. 4:3, 6), and all other subtlety of argument, making instead a frontal assault upon Jesus' commitment to God, proposing 'a transfer of allegiance on Jesus' part from God to Satan.'[11] Jesus once again appealed to Deuteronomy, this time to the statement in 6:13, 'It is the LORD your God you shall fear. Him you shall serve....' Jesus added the word 'only', correctly reflecting the prohibition that follows in verses 14 and 15 of Deuteronomy 6: 'You shall not go after other gods,... for the LORD your God in your midst is a jealous God.'

As Vos points out, Satan in this temptation appealed to Jesus' innate human need to worship and to Messiah's destiny to rule the nations (which had been promised to Him; see Ps. 2:8-9; Rev. 11:15), neither of which was sinful in itself.[12] What would have been sinful in following Satan's proposed course of action was the reversal of the object to whom worship was rendered (i.e., not the true God; this fact, Vos notes, overturns the modern subjective notion of religion which approves religious expression regardless of the object of worship, emphasizing only the sincerity with which it is offered, p. 339) and the means by which the rule over the nations was to be gained (autonomy from God, subjection to Satan). Jesus' messianic mission designated Him as the agent of God's revelation, redemption and rule; and He determined to remain faithful to that calling, even though it would be more painful for Him in the short run to accomplish these divine objectives by the divinely-appointed means.[13]

---

11 Vos, *Biblical Theology*, p. 339.

12 Vos, *Biblical Theology*, pp. 339, 341.

13 Harrison takes a similar view of the temptations to that of Vos and that which is adopted here; *Short Life of Christ*, pp. 80-92.

From this vantage point it is possible to observe that not only do all three temptations involve the proposal of autonomous action on Jesus' part, they also involve an increasing degree of proposed autonomy over against God as the temptations advance through the three phases. The first proposal involves Jesus taking action *Himself* to supply His necessary provision; the second involves Jesus *forcing God to act* to protect Him; the third involves *complete independence from God* in attaining the messianic reign. In successfully resisting these proposals, Jesus demonstrated His commitment, as man and as Messiah, to a course of life and action which rejected the adoption of a stance of human autonomy and to the adoption of a stance incorporating dependence upon God and submission to His government. By acting thus He set Himself on the path of reversing the direction chosen by Adam and the damage it had wrought and of fitting Himself to become the spotless sacrifice which would secure forgiveness for rebellious humans and to become the personal agent of the government of God.

APPLICATORY OBSERVATIONS

1) We are now in a position to admire the accomplishment of Jesus in His temptation. (a) It confirmed Jesus in his commitment to God's purpose for Him as Messiah (a commitment He had made at his baptism). (b) It gave Jesus victory over Satan on which to base his later ministry (Matt. 12:29). (c) It established the proper pattern of humans' relationship to the government of God, which is one of willing submission ('I seek not my own will but the will of him who sent me,' John 5:30b). (d) It fitted Jesus to be the Redeemer of God's people: as a spotless, sinless sacrifice (Eph. 5:2; 1 Cor. 5:7; 2 Cor. 5:21; 1 Pet. 2:22); and as a sympathetic high priest and intercessor (Heb. 4:15-16; 2:17-18). But mere admiration is not enough to benefit us; we must trust in the powerful efficacy of Jesus' priestly work in order to partake of its benefits.

2) Jesus' temptations were both like and unlike ours. They were *like our own* in that (a) they related to common human needs and desires such as we experience; (b) they related to legitimate human needs and desires, i.e. those for provision, protection, and power; (c) they related to the reality that human sin often arises from the effort to meet these needs

and desires in illegitimate ways (1 John 2:16). Thus Jesus identified with us in His temptation. However, there were also ways in which Jesus' temptations were *not like our own*: (a) they related to the offices that belonged uniquely to Jesus as representative Man, as representative Israelite, and as Messiah; (b) the outcome would affect the entire future of the human race and the redemptive purpose of God; (c) Jesus' temptations did not arise from evil desire while ours often do (pride, ambition, envy, malice, hatred, anger, jealousy, avarice, gluttony, voluptuousness, drunkenness).[14] In that Jesus' temptations related to His messianic office, they were unique to Him; in that they related to common human desires, they are shared with other humans. The former gives us just reason to trust Him as we come to God; the latter makes Him sympathetic with our weaknesses and able to help us.

3. Jesus' Express Submission to the Will of God

In order for Jesus to serve effectively as a priest on behalf of His people and to offer Himself as a perfect sacrifice to secure their forgiveness He had to overturn the pattern of autonomous human action as set by Adam and followed by his descendants. Accordingly, Jesus took it as His mission to submit Himself to the will of the Father in an absolute way: no action He engaged in would be His own autonomous deed but would be performed out of obedience to God.

The strongest witness to Jesus' commitment to this aim is found in the fourth Gospel. The Gospel according to John is replete with Jesus' statements of His absolute submission to the will of the Father.

1. John 5:19: So Jesus said to them, 'Truly, truly, I say to you, *the Son can do nothing of His own accord*, but only what he sees the Father doing.'

2. John 5:30: '*I can do nothing on my own*. As I hear, I judge, and my judgment is just, because *I seek not my own will but the will of Him who sent me*.'

---

14   The list is that of W. G. T. Shedd, *Dogmatic Theology*, 3rd ed., ed. Alan W. Gomes (Phillipsburg, NJ: Presbyterian and Reformed, 2003), p. 666.

3. John 6:38: 'For *I have come down from heaven, not to do my own will, but the will of him who sent me.*'

4. John 7:16: So Jesus answered them, '*My teaching is not mine, but His who sent me.*'

5. John 7:28: 'But *I have not come of my own accord.* He who sent me is true, and him you do not know.'

6. John 8:28-29: So Jesus said to them, 'When you have lifted up the Son of Man, then you will know that I am he, and that *I do nothing on my own authority, but speak just as the Father taught me.* And he who sent me is with me. He has not left me alone, for *I always do the things that are pleasing to him.*'

7. John 8:42: Jesus said to them, 'If God were your Father, you would love me, for *I came from God* and I am here. *I came not of my own accord,* but he sent me.'

8. John 8:54-55: 'It is my Father who glorifies me.... I do know him and *I keep His word.*'

9. John 12:49-50: 'For *I have not spoken on my own authority,* but *the Father who sent me has himself given me a commandment – what to say and what to speak.* And I know that His commandment is eternal life. *What I say, therefore, I say as the Father has told me.*'

10. John 14:10: '*The words that I say to you, I do not speak on my own authority,* but the Father who dwells in me does His works.'

11. John 14:24: 'Whoever does not love me does not keep my words. And *the word that you hear is not mine but the Father's who sent me.*'

12. John 14:31: '... *I do as the Father has commanded me,* so that the world may know that I love the Father.'

These dozen statements by Jesus exhibit some interesting features. (1) In most of them (eight of the twelve), Jesus speaks of the Father as having sent Him, emphasizing a designated mission. (2) In some of them, Jesus uses the language of authority (8:28;

137

12:49), emphasizing that He acted not on His own authority but on that of the Father. (3) In some of them Jesus speaks of the Father commanding Him (12:49-50; 14:31), an expression of authority and of Jesus' submission to it. (4) Jesus specifically claimed that His teaching was from the Father (7:16; 8:28; 12:49-50; 14:10, 24). In all of this, Jesus was testifying to His refusal to claim autonomy and to act autonomously. This was necessary not only for the fulfilling of His messianic ministry generally but also for the representative renunciation of autonomy which was specifically a function of His priestly office as He became the perfect and last Adam. Unlike the first Adam, He would not seek to act independently of God.

4. Jesus' Struggle in Gethsemane

The Gospel accounts narrate that Jesus engaged in a monumental spiritual struggle in the hours just before His arrest, trial and crucifixion (Matt. 26:36-46). The issue was the same as in His earlier temptation: would He assert personal autonomy or submit Himself to the will of the Father? The momentous nature of the struggle and its outcome is seen in several features of the text.

1) Jesus took the inner circle of three disciples with Him to support Him (Matt. 26:36-38). The fact that the disciples were uncomprehending and failed in their support of Him does not lessen the fact that Jesus felt the need of and sought their support at this crucial moment.

2) The gospel texts use the strongest terms to describe Jesus' inner turmoil on this occasion. The language is quite vivid. 'He began to be sorrowful and troubled. Then he said to them, "My soul is very sorrowful, even to death"' (Matt. 26:37-38). He 'began to be greatly distressed and troubled' (Mark 14:33). 'Being in an agony he prayed more earnestly; and His sweat became like great drops of blood falling down to the ground' (Luke 22:44). This suggests that the stress He felt at this time was particularly severe.

3) Jesus expressed His desire to be delivered from having to drink the 'cup' that He knew was facing Him (Matt. 26:39). The reason for His reluctance was likely that Jesus knew the cup He was to drink held the wrath of God. The 'cup' was a not uncommon Old Testament metaphor for the wrath of God, as, for example, God spoke to Jeremiah: 'Take from my hand this cup of the wine of wrath, and make all the nations to whom I send you drink it' (Jer. 25:15; the figure continues through verse 28). Everett Harrison has provided the explanation:

> What convulsed the Savior was the fear of separation from God due to becoming the sin-bearer for men. He had long contemplated from afar what this would mean to him, but now the hour was upon him and it was overwhelming. He began to gaze into that cup and discern its awful contents. He had gladly companied with sinners and gloried in it, but now he was to be counted a sinner, standing in the sinner's place, bearing the sinner's curse. The darkness of Gethsemane's night presaged the blackness that would enshroud Golgotha. The awfulness of the prospect before the Savior began powerfully to affect him.

In support of this understanding, Harrison points to Jesus' quotation of Isaiah 53:12 just before making His way to Gethsemane: 'I tell you that this Scripture must be fulfilled in me: "and he was numbered with the transgressors." For what is written about me has its fulfillment' (Luke 22:37). For Jesus, realizing that 'death in the place of sinners would entail separation from a holy God (cf. Matt. 27:46), the cup must indeed have seemed too bitter to drink.' The upshot of this realization was that, given His personal preference, Jesus would rather not take this cup from the Father's hand.[15]

4) Jesus prayed thus not once but three times (Matt. 26:42, 44). It was not a struggle that He endured without pitiable anguish of soul and continued petition of the Father for relief.

5) The ultimate resolution of the issue was Jesus' personal submission to the will of the Father (Matt. 26:39, 42, 44). Rather than assert in practice His undeniable personal desire to be delivered from partaking the contents of this cup – which would have been an act of autonomy – Jesus gave up His self-will and gave Himself unto the will of His Father. He knew

---

15 Harrison, *Short Life of Christ*, pp. 195-96. This interpretation is supported by J. I. Packer, *Knowing God* (Downers Grove, IL: Inter-Varsity, 1993 [1973]), pp. 192-94.

that His death for the redemption of a people for God's own possession would bring upon Himself unspeakable darkness and a terrible isolation, a break in that perfect fellowship which the Son had from eternity enjoyed with the Father. Yet, in the words of the Epistle to the Hebrews, He 'for the joy that was set before him endured the cross, despising the shame' (12:2), and not only the shame, but discounted His own personal pain of soul as well. As Harrison put it, 'Gethsemane was the Savior's preparation for Calvary. On the cross he yielded up His body [and soul, Isa. 53:12] as a sacrifice for sin, but here in the garden he anticipated that hour by yielding up His will.' Jesus' abandonment of self-will in Gethsemane may be seen as the universe's ultimate act of disavowing personal autonomy in the interests of the kingdom of God. Eventually He would be seated at the right hand of God (Heb. 12:2), but the path that led Him there was indeed a sorrowful one.[16]

Having resolved the issue, Jesus from this point on would not hesitate or flinch; He moved with calmness and confidence through His arrest, legal hearings, and crucifixion. His atoning death had yet to be accomplished on the cross, but His commitment to it was established in Gethsemane.

APPLICATORY OBSERVATIONS:

1) Christians may be grateful for Jesus' complete submission and obedience to the will of the Father, for this was essential to His priestly work of atonement. 'Christ suffered once for sins, the righteous for the unrighteous, that he might bring us to God' (1 Pet. 3:18). Without His life of perfect righteousness, His death could not have accomplished atonement for His people, for He would not have been a spotless sacrifice.

2) Jesus' submission to God's will provides an example for Christians to follow. 'Christ suffered for you, leaving you an example, so that you might follow in His steps' (1 Pet. 2:21), that is, His steps of willingness to suffer for the will of God (vv. 19-20; see 4:19).

3) Jesus' experience in Gethsemane shows that it is not always easy to do the will of God. He achieved the death of

---

16 Harrison, *Short Life of Christ*, p. 196.

His own self-will only through tremendous struggle. So it may be with His disciples: the death of self-will is mandatory but often difficult. Even Jesus is said to have 'learned obedience through what he suffered' (Heb. 5:8).

II. Jesus' Vicarious Atonement on behalf of Rebels against God's Lordship

A second and decisive aspect of Jesus' priestly messianic function was His deliberate death in order to secure the redemption and forgiveness of humans who were in rebellion against God's rule. There are two passages in the synoptic Gospels which explicitly deal with this function.

1. Matthew 20:28: Jesus' Death as Providing a Ransom

As Jesus and His disciples were approaching Jerusalem He told them for the third time of His impending arrest, crucifixion and resurrection (Matt. 20:17-19). Two of the disciples and their mother, either oblivious to the reality now facing Jesus or anticipating His future victory, asked for positions of honor in His kingdom (20:20-21). After a brief exchange, Jesus declared that it was not His prerogative to grant such positions (20:22-23). The other disciples became indignant at the two who had made such a request (20:24), and Jesus used the moment to teach all of them about the contrary values of the kingdom of God. While the rulers of the Gentiles may indeed 'lord it over' their subjects and perhaps oppress them through the use of their authority (20:25), yet among His disciples 'it shall not be so'; rather, status in the disciple community is to be measured in terms of service to others (20:26-27). Then Jesus gave His own ministry as an example: 'even as the Son of Man came not to be served but to serve, and to give His life as a ransom for many' (20:28). Various aspects of this statement may be observed.

1) Jesus' ministry provides a pattern of servanthood. Jesus made an 'I came' assertion (more commonly found in John's Gospel) concerning His messianic mission. He came, He said, not to 'be served' (passive voice) but 'to serve' (active voice). The very point of the mission of Messiah was to serve, not to receive service – and thus it should be as well for the disciples in their own lives. They, no less than he, should have it as their aim not to 'lord it' or rule over others but to serve them. This is the criterion of greatness in the kingdom of God.

2) Jesus' ministry provides a life given in death. Jesus further explained the messianic mission as involving the giving of His life. This indicates that it was a major purpose of the incarnation of God the Son as Jesus of Nazareth that He should give Himself to die. Here Jesus fleshes out slightly His earlier enigmatic statement that He 'must' die (16:21). It is part of the divine purpose for Him that He give Himself in death, and it was His deliberately adopted mission as well; the clause 'and to give His life' follows upon and completes the 'I came' found earlier in the verse.

3) Jesus' ministry provides a ransom for others. There is no break between 'give His life' and the following words, 'a ransom for many.' The term translated 'ransom' (*lytron*) refers to a price paid to secure the freedom of another, and this idea may be heightened by the Greek preposition *anti*, translated 'for' and characteristically meaning 'in the place of' or 'instead of.'[17] This means that Jesus' life, given in death, will secure the freedom or liberation of those for whom He died. The precise mechanism involved in this transaction is not here explained, but it carries the overtones of a vicarious, substitutionary atonement. Such a significance is strengthened by the allusion to Isaiah 53 in the statement that Jesus will give His life as a ransom for 'many'. Similar language is used in Isaiah 53:11, to the effect that the Servant will 'make many to be accounted righteous', and in 53:12, that 'he bore the sin of many'. R. T. France has indicated that it is now commonly accepted that the image of the Suffering Servant of Isaiah 52:13–53:12 forms the background to this saying of Jesus.[18]

New Testament scholar Herman Ridderbos points out how Jesus' willingness to die for others served the interests of the government of God:

---

17 For a defense of this understanding of the Greek terms, see Leon Morris, *The Apostolic Preaching of the Cross*, 3rd ed. (Grand Rapids: Eerdmans, 1965), pp. 29-38.

18 France, *Gospel of Matthew*, NIC, pp. 762-63, n. 26.

In the whole of His suffering and death Jesus serves *God*. God desires His Son to suffer. It is God to whom, of course, the price must be paid, whose rights have been violated and must be restored. The possibility of such restoration is a proof of grace. But the terrible nature of sin must be exposed, and God's rights must be asserted in opposition to sin.[19]

That is, Jesus honored the government of God in personally submitting to God's will for Himself, and He served the interests of the government of God in meeting the demands of God's righteousness and justice by suffering the penalty which human sin merited in order that God might justly forgive sinners who deserved death (see Rom. 3:25-26).

2. Matthew 26:28: Jesus' Death as Securing Forgiveness of Sins

The fullest explanation which Jesus gave concerning the meaning of His death is found in His words spoken while observing the Passover with His disciples. After indicating that one of the disciples would betray Him Jesus proceeded to use the elements of the Passover meal to set forth the significance of His impending death (26:20-30).

The entire exchange is to be understood as relating to Jesus' death, that is, the bread is included as well as the wine, although it is the latter which will be treated more fully here. As France points out, 'in telling His disciples to take the bread and eat it ... Jesus implies that His death is in some sense for their benefit.'[20] However, it is Jesus' words relating to the wine – symbolizing Jesus' shed blood – which are most explicit and deserve the most attention.[21] His assertion was 'this is my blood of the covenant, which is poured out for many for the forgiveness of sins' (26:28). Three aspects of His shed blood are here emphasized.

1) Jesus' shed blood is the blood of the covenant. Jesus' reference to the 'blood of the covenant' calls to mind the similar phrase

---

19 Ridderbos, *Coming of the Kingdom,* p. 168.

20 France, *Gospel of Matthew,* NIC, p. 992.

21 See Morris, *Apostolic Preaching of the Cross,* pp. 112-28, for the argument that 'blood' in the Bible typically refers to 'life given up in death' (p. 117).

used by Moses in Exodus 24:8 as he instituted the Sinaitic Covenant between Jehovah and the nation of Israel. As he sprinkled the people with the blood of the sacrificial animals used in this ceremony, Moses said, 'Behold the blood of the covenant that the LORD has made with you....' It was this blood which formally established the covenant with Israel. The translators of the Holman Christian Standard Bible apparently saw a parallel in Jesus' words, which they translate: 'this is My blood [that establishes] the covenant', with the brackets indicating words supplied by the translators which are not explicitly found in the Greek text but implied by it. The mention of 'covenant' also seems to reflect Jeremiah 31:31-34, where a 'new covenant' is mentioned which includes forgiveness of sins (some Greek manuscripts insert the word 'new' before 'covenant,' as does Luke 22:20).

2) Jesus' shed blood is poured out for many. He will shed His blood for the benefit of others, the 'many'. As noted above, this terminology is used in Isaiah 53:11-12 of the beneficiaries of the Servant's death. And as France points out, 'the Isa 53 allusion is further suggested by the verb "poured out", which is used in Isa 53:12 of the servant "pouring out His life unto death".'[22]

3) Jesus' shed blood secures forgiveness of sins. The blood of Jesus is to be shed 'for the forgiveness of sins'. This is a theme found throughout Isaiah 53 (vv. 5-6, 8, 10, 11, 12), and one prominently mentioned in the 'new covenant' passage of Jeremiah 31:34, where God says, 'I will forgive their iniquity, and I will remember their sin no more.' It also reflects back on the stated purpose of the mission of Messiah in Matthew 1:21, which is that 'he will save His people from their sins.'

The result of this accumulation of suggestive phrases is 'the most comprehensive statement in Matthew's gospel of the redemptive purpose and achievement of Jesus' death'[23] – and it is found on the lips of Jesus Himself. For purposes of the present study, it is helpful to consider the translation of Isaiah 53 offered in the Holman Christian Standard Bible:

---

22 France, *Gospel of Matthew*, NIC, p. 994.

23 France, *Gospel of Matthew*, NIC, p. 994.

'He was struck because of My people's rebellion' (Isa. 53:8d); He 'submitted Himself to death, and was counted among the rebels; yet He bore the sin of many and interceded for the rebels' (53:12b). It was on behalf of those who had rebelled against God's lordship that Jesus gave Himself in death. His death absorbed that penalty which their rebellion deserved and secured that forgiveness which their rebellion did not deserve. It was indeed an expression of God's love and grace, but it had as its end to make people right before the justice of a holy God, that is, it served the interests of His righteous government.

Herman Ridderbos has once again expressed the heart of the matter in succinct fashion. 'The new covenant God had promised to make with His people when he would forgive their sins and write His law in their hearts (Jer. 31:31, 34), has been inaugurated by [Jesus'] blood and has thus become possible and legally valid.'[24] The new covenant was thus formally instituted by Jesus' death (represented by the language about His 'blood').[25] By means of this covenant those who were rebels against God's lordship may receive forgiveness and reinstatement in good standing before Him by simply abandoning their rebellion and receiving these gifts through faith in the accomplishment of Jesus.

APPLICATORY OBSERVATIONS:

1) It was a central purpose of the incarnation that it should lead to Jesus' death as an atoning sacrifice. Jesus' death was not a terrible mishap but the purpose for which He 'came'. In fulfilling that purpose, He not only purchased redemption for His people, for which they may be everlastingly grateful and devoted to Him, but He also provided a model of 'living unto God', a pattern of self-sacrifice in the interests of God's purposes and for the benefit of others. This is how every disciple of Jesus is called upon to live.

---

24 Ridderbos, *Coming of the Kingdom*, pp. 172-73.

25 For a treatment of the biblical concept of 'covenant' and its connection with forgiveness and Jesus' death, see Morris, *Apostolic Preaching of the Cross*, pp. 65-111, especially pp. 107-09.

2) The justice of God is not a trifle. The redemption of a people for God's possession required that God's justice be satisfied, and it was satisfied through the death of Jesus. This reality informs us of the heinousness of sin and of the extent to which God was willing to go to save a people for Himself: the giving of His Son expressed the height of divine love. Christians rightly may do no less than love Him supremely in return.

6

The Kingly Function of Jesus the Messiah:

Serving as Agent of God's Lordship

It would be one of the functions of Messiah to rule, that is, to exercise kingly authority on God's behalf. From early on in the Old Testament revelation of God's purpose for Messiah it was indicated that He would descend from the tribe of Judah and that He would wield the 'scepter' and the 'ruler's staff' and that the 'obedience of the peoples' would be rendered to Him (Gen. 49:10). Indeed, the chief image of Messiah presented in the Old Testament was that of a king or ruler, as the earlier argument has shown. Thus it is not surprising that such a function should appear in the historical accounts of the life and ministry of Jesus of Nazareth, even before His resurrection and ascension (when He entered into the exercise of His kingly rule).

I. Preliminary Expressions of Jesus' Lordship
Some events early in the life and ministry of Jesus gave an indication of His destiny to rule in kingly glory.

1. At Jesus' Birth (Luke 1:32-33)
Prior to Jesus' conception and birth He was introduced as a king. The angel Gabriel announced to Mary His mother that she would conceive and bear a son whose name would be 'Jesus' (1:31; the meaning of the name is not expanded upon here as it is in Matthew 1:21). Then the angel said, 'He will be great and will be called Son of the Most High. And the Lord God will give to him the *throne* of His father David, and he will *reign* over the house of Jacob forever, and of His *kingdom* there will be no end' (1:32-33). Concerning this pronouncement, several relevant points may be made.

1) Jesus will be a regal person. The language 'Son of the Most High,' says Darrell Bock, 'is simply another way of saying "Son of God," since *hypistou* ["most high"] is another way to refer to God's supreme authority as "the Most High".'[1] The use of this term in one of the Dead Sea Scrolls (4Q246) of a ruling figure leads Bock to argue for 'the regal context in which the term operates. A king is about to be born.' The term 'son', used of the Davidic king's sonship to God in 2 Samuel 7:14, also suggests a regal connection. 'As Jesus' birth is announced, regal imagery abounds to describe the coming Messiah.'[2] I. Howard Marshall concurs: 'The use of *pater* ["father": "his father David"] indicates that the child will be the royal messiah inasmuch as he is descended from David – hence the significance of the earlier reference to Joseph's descent [v. 27].'[3]

2) Jesus will occupy David's throne by the grant of God. The angel affirms that God will give to Jesus the throne of 'his father David.' Jesus' legal connection to David is through Mary's betrothed husband (1:27), though Mary is also most likely a descendant of David. As Bock again observes, 'He is to receive the throne of his father David, a picture of majestic rule'; and 'The Davidic throne is clearly a regal image drawn from the Davidic covenant's promise of a son, a house, and an everlasting rule (2 Sam. 7:8-16, esp. vv. 13, 16 ...).' While Solomon was the immediate fulfillment of this promise, ultimately it referred to Messiah. Bock claims that 'Jesus' regal Davidic connection is the basic Christological starting point for Luke's presentation of the person of Jesus,' and leads to the presentation of Jesus and the kingdom of God found in the book of Acts.[4]

3) Jesus will reign over a kingdom which will never end. The emphatic (because repeated) assertion of verse 33 is that Jesus' reign shall last forever and shall have no end. The affirmation

---

1 Darrell L. Bock, *Luke*, vol. 1. Baker Exegetical Commentary (BEC) on the New Testament (Grand Rapids: Baker, 1994), p. 113.

2 Bock, *Luke*, BEC, 1:113-14; citations from p. 114.

3 I. Howard Marshall, *Luke*, NIGTC, p. 68.

4 Citations and argument in Bock, *Luke* (BEC), 1:114-15.

that Jesus will reign over the 'house of Jacob' (Israel) does not preclude the possibility that the notion of 'Israel' could be expanded by the extension of the gospel to Gentiles. Both clauses of this verse utilize the language of kingship: the first uses a verb meaning 'reign as king', the second uses the noun 'kingdom'. The second clause of the verse is most emphatic in asserting that 'of his kingdom there shall not be an end'. Marshall points out that the angel's assertion 'says nothing about the commencement of the reign', and though Luke shared the early church's understanding which 'associated the reign of Jesus with his resurrection and exaltation and linked this with the Davidic promises (Acts 2:30-36)', yet at the same time Luke was 'also conscious that the kingdom of God could be said to have arrived in the ministry of Jesus, so that the exaltation was the open recognition of One who had already acted in his earthly life with kingly power as the representative of God.'[5]

Clearly, the features of this passage warrant Bock's conclusion: 'The ruling position and activity of Jesus in God's plan is the fundamental point of the angelic description of Jesus.'[6]

2. At Jesus' Transfiguration (Matthew 17:1-8)

Another point at which Jesus' future status as glorified Lord is suggested before the occurrence of His resurrection and ascension is the event commonly known as the 'transfiguration' (Matt. 17:1-8; Mark 9:2-8; Luke 9:28-36). As described in the Gospels, Jesus took with Him Peter, James and John to the top of a mountain where He was transformed in their presence, radiating an intense light from His person and His clothing. There also appeared Moses and Elijah, talking with Jesus. A voice from an overshadowing cloud told the disciples, 'This is my beloved Son, with whom I am well pleased; listen to him' (Matt. 17:5).

The command to 'listen' to Jesus probably referred back to His previous disclosure that He 'must go to Jerusalem and

---

5   Marshall, *Luke*, NIGTC, p. 68.

6   Bock, *Luke*, BEC, 1:116.

suffer many things from the elders and chief priests and scribes, and be killed, and on the third day be raised' (Matt. 16:21). This disclosure provoked a sharp rebuke from Peter, to which Jesus replied with an even sharper rebuke that Peter's thinking was far from agreement with God's purposes (16:22-23). Jesus continued to explain that discipleship meant following the same principle that He was pursuing, self-denial and the death of self-will (16:24-26). Then Jesus spoke of the more distant future, when 'the Son of Man is going to come with his angels in the glory of his Father, and then he will repay each person according to what he has done' (16:27). This seems to speak of His coming in glory and His function of fulfilling the role of the Judge of humanity. This claim is followed by the enigmatic statement, 'Truly, I say to you, there are some standing here who will not taste death until they see the Son of Man coming in his kingdom' (16:28; most interestingly, while Matthew speaks of the kingdom of the Son of Man, Mark 9:1 and Luke 9:27 quote Jesus as speaking of the coming of the 'kingdom of God', suggesting that the kingdom of the Son of Man and the kingdom of God are equivalent expressions: Jesus is truly to be God's agent in ruling over God's kingdom, which is Jesus' kingdom as well).

The argument of R. T. France carries considerable persuasive power that this last statement (16:28) refers not to Jesus' return or *parousia* but to His installation at the right hand of God as reigning Lord of the universe. France observes that the language of verse 28 is reminiscent of that of Daniel 7:13-14: 'I saw in the night visions, and behold, with the clouds of heaven there *came* one like a *son of man*, and he *came* to the Ancient of Days and was presented before him. And *to him was given* dominion and glory and *a kingdom* ...' The italicized language fairly closely parallels that of Jesus' claim in Matthew 16:28 and suggests the source of his allusion. The event in view in this understanding is not Jesus' return to earth (as it is in 16:27) but His prior ascension, exaltation, and installation as the reigning Son of Man.[7] This reality should have served to encourage the disciples that Jesus' death would

---

7   France, *Matthew*, TNTC, p. 261.

not mean the end for Him, but is a necessary passageway to greater glory. The disciples would 'see' Jesus' entry into His kingdom in beholding His resurrected glory (see the next section below), in witnessing Jesus' ascension (Acts 1:9), and would observe its effects in His outpouring of the Holy Spirit on the Day of Pentecost (Acts 2:32-33), which Spirit would effectuate the advance of the kingdom in the world during this present age. Thus Peter concluded his message on that day, 'Let all the house of Israel therefore know for certain that God has made him both Lord and Christ, this Jesus whom you crucified' (Acts 2:36), that is, God has made Him Sovereign Lord of the universe and reigning Messiah. But before that time, a few of Jesus' disciples would experience a foretaste of His exalted glory in the event of His transfiguration.

This understanding of the transfiguration as a foregleam of future glory is supported by Everett Harrison. Harrison points out that, according to Luke's account, the conversation of Jesus with Moses and Elijah concerned His impending *exodus* (a 'going-out'), meaning His death at Jerusalem (Luke 9:31). While this could mean merely the end of Jesus' life, two considerations suggest 'a deeper meaning'. First, the language of Luke refers to Jesus' *accomplishing* of this exodus, 'which is rather strange language for such an ordinary experience as death', thus suggesting that something more is meant. Second, 'on the way down the mountain, Jesus spoke of his resurrection' (Matt. 17:9; Mark 9:9). Hence, Harrison concludes, 'it may well be that the word *exodus* in this setting is designed to point to death as a victorious event, despite the appearance of weakness and defeat, holding in itself the prospect of glorious resurrection.'[8]

Harrison connects the transfiguration with the earlier pronouncement of Jesus concerning some of His disciples beholding the kingdom coming with power (Matt. 16:28; Mark 9:1; Luke 9:27). That earlier statement, followed immediately by the transfiguration in the Gospel accounts, 'seems to suggest that the transfiguration was intended as a foregleam of the glory of the Son of man as he would be

---

8   Harrison, *Short Life of Christ*, p. 157.

in his consummated kingdom.'[9] Thus the transfiguration arguably stands as a preview or foretaste of Jesus' kingly status in his resurrection and exaltation.

APPLICATORY OBSERVATIONS

1) From the very first of the events relating to the incarnation of God the Son, even before His conception in the womb of Mary, Jesus of Nazareth was intended for kingship. His rule was not an afterthought in the divine program but was central in the Old Testament portrayal of Messiah and in the angelic announcement to Mary. To omit His kingship from the message of the New Testament accounts is to violate the spirit of the documents and would constitute as great a blunder as to omit His priesthood. Those who receive Him as priest must also reckon with the fact that He is king and acknowledge Him as such.

2) If Jesus' first disciples needed encouragement concerning His future glory as king, those disciples who live now also need to be reminded of His present kingship, His overruling of all the affairs of earthly life, and His future final victory. This is a most encouraging and fortifying truth for God's people, and one of which they may remind themselves often.

II. The Concrete Accomplishment of Jesus' Lordship: Resurrection and Exaltation

Jesus the Messiah's kingly reign or lordship was not only predicted at His birth, hinted at and then proclaimed in His teaching, and foreshadowed by His transfiguration, but it was also historically established through specific events in His messianic career. Jesus the Messiah entered upon the full status and exercise of His kingly function through the historical events of His resurrection and ascension.

1. The Resurrection of Jesus

The beginning of Jesus' exaltation as Lord is to be found in His resurrection from the dead. The testimony to His resurrection (which evidently was not itself witnessed by any humans) is set forth in the Gospel accounts of the empty tomb and of his post-resurrection appearances to his disciples (Matt. 28:1-20;

---

9   Harrison, *Short Life of Christ*, p. 163.

Mark 16:1-8; Luke 24:1-49; John 20:1-21:25). Jesus' resurrection served several functions.

1) The resurrection constituted Jesus' victory over death. Death has been a great affliction upon the human race ever since the fall in the Garden of Eden (although it is also a mercy). Humans have been attempting to overcome death ever since (or dreaming of overcoming it) but to no avail. In the resurrection of Jesus, death was overcome by and for Jesus personally (as Peter said on the Day of Pentecost, 'God raised him up, loosing the pangs of death, because it was not possible for him to be held by it,' Acts 2:24) and in principle for the human race more generally. As 'the firstborn from the dead' (Col. 1:18), Jesus incorporated in His own resurrection the eventual raising of His own people as well (1 Cor. 15:23: 'Christ the firstfruits, then at his coming those who belong to Christ'). If Jesus is not raised from the dead, then death has not been overcome and the Christian faith is a great hoax (1 Cor. 15:12-19).

2) The resurrection validated and made effective Jesus' death as an atoning sacrifice. As Everett Harrison has suggested, 'The resurrection testified to the success of his mission.... The resurrection served notice on all that this redeeming mission had in fact been successfully carried out.' Harrison points out the significance of Romans 4:25. 'Jesus was raised on account of our justification (as 4:25 should probably be translated), to make it plain that a new relationship had been set up by the cross for all sinners who were willing to come to God through him.'[10] But it is difficult to conceive of the cross having this effectiveness *apart from* the resurrection of Jesus; the New Testament conception of salvation is inconceivable and incomprehensible without this climax to its accomplishment.

3) The resurrection vindicated Jesus' claims regarding His person and mission. Peter proclaimed to his Jewish audience concerning the healing of a lame man, 'by the name of Jesus Christ of Nazareth, whom you crucified, whom God raised from the dead – by him this man is standing before you well. This Jesus is the stone that was rejected by you, the builders, which has become the cornerstone' (Acts 4:10-11). This

---

10   Harrison, *Short Life of Christ*, p. 244.

suggests that the resurrection served as God's affirmation of Jesus as the Messiah and as the One through whom salvation had been wrought (v. 12).

4) The resurrection constituted the initial phase of Jesus' exaltation to supreme lordship (Matt. 28:18). His exaltation to supreme lordship began with His resurrection, as demonstrated by His claim in Matthew 28:18, one of the most forceful claims to authority uttered by Him: 'All authority has been given to Me in heaven and on earth.' Several observations are pertinent to our present discussion.

(a) *The authority that Jesus here speaks of is an authority which was given or granted to Him.* The meaning of the Greek verb *didomi* (give) as used in this context is 'to grant by formal action, *grant, allow,* frequently of God'.[11] The aorist passive verb indicates the passivity of Jesus in being granted this authority (it was conferred upon Him by God) as well as the definiteness of the point in time when He received it (implying perhaps that there was a time – in His incarnate existence – when He did not possess it). All this is further emphasized by the occurrence of the verb and the pronoun at the beginning of the sentence, giving a majestic and authoritative ring to the whole pronouncement, so that it reads literally: '*It has been given to me* all authority in heaven and on earth.' The implication of this claim is that the authority with which Jesus has been invested is *divine authority* – He is invested with the authority of God, He speaks with the authority of God, He will reign (after His ascension) with the authority of God and as the agent of God.

(b) *It is significant that this pronouncement was made by Jesus after His resurrection.* While Jesus certainly claimed authority for Himself on other occasions, it is significant that nothing approaching the comprehensiveness of this claim is to be found prior to the resurrection.[12] It is thus reasonable

---

11 BDAG 243, meaning 13.

12 See Mark 2:10; John 17:2. The claim found in Matthew 11:27 should be understood as limited to the concerns of the immediate context, that is, the sovereign bestowal of salvation. See John A. Broadus, 'Commentary on the Gospel of Matthew', in Alvah Hovey, ed., *An American Commentary on the New Testament*, 7 vols. (Valley Forge: American Baptist Publication Society, 1886), 1:252.

to infer that the authority claimed by Jesus in this verse was bestowed on Him when He was raised from the dead. This suggests that a fundamental change in Jesus' status took place at His resurrection and exaltation: He was transferred from the position of one who willingly placed Himself under the authority of men to a position of supreme authority over men and over the universe.

(c) *Jesus claimed for Himself a universal authority.* Jesus' authority encompasses no less than 'heaven and earth', a phrase which may speak of heaven as 'standing independently beside the earth' (as BDAG suggests) but which rather seems to imply 'the totality of creation'.[13] In any case it must certainly be a most comprehensive authority which is in view; there is no part of creation that does not come under its sway. The supremacy of this authority is heightened by the phrase 'all authority' (*pasa exousia*), which may be understood as 'absolute authority', specifically 'Jesus' total authority',[14] indicating that there is (under God) no authority superior to that possessed by Jesus. This affirmation by Jesus is nothing less than a claim to absolute lordship: 'He who has *exousia* is *kyrios*,' writes W. Foerster, who elsewhere concurs that the *exousia* claimed by Jesus in Matthew 28:18 refers to His exaltation as Lord and Christ, parallel to Acts 2:36.[15]

It may be objected that the authority claimed by Jesus in Matthew 28:18 could not be that authority attaching to His mediatorial lordship (that which He exercises as the God–man) because that mediatorial authority is commonly represented in the New Testament as having been bestowed at the time of Jesus' ascension to the right hand of God (Acts 2:33-36; see Eph. 1:20-23). To this it may be replied that Jesus' resurrection was the first stage of, and implied the whole of, the exaltation. As A. B. Bruce has written, the ascension is 'conceived as involved in the resurrection'.[16] A fine note on

---

13   BDAG 737; compare the suggested meanings in the first two sections under 1.a.

14   BDAG 353, meaning 3.

15   TDNT 3:1089; 2:568.

16   A. B. Bruce, 'The Synoptic Gospels', in W. Robertson Nicoll, ed., *The Expositor's Greek Testament*, 5 vols. (reprint ed., Grand Rapids: Eerdmans, 1967), 1:339.

the theology of Matthew 28:18, including the relationship between the resurrection and ascension, may be found in J.P. Lange's commentary on Matthew in the series bearing his name. Lange writes:

> According to the true conception, the ascension is essentially implied in the resurrection. Both events are combined in the one fact of Christ's exaltation. The resurrection is the root and the beginning of the ascension; the ascension is the blossom and crown of the resurrection.... But this [resurrection] life, as regards its essence, is the heavenly life; and, as regards its character, the entrance into that estate was accordingly the beginning of the ascension. The resurrection marks the entrance into the heavenly *state*; the ascension, into the heavenly *sphere*.[17]

Bruce Metzger similarly points out, 'the apostolic teaching did not always sharply differentiate the ascension or glorification of Christ from his resurrection. Apparently in some parts of the early church the resurrection and ascension were regarded as two episodes in the same process of the exaltation of Christ.'[18] Thus, while the exaltation is generally regarded in the New Testament as having occurred when Jesus ascended to the right hand of the Father, it is not improper for Jesus to speak of His being granted mediatorial authority even before the ascension; for His investiture with authority began immediately upon His entrance into the glorified state, that is, at the resurrection.

(d) *It is on the basis of the authority claimed by Jesus that He issued the command found in verses 19-20.* The particle *oun* ('therefore') occurs near the beginning of verse 19,[19] linking it with verse 18, indicating thus both the authority

---

17 John Peter Lange, *Commentary on the Holy Scriptures: Critical, Doctrinal and Homiletical,* trans. and ed. Philip Schaff, 24 vols. in 12 (reprint ed., Grand Rapids: Zondervan, 1960), vol. 8, 'Matthew', pp. 561-62. Lange's whole note is worthy of attention.

18 Bruce M. Metzger, 'The Ascension of Jesus Christ', in *Historical and Literary Studies: Pagan, Jewish, and Christian* (Grand Rapids: Eerdmans, 1968), p. 82.

19 The word *oun* is omitted by some Greek manuscripts, but the weight of evidence favors its inclusion.

by which Jesus speaks and the authority by which His disciples are to act. He speaks as one who has been given all authority in heaven and earth, and thus He commands His church; His disciples are to go, preach, baptize and teach in that same authority, as those who have been duly authorized by Him. Jesus is seen here in the actual exercise of that authority which is His as exalted Lord; it is to be understood as involving not only His right to rule the universe in a cosmic sense, but also the right to direct His church as He sees fit. John Broadus observes, 'It is on the basis of this mediatorial authority, in heaven and on earth, that the Savior issues his commission to his followers.'[20]

APPLICATORY OBSERVATIONS:

1) A dead king is not a triumphant king or a ruling king. The only way to speak meaningfully about the lordship of Jesus Christ is on the basis of His bodily resurrection. Those who attempt to maintain His 'lordship' apart from His resurrection are dealing in nonsense.

2) The reality of Jesus' resurrection and investiture with authority means that He must be recognized as rightly exercising legitimate authority and lordship over every

---

20 Broadus, 'Matthew', p. 592. Larry W. Hurtado has such a fine statement of the 'specific convictions' engendered in Jesus' disciples by His post-resurrection appearances that it is worth repeating in full: 'The earliest indications are that these convictions were the following: (1) that God had released Jesus from death, so that it really is Jesus, not merely his memory or influence, who lives again; (2) that God has bestowed on Jesus uniquely a glorious new form of existence, immortal and eschatological bodily life; (3) that Jesus has also been exalted to a unique heavenly status, thus presiding by God's appointment over the redemptive program; and (4) that those who were given these special encounters with the risen Jesus were divinely commissioned to proclaim Jesus' exalted status and to summon people to recognize in his resurrection/exaltation the signal that the eschatological moment of redemption has arrived. The experiences, therefore, likely involved an encounter with a figure recognized as Jesus but also exhibiting features that convinced the recipients that he had been clothed with divinelike glory and given a unique heavenly status' (Hurtado, *Lord Jesus Christ: Devotion to Jesus in Earliest Christianity* [Grand Rapids: Eerdmans, 2003], pp. 71-72).

professing Christian and over every congregation that claims to be Christian. This truth has implications for personal lifestyle and congregational order, implications which it requires the rest of the New Testament to explain adequately.

So the concrete establishment of Jesus the Messiah's kingly reign was begun in His resurrection from the dead. That event, even before His ascension, led Him to claim His investiture with 'all authority' by God (Matt. 28:18). But there was more to come. The full investiture with supreme lordship over all the universe is represented by the New Testament as occurring upon Jesus' ascension and exaltation to the 'right hand of God' (Acts 2:33). As this is one of the more common themes of the New Testament writings, it is worthy of serious and separate consideration.

2. The Ascension of Jesus

The bodily ascension of Jesus is described in two passages of the New Testament but it is presupposed in many other passages. The two direct descriptions are in Luke's writings, Luke 24:50-51 and Acts 1:9-11. The former says: 'Then he led them out as far as Bethany, and lifting up his hands he blessed them. While he blessed them, *he parted from them and was carried up into heaven.*' The Acts passage reads as follows: 'And when he had said these things, as they were looking on, *he was lifted up, and a cloud took him out of their sight.* And while they were gazing into heaven as he went, behold, two men stood by them in white robes, and said, "Men of Galilee, why do you stand looking into heaven? This *Jesus, who was taken up from you into heaven,* will come in the same way as you saw him go into heaven."' While both passages describe Jesus as ascending into the heavenly sphere, the Acts passage also has the angels saying explicitly that Jesus was 'taken up into heaven', leaving little doubt about the claim expressed by the narrative as to the historical nature and reality of the event.[21]

1) The Nature of the Ascension. The ascension of Jesus, as described by Luke and assumed throughout the New

---

21 For a recent defense of the historicity of Jesus' ascension, see Reymond, *Systematic Theology,* pp. 575-78. The objective historical reality of the event is emphasized by Metzger, 'The Ascension of Jesus Christ,' pp. 82, 85.

Testament, involved the bodily removal of Jesus after His resurrection from the earthly sphere to the heavenly realm. Two observations here seem relevant. First, as earth-bound creatures we must acknowledge our own ignorance of much of the reality concerning the universe and must not judge the biblical accounts in terms of the assumed 'knowledge' of modern science. Indeed, scientific thought suggests that there may be several dimensions of reality, and it is thus entirely possible that Jesus was transferred to a different dimension of reality which is not currently visible to us. We are not warranted by the phenomenological language of Scripture to conclude that the biblical accounts naively assume a mere 'up' and 'down' in the relationship between heaven and earth. The Bible as a whole leads us to think there is a 'place' where God most fully manifests His presence, that this place is called 'heaven' (not merely the realm of the stars and planets), and that Jesus was taken there bodily.[22]

Second, something like the ascension was a necessary counterpart to the incarnation. If the second person of the eternal Godhead truly assumed a complete human nature at the incarnation and He continues to possess a human nature (including a body) after His resurrection, then the only way for Him to remove Himself from this earthly sphere was by means of a bodily transference from the earthly sphere to the heavenly one (this assumes also His possession of a glorified body, suitable for dwelling in the heavenly realm, provided Him at His resurrection). Just as the Son permanently took on humanity when He entered the earthly sphere, so He must take His humanity with Him when He entered the heavenly sphere, requiring some kind of physical removal from earth such as the ascension provided.[23]

---

22 Metzger has similar emphases, 'The Ascension of Jesus Christ', pp. 83-85. For a discussion of related themes, see Wayne Grudem, *Systematic Theology: An Introduction to Biblical Doctrine* (Grand Rapids: Zondervan, 1994, printing of 2000), pp. 617-20, 1159-60.

23 Metzger argues that the act of physically ascending was not necessary for Jesus to enter heaven (as His post-resurrection appearances suggest that His presence and movement were 'not subject to the ordinary laws of nature') but was didactic in purpose, intended to instruct Jesus' disciples concerning His definitive removal from the earthly sphere and the termination of His post-resurrection appearances ('The Ascension of Jesus Christ', pp. 83-84, [citation from p. 83], pp. 85-86).

2) The Significance of the Ascension. Acts 1:1-2 would seem to be a crucial text for reaching a proper understanding of the ascension of Jesus: 'In the first book, O Theophilus, I have dealt with all that Jesus *began* to do and teach, *until the day that he was taken up....*' This statement suggests that Jesus' ministry continued after His ascension, but with the difference that it was now conducted in a different manner than during His earthly career. As Harrison points out, Jesus' earthly post-resurrection appearances to His disciples ended at this point (those appearances to Stephen [Acts 7:56], to Saul [Acts 9:4-6], and to John [Rev. 1:12-16] apparently display Jesus in His heavenly state).[24] He now would exercise His messianic ministry in and from the heavenly realm; and to this the Book of Acts bears frequent testimony (2:33; 4:10; 7:55-56; 9:3-6, 10-16; 18:9-10; etc.). In the terms which have been used thus far, this truth could be stated as follows: 'The ascension of Jesus involved a continuation in the heavenly sphere of Jesus' messianic ministry in his prophetic function, in his priestly function and in his kingly function.' This statement can be enlarged upon in order to express more fully its meaning.

(a) After His ascension Jesus continued His prophetic function. After His resurrection and ascension Jesus continued His messianic prophetic ministry by sending the Holy Spirit upon His disciples (Acts 2:33), which accomplished two things. First, the Spirit brought to the disciples' memory all that Jesus had taught them (John 14:26), enabling them to record Jesus' proclamation as we have it in the Gospels. Second, just as Jesus inaugurated His public messianic ministry by proclaiming the near arrival of the kingdom of God (Matt. 4:17; Mark 1:14-15); gave instruction to His disciples concerning the demands and nature of the kingdom (Matt. 5–7; 13); and after His resurrection He appeared to His disciples for forty days, 'speaking about the kingdom of God' (Acts 1:3), so after His ascension, in sending the Holy Spirit upon the disciples (Acts 2:33), He empowered them to proclaim the kingdom of God (Acts 8:12; 14:22; 19:8; 20:25; 28:23, 31). Both of these constituted the

---

24 Harrison, *Short Life of Christ,* p. 252.

continuation of Jesus' own prophetic proclamation, in His name, by His authority, and in His power.

Paul was likely referring to such activity of Jesus when he wrote in Ephesians 4:8 that, 'When he ascended on high he led a host of captives, and *he gave gifts to men.*' Paul goes on to speak of apostles, prophets, evangelists, and pastors and teachers (4:11) as included among those gifts. The office of apostle especially should be seen as the authoritative continuation of Jesus' prophetic ministry.

(b) *After His ascension Jesus entered a new phase of His priestly function.* Harrison highlights the consequences of Jesus' ascension which involve His ministry as High Priest of His people.[25] (i) The ascension *certifies the completed atoning work* which Jesus had accomplished in His death. Hebrews 1:3 says, 'After making purification for sins, he sat down at the right hand of the Majesty on high.' Thus the ascension testifies to the perfect acceptability to the Father of Jesus' atoning work on the cross as well as the completed nature of that work, of which Hebrews abundantly speaks (7:27; 9:12, 28; 10:10, 12, 14, etc.).

(ii) The ascension *affirmed and enabled Jesus' present work as the great high priest* of His people. Hebrews asserts that 'we have a great high priest who has passed through the heavens, Jesus, the Son of God' (4:14). This is a theme which continues through the tenth chapter of Hebrews. He has 'entered ... into heaven itself, now to appear in the presence of God on our behalf' (9:24).

(iii) The ascension of Jesus *gives assurance to Christians of their own expectation of full and final redemption.* Hebrews 9:12 states that Christ 'entered once for all into the holy places ... by means of his own blood, thus securing an eternal redemption.' The current priestly ministry of Jesus is thus the guarantee of the final eschatological redemption which is promised to His people. In sum, the continued efficacy of Jesus' priestly work is dependent on His having entered into the very presence of God as the representative of His people, accomplished by means of His ascension.

---

25   Harrison, *Short Life of Christ*, pp. 253-54.

(3) *After His ascension Jesus entered more fully into His kingly function.* Peter proclaimed on the Day of Pentecost that Jesus had been 'exalted at the right hand of God' and that 'God has made him both Lord and Christ, this Jesus whom you crucified' (Acts 2:33, 36). As will be shown later, this means that Jesus entered into His active reign as Messiah and the exercise of universal lordship upon His ascension to the right hand of God the Father. Metzger claims that 'his act of ascending conveyed the clear impression that he had gone to his Father and that all power was put into his hands.... [H]e parted from his followers in such a way that they thereby became even more certain of his royal power and rule.' The language of Jesus being at the 'right hand of God' 'is metaphorical language for the divine omnipotence.... it affirms that he is reigning as king, wielding the power of divine omnipotence.'[26]

A fact which needs continually to be kept in mind when considering the exaltation of Jesus is that this exaltation involved the seating on the throne of the universe not merely God the Son considered simply in His deity but the God-Man Jesus of Nazareth. Jesus retained His human nature when He was exalted to heaven. As Harrison points out, 'the incarnation persists in the person of the man Christ Jesus.' He quotes John Duncan: 'The dust of the earth is on the throne of the majesty on high.'[27] A human being sits on the throne of the universe and exercises divine prerogatives.

---

26 Metzger, 'The Ascension of Jesus Christ,' pp. 86-87. Donald Guthrie sets forth a helpful statement of the theological meaning of the ascension of Jesus in eight points: The ascension is/means (1) The completion of the resurrection; (2) the beginning of exaltation and enthronement; (3) the inauguration of the ministry of intercession; (4) the fulfilment of the divine mission; (5) the filling by Christ of all things; (6) the bestowing of the gift of the Spirit; (7) the opening up of access for believers; (8) the start of the new age. 'This age is the age of the risen and enthroned Lord' (*New Testament Theology* [Downers Grove, IL: InterVarsity, 1981], pp. 398-401, citation from p. 401).

27 Harrison, *Short Life of Christ,* p. 252.

Much of the remainder of this study will be concerned to show, as stated by Robert Reymond, 'that upon his resurrection and ascension (these two events may be construed quite properly together ... as the collective two-stage means to his exaltation to Lordship), as the fruit and reward for his labors on earth, Jesus the Messiah was granted supreme lordship and universal dominion over men.' And Reymond points out as well the feature of Jesus' exaltation mentioned above: 'It was as the divine–human Messiah, then, that he "acquired" or "was given" at his ascension *de facto* authority to exercise mediatorial dominion.'[28] It was not simply as God that He was exalted and enthroned, but as the God–Man.

APPLICATORY OBSERVATIONS

1) The entire Christian scheme of redemption depends upon Jesus' ascension into heaven; hence, it is not an optional part of the story. It is not a dead and buried Savior on whom Christians rely but a living and exalted one who represents them before God. If a so-called Christian theology stops short of this it does not portray the full biblical picture of salvation.

2) Jesus' ascension provides the basis for His return to earth. Although Jesus the Messiah has accomplished redemption and has been exalted to supreme authority, that redemption will not be experientially completed in His people and that authority will not be universally acknowledged until He appears 'a second time' (Heb. 9:28). His bodily departure is the prerequisite for His bodily return.

---

28 Reymond, *Systematic Theology*, pp. 579, 580. For a fuller treatment of this reality, see Appendix 2.

PART THREE

THE PROCLAMATION
AND CONFESSION
OF JESUS' LORDSHIP

7

The Apostolic Proclamation
of Jesus' Lordship:
The Book of Acts

The earliest Christian preaching of which we have any record is that recorded in the Book of Acts in the New Testament. What is found there is that the apostles consistently set forth Messiah Jesus as the risen and exalted Lord and as the proper object of faith for their hearers. That is, the gospel message of the early Christian preachers centered on the person and position of Jesus the Messiah in the fullness of His present lordship. The first example of apostolic preaching is foundational and is supported by the preaching recorded in the remainder of Acts.

I. Acts 2:36: Jesus is Risen Lord and Exalted Messiah

Acts 2:36 is a passage of fundamental importance for establishing the New Testament teaching on the lordship of Jesus. The occasion was that of Peter's address on the day of Pentecost, and it thus places us at a very early point in the developing theology of the young church.

Peter's affirmation is that 'God has made him both Lord and Christ, this Jesus whom you crucified.' Concerning this declaration and the context in which it is made, a few relevant observations may be noted (dealing first with the title 'Lord' and then with the more problematic title – in this context – 'Christ').

1. Peter affirms that Jesus was 'made' Lord, indicating a new and distinctive phase of Messiah's career.

The verb *poieo* ('made'), used in this particular construction, means 'making someone (into) something',[1] that is, in this

---

1   BDAG 840 (2.h.beta). Darrell Bock weakens the force of the verb when he seeks to interpret it as merely 'a designation or role that God had made evident,' in *Acts*, Baker Exegetical Commentary (Grand Rapids: Baker Academic, 2007), p. 136.

instance, Jesus was made to be Lord. As Joseph Addison Alexander has pointed out, *poieo* 'is never a mere synonym of *showed, declared*,'[2] and thus the meaning cannot be weakened to indicate the mere declaration or demonstration of Jesus' lordship, but must refer to His actual installation into the office of 'Lord'. The action of God mentioned in this verse relative to Jesus' lordship is, as Alexander contends, not a 'declaratory act' but a 'constituting act'.[3]

2. **The term 'Lord,' as used in Acts 2:36, refers not to Jesus' essential deity but to the office of sovereign authority into which He was installed at His exaltation.** Alexander again has an appropriate comment: '*Lord* cannot mean a divine person ... for the Father did not make the Son to be God, but must mean a mediatorial sovereign.'[4] Once the meaning 'made' is acknowledged for *poieo*, then unless we are prepared to concede an adoptionist Christology here (which would contradict the rest of the New Testament), *kyrios* must be recognized as the title of the office into which Jesus was installed. The necessity for this understanding of *kyrios* is clearly demanded by the fact that God *made* Jesus to be such, which of course could not be predicated of His deity, which He already possessed and which is not, at any rate, an acquired quality. And this further underscores the need for the careful distinction that it was *as the God–man* that Jesus was exalted and invested with mediatorial lordship, a role which He had not previously enjoyed *as the God–man* and which stands in sharp contrast with His former (pre-resurrection) status of humility and servanthood.

3. **The appointment of Jesus to lordship by God the Father occurred in conjunction with the resurrection and exaltation of Jesus.**
Peter devoted considerable attention to the resurrection of Jesus in Acts 2:24-32, leading directly to the mention of His

---

2   Joseph Addison Alexander, *A Commentary on the Acts of the Apostles*, 2 vols. in 1 (reprint ed., London: Banner of Truth Trust, 1963), 1:82.

3   Alexander, *Acts* 1:82.

4   Alexander, *Acts* 1:82.

exaltation in verse 33 and His lordship in verse 36. In fact, the exaltation of Jesus and His installation as Lord could almost be said to define each other: the exaltation of Jesus means His installation as Lord, and His installation as Lord is called His exaltation. The connecting link between these two concepts is supplied by the quotation from Psalm 110 in Acts 2:34-35. Falling as it does between the mention of Jesus' exaltation to God's right hand in verse 33, and His installation as Lord in verse 36, the citation of Psalm 110:1 brings both of these elements together in a single thought: David's Lord (*kyrios*, v. 34) is installed at God's right hand (v. 34) in a position of absolute authority (v. 35). This intimate connection of Jesus' present lordship with His resurrection and exaltation indicates that it was indeed a new phase of His ministry into which He entered when He was invested with authority as Lord. His mediatorial lordship is a bestowed position (as will be seen in the treatment of Philippians 2:9-11 later in this study) grounded in the redemption accomplished by His atoning death and brought about through His resurrection in glory and exaltation to the right hand of God. It is something which He is not said to possess before His resurrection.

4. Against this background the difficulties attending the interpretation of the title 'Christ' in verse 36 are not insuperable.

The most plausible explanation of the statement that God 'made him Christ' is that offered by George Ladd: 'Peter means to say that Jesus has entered in upon a new stage of his messianic mission. He has now been enthroned as messianic King.' Ladd rejects the view that an adoptionist Christology is evidenced here (the view that 'Jesus *became* Messiah at his exaltation'), for other passages in Acts show that Peter knew otherwise: 'In the days of his flesh [Jesus] has been anointed (4:27; 10:38), and it was as the Messiah that he had suffered (3:18).' The meaning is, rather, that 'in his exaltation Jesus becomes the Messiah in a new sense: he has begun his messianic reign as the Davidic king.'[5] It is thus the regal aspect of Jesus' messiahship

---

5   Ladd, *New Testament Theology*, p. 336.

that Peter refers to, as contrasted with His previous suffering and humiliation.

5. Verse 33 shows that Jesus was actively engaged in the exercise of His lordship in the bestowal of the Holy Spirit.

It is Jesus Himself who is the subject of the verbs in verse 33; it was He who bestowed on the infant church the promised Holy Spirit. It was Jesus, 'having been exalted to the right hand of God, and having received from the Father the promise of the Holy Spirit', who 'poured forth' that Spirit with its miraculous manifestations at Pentecost. He was indeed Lord – over the church as well as over the earth. If the outpouring of the Spirit was a sign of the messianic age – as Peter suggested in quoting Joel 2 in verses 17-21 – then it is appropriate that He who has now been made the ruling messianic king should be the active agent in pouring forth that Spirit.

We have found then in Acts 2:36 that the exaltation which Jesus experienced subsequent to His resurrection consisted of His being granted, as the God–man, a position of supremacy and authority at God's right hand, a position to which is attached the title 'Lord', with all the rights and prerogatives which that title implies. This teaching is furthermore seen to be fundamental to the theology of the early New Testament church, climaxing as it does the first apostolic proclamation of the gospel after the descent of the Holy Spirit.

APPLICATORY OBSERVATIONS

1) The bestowal of the Holy Spirit was as much the work of Jesus the Messiah as it was the work of the Father (both are mentioned in John 15:26; 16:7; the Father acts in Jesus' name, 14:26). It was an act of the risen and exalted Messiah, and thus the Holy Spirit could be called 'the Spirit of Christ' (Rom. 8:9).

2) The work of redemption is a Trinitarian work. It is accomplished and applied by the harmonious and united working of the Father (who in this text exalted Jesus), the Son (who poured out the Spirit), and the Holy Spirit (who comes to indwell, confirm, and equip believers).

3) Jesus' mediatorial lordship (that which He exercises as the God–man) began in its fullness as soon as He was exalted to the Father's right hand. While it will later be openly manifested and acknowledged (Phil. 2:9-11), He is now fully Lord, and He should be acknowledged and received as such by professing Christians.

II. The Remainder of the Book of Acts

We have found in Acts 2:33-36 a crucial text, teaching us that the exaltation which Jesus experienced subsequent to His resurrection consisted in His being granted, as the God–man, a position of supremacy and authority at God's right hand, a position to which is attached the title 'Lord', with all the rights and prerogatives which that title implies. This teaching is furthermore seen to be fundamental to the theology of the early New Testament church, climaxing as it does the first apostolic proclamation of the gospel after the descent of the Holy Spirit.

This emphasis on the exaltation and lordship of Jesus in Peter's Pentecost sermon was no accident or fluke but was characteristic of the preaching of the early church. Virtually every evangelistic address found in Acts includes mention of the exaltation and lordship of Jesus. Those which do not refer specifically to Jesus' lordship do speak of His resurrection, which, as we noted earlier, is the first stage of His exaltation and which, even before the ascension, involved the conferment of mediatorial authority (Matt. 28:18).

Besides Acts 2:33-36 we may note the following passages in Acts.

1. Acts 3:20-21. In Peter's evangelistic address at the temple recorded in chapter 3 Jesus is referred to as 'the Christ appointed for you, Jesus, *whom heaven must receive* until the time for restoring all the things about which God spoke' (Acts 3:20-21), an obvious allusion to the ascension and present exalted state of Jesus. Until the time for the 'restoring' of all things concerning which God has made promise, 'the glorified body of the risen and ascended Christ not only may but *must*, as an appointed means of that accomplishment, be resident in heaven, and not on earth.'[6]

---

6   Alexander, *Acts* 1:118 (emphasis added).

2. Acts 5:31. When, in Acts 5, Peter replies to the Sanhedrin's demand that the apostles stop preaching in Jesus' name, he tells them that '*God exalted him* [Jesus] at his right hand as *Leader* [*archegos*, 'leader, ruler, prince'[7]] and Savior', a reference to Jesus' position of authority as exalted Lord. Alexander argues that the term [God's] 'right hand' is ambiguous, and could mean both '*With his right hand*, by the exertion of his power, and *to his right hand*, i.e. to a share in that power and in the dignity connected with it.'[8]

3. Acts 7:56. Later, when Stephen is on trial before the same group, he speaks (at the risk of his life) of Jesus' exaltation: 'Behold, I see the heavens opened, and the *Son of Man* standing *at the right hand of God*' – which utterance led immediately to his being stoned by his Jewish hearers (7:57-58). The cause of the Jews' rage is perhaps explained by Alexander:

> *The Son of Man*, which here replaces *Jesus* in the foregoing verse, is nowhere else in Scripture applied to Christ, except by himself. Stephen's use of the phrase is not sufficiently explained ... unless we furthermore suppose a reference to his Messianic claims and honors. 'I see the heavens opened to my view, and him who used to call himself the Son of Man on earth, now standing as the Son of Man in the highest place of honour and authority.'[9]

4. Acts 10:36, 42. When Peter preached to the household of Cornelius, he declared that Jesus is '*Lord* of all' (Acts 10:36), which in this context, Alexander argues, means that the gospel is 'not designed for them [Jews] alone, since Jesus Christ, through whom it is proclaimed, is Lord of all men, not of the Jews only', that is, the gospel is intended for Gentiles as well. Later in the same address Peter declared that Jesus in His exalted state 'is the one appointed by God to be *judge* of the living and the dead' (Acts 10:42). Both of these terms, 'Lord' and 'judge', referred to Jesus' exalted status as the

---

7   BDAG, p. 138.

8   Alexander, *Acts*, 1:228; for his full argument concerning the ambiguity of the term, see 1:79.

9   Alexander, *Acts*, 1:308.

one who currently exercises authority on God's behalf and who in the future will serve as judge of humanity. Alexander suggests that Jesus' status as judge of the human race must have been thought to have particular relevance to Gentile audiences, as it is mentioned here by Peter and at Athens by Paul (Acts 17:31).[10]

5. *Acts 11:20.* When those who were scattered by 'the persecution that arose over Stephen' reached Syrian Antioch they 'spoke to the Hellenists also, preaching the *Lord* Jesus' (Acts 11:20). The message included not only the reality of 'Messiah crucified' (a constant theme of apostolic preaching in Acts to this point; see 1 Cor. 2:2), but also of Messiah Jesus as exalted Lord.

6. *Acts 13:32-37.* The first of Paul's evangelistic addresses to be recorded in Acts is found in chapter 13. Preaching in Pisidian Antioch to a predominantly Jewish audience, Paul gave heavy emphasis to the resurrection of Jesus (Acts 13:30-37), a passage which may contain an oblique reference to the exaltation: in verse 33 he possibly offers Old Testament support for the resurrection of Christ by quoting Psalm 2:7, a psalm which speaks above all else of Messiah's installation as Jehovah's appointed King (Ps. 2: 6-9). If the context of Psalm 2:7 is thus taken into account, as well as the role of the resurrection in the exaltation of Jesus, then a reference by Paul to the exaltation would seem to be implied if this is a reference to the resurrection.[11]

7. *Acts 16:31.* Later, in Acts 16, when Paul was asked by the jailer at Philippi concerning the way of salvation, he replied, 'Believe in the *Lord* Jesus, and you will be saved'. Trusting in Jesus is to put one's faith in Him who is nothing less than Lord.

8. *Acts 17:7.* When some Christians in Thessalonica were dragged before the city authorities by a Jewish-organized mob they were accused of acting 'against the decrees of Caesar, saying that there is another *king*, Jesus.' It is significant that

---

10 Alexander, *Acts,* 1:414.

11 The verb 'raised' is ambiguous in this verse; for a defense of 13:33 as a reference to the resurrection of Jesus, see Robert Duncan Culver, *Systematic Theology: Biblical and Historical* (Christian Focus, Rossshire, UK: 2005), p. 604; for its denial, see Alexander, *Acts,* 2:29.

here the Christian message is characterized by its enemies (though admittedly without full understanding) as asserting that Jesus is king (*basileus*), a title which, in the words of Cullmann, is 'a variant of the *Kyrios* title'.[12]

9. *Acts 17:31.* The record of Paul's speech at Athens (17:22-31) is the fullest account in Acts of a message delivered to a pagan (non-Jewish) audience (see 14:15-17 for a summary of a briefer impromptu message). This speech seems to contain a reference to the exaltation of Jesus. In Acts 17:31 Paul offered the historical reality of the resurrection of Jesus as evidence of his assertion that God had appointed Jesus as that Man through whom God will judge the world. God 'has fixed a day on which he will *judge* the world in righteousness *by a man* whom he has appointed; and of this he has given assurance to all by raising him from the dead.' The exercise of judgment on God's behalf is certainly the prerogative only of one who possesses supreme authority, an idea which presupposes the exaltation of Jesus subsequent to His resurrection.

10. *Acts 20:21.* This passage is not a direct evangelistic address but a description by Paul of his preaching ministry in Ephesus. He characterized his evangelism as one of 'testifying both to Jews and Greeks of repentance toward God and of faith in our *Lord* Jesus Christ.' The matter of repentance is quite germane to the present study and will be addressed later; for the moment, however, is it sufficient to note that Paul recalled his preaching as that which encouraged people to put their trust in none other than Him who is designated 'Lord', namely, Jesus the Messiah.

11. *Other indications of Jesus' Lordship.* The rest of the major addresses in Acts are not evangelistic in nature (Paul's farewell to the Ephesian elders, 20:17-35, must be included here; and his defense of himself before various bodies, 22:1-21; 24:10-21; 26:1-23), but it may be noted that the emphasis on Jesus' resurrection continues (Acts 25:19; 26:8). Indeed, Paul's conversion experience, which he recounted in his speeches in Acts 22 and 26, was nothing less than a vision of the risen, glorified and exalted Lord Jesus.

---

12 Cullmann, *Christology*, p. 220.

Besides the more direct references to Jesus' exaltation, there are found in Acts several descriptions of early Christian preaching which mention the kingdom of God as the subject matter of such preaching. A number of these link the name of Jesus with the proclamation of the kingdom. For example, Philip is said to have 'preached good news about the *kingdom of God* and the name of *Jesus Christ*' (Acts 8:12), closely connecting the two. Likewise, at the end of the book, a similar proclamation is said to have characterized the ministry of Paul in Rome. Gathering the leaders of the Jewish community to his rented quarters, Paul 'expounded to them, testifying to the *kingdom of God* and trying to convince them about *Jesus* both from the Law of Moses and the Prophets' (28:23). As Luke closed the book he described Paul as continuing his ministry in Rome for two years, 'proclaiming the *kingdom of God* and teaching about the *Lord Jesus Christ* with all boldness and without hindrance' (28:30-31). It is at least likely that in the connecting of Jesus with the proclamation of the kingdom of God (and in the last instance calling Jesus 'Lord'), it is intended that we are to understand that Jesus was set forth in the message as having a crucial role in the kingdom of God, namely, as the agent of God's rule.

The other three instances of the proclamation of the kingdom in Acts are found in 14:22, 19:8 and 20:25. In Acts 14:22 Luke summarizes Paul's exhortation to the new believers who were converted on the first missionary tour as 'saying that through many tribulations we must enter the *kingdom of God*', which suggests that the kingdom of God had been an integral part of Paul's message in his original preaching there. Acts 19:8 describes Paul's initial ministry at Ephesus as one of 'reasoning and persuading them about the *kingdom of God*.' And Paul bore similar testimony to his proclamation in Ephesus in Acts 20:25, where he reminded the elders of the Ephesian congregation that he had 'gone about proclaiming the *kingdom*'. These incidental notices suggest that the kingdom of God – a manifestation of God's government, exercised through Messiah Jesus – played a significant role in the apostolic proclamation.

This brief survey of Acts suggests that there is no element of apostolic preaching more prominent than the resurrection, exaltation and lordship of Jesus the Messiah. Even the preaching about Jesus' death did not overshadow this element, for the apostles were quick to declare that the One who was crucified is now the exalted Lord, and it was as the exalted Lord that He was presented to their hearers.

APPLICATORY OBSERVATION
The apostles and other early Christian preachers, under the leadership of the Holy Spirit, saw fit to proclaim consistently a message which included God's kingship (now to be acknowledged by humans), and Jesus' lordship (to be acknowledged as well) as a result of His exaltation to the right hand of the Father. They engaged in this proclamation against opposition and at the risk of their freedom and even their lives. Can the faithful communication of the gospel in our own day do any less than proclaim the same message?

III. The Pattern of the Apostolic Proclamation
The foregoing brief survey of the apostolic preaching in Acts (along with elements found especially in the Pauline letters, to anticipate some of the findings of the next chapter) suggests that it can at least be said that there is no element of apostolic preaching more prominent than the resurrection, exaltation and lordship of Jesus. Other research on the content of the apostolic *kerygma* (a Greek word meaning proclamation or message) confirms this impression.

1. New Testament students have observed a pattern in the early apostolic proclamation of the gospel.
1) C. H. Dodd. In the 1930s British New Testament scholar C. H. Dodd produced a study entitled *The Apostolic Preaching and Its Developments.* He surveyed relevant passages in Acts and the Pauline letters, and summarized the results for each body of literature. Dodd utilized the Greek term *kerygma* to refer to the content of the message of the early church. According to Dodd, an outline of the early *kerygma* in Acts would look something like this:

1. The age of fulfillment has dawned.

2. This has occurred through the ministry, death, and *resurrection* of Jesus.

3. *Jesus has been exalted at the right hand of God.*

4. The presence of the Holy Spirit in the church is the sign of Christ's present power and glory.

5. The Messianic age will shortly reach its consummation in the return of Christ.

6. Appeal for repentance, offer of forgiveness and of the gift of the Holy Spirit, and promise of salvation.[13]

The pattern of Paul's message is very similar:

1. Prophecies are fulfilled and the new age is inaugurated by the coming of Christ.

2. He was born of the seed of David.

3. He died according to the Scriptures, to deliver us out of the present evil age.

4. He was buried.

5. *He rose on the third day* according to the Scriptures.

6. *He is exalted at the right hand of God, as Son of God and Lord of the dead and the living.*

7. He will come again as Judge and Savior of men.[14]

For purposes of the present study the crucial point to observe is that Jesus' resurrection, exaltation and lordship were essential elements in both the early preaching found in Acts and in Paul's characterization of His own message. While other aspects of Dodd's argument in the book mentioned above and in his broader work may certainly be called into question, on this matter his conclusions seem generally to be well-founded.

---

13 C. H. Dodd, *The Apostolic Preaching and Its Developments* (reprint ed.; New York: Harper & Row, 1964), pp. 21-24.

14 Dodd, *Apostolic Preaching*, p. 17. In this and the previous summary, some points are taken verbatim from Dodd but not put in quotation marks to avoid their excessive use. Italics added for emphasis.

2) *Robert H. Mounce.* In a later study Robert H. Mounce offered a formulation of the early *kerygma* that refines that of C. H. Dodd. Mounce suggests that the *kerygma* consisted of three elements: 'a historical proclamation, a theological evaluation, and an ethical summons.'[15] These are respectively: (1) a proclamation of the death, resurrection and exaltation of Jesus, seen as the fulfilment of prophecy and involving man's responsibility; (2) the resultant evaluation of Jesus as both Lord and Christ; (3) a summons to repent and receive forgiveness of sins.[16]

Mounce's formulation is based primarily on the examples of apostolic preaching found in Acts but he shows that it is also in harmony with those kerygmatic passages in the Pauline Epistles which are possibly pre-Pauline in origin and which thus indicate the nature of the message handed down to Paul (1 Cor. 15:3-5; Rom. 10:9; 1:3-4; 4:24-25; 8:34).[17]

It may be noted that Mounce, in his outline of the characteristic elements of the *kerygma,* refers in his first point to the proclamation of the resurrection and exaltation of Jesus (which is so obvious in Acts as to need no demonstration here) leading on to the announcement of Jesus' lordship and messiahship, in support of which Mounce adduces Acts 2:34, 36; 3:19-20 and 10:36, passages from the major evangelistic addresses of Peter. Mounce concludes, 'No matter how far we move back into the dawn of apostolic preaching, there we find as its very heart and core the proclamation that Jesus of Nazareth is "both Lord and Christ."'[18] In a similar vein is the comment by F. F. Bruce, offered in another connection but relevant here: 'From the earliest days of the apostolic preaching the resurrection and enthronement of Christ were proclaimed side by side as integral to the good news.'[19] It would seem that

---

15 Robert H. Mounce, *The Essential Nature of New Testament Preaching* (Grand Rapids: Eerdmans, 1960), p. 110.

16 Mounce, *Essential Nature*, p. 77.

17 Mounce, *Essential Nature*, pp. 88-109.

18 Mounce, *Essential Nature*, p. 108.

19 F. F. Bruce, *The Epistle to the Ephesians* (Westwood, NJ: Fleming H. Revell Co., 1961), p. 41.

a careful perusal of the book of Acts could lead to no other conclusion.

3) Bruce M. Metzger. The esteemed New Testament scholar Bruce Metzger likewise offers a synopsis of apostolic preaching in Acts which draws attention to these elements of the message. According to Metzger, the 'common core' found in all the apostolic preaching is as follows:

(a) The promises of God made in Old Testament days have now been fulfilled, and the Messiah has come:

(b) He is Jesus of Nazareth, who (a) Went about doing good and executing mighty works by the power of God; (b) Was crucified according to the purpose of God; (c) *Was raised by God from the dead*; (d) *Is exalted by God and given the name 'Lord'*; (e) Will come again for judgment and the restoration of all things.

(c) Therefore, all who hear the message should repent and be baptized.[20]

Perhaps it is worthy of note that Metzger accurately reflects the apostolic emphasis on the present exalted status of Jesus: He *is* exalted by God and given the name 'Lord' – it is the identity of Jesus as the crucified one who is now the exalted Lord which is the focus of the apostolic message. He is the present reality with whom the apostles' hearers must deal in the present moment of their lives.

4) More recent studies. More recent examinations of the matter of apostolic preaching reach similar conclusions. Thus a recent reference work reports:

The sermons recorded in Acts tend to have a general common structure and message. Jesus is described as the Son of God (9:20), who fulfilled OT prophecies concerning the Messiah (cf. 2:25-35; 3:24-26; 10:43; 13:32-37). He went about doing good (10:37-38), was crucified but *rose from the dead* (e.g., 2:32; 4:10), and *is now exalted at God's right hand*

---

20 Bruce Manning Metzger, *The New Testament: Its Background, Growth, and Content* (Nashville: Abingdon, 1965), p. 177. Italics added for emphasis.

(2:33; 3:21; 10:42). In his name alone forgiveness of sins can be realized (2:38; 3:19; 10:43).[21]

2. Examination of the messages in Acts reveals a pattern in the apostolic preaching.

We are not dependent, however, on the secondary work of later students of the New Testament for the demonstration of a discernable pattern in the preaching found in Acts. Such a pattern can be demonstrated from the text of Acts itself. For the purposes of this study we shall limit ourselves to the major evangelistic messages of Acts in which a full gospel presentation is directed to Jewish or 'devout' (Gentile partial adherents of Judaism) audiences, namely, those found in Acts 2, 3, 10 and 13 (other speeches not covered here include defenses before Jewish authorities in Acts 4, 5 and 7; Paul's speeches to pagan audiences in Acts 14 and 17, which take a different starting point and different form; and Paul's apologetic accounts of his conversion in Acts 22 and 26).

An examination of these four messages reveals a pattern in which five distinct elements generally appear (with one exception). These elements are:

(i) The claim that gospel events constitute the fulfillment of prophecy

Acts 2:16-21	3:13a, 18, 21-25	10:43	13:16-23, 27

(ii) Presentation of historical data of Jesus' life, ministry and death

Acts 2:22-24	3:13b-15a	10:36-39	13:24-29

(iii) The claim that God raised Jesus from the dead

Acts 2:24-32	3:15b	10:40-41	13:30-37

---

21 Verlyn D. Verbrugge, *New International Dictionary of New Testament Theology: Abridged Edition* (Grand Rapids: Zondervan, 2000), p. 306; italics added (it should be noted that this work is an abridgment of work originally done in the 1960s and 1970s, but it still stands as authoritative). Likewise, Fred B. Craddock acknowledges Dodd's work and does not dispute the idea of a pattern in early Christian proclamation, in 'Preaching', *Anchor Bible Dictionary*, ed. David Noel Freedman (New York: Doubleday, 1992), 5:451-54, esp. pp. 452-53.

(iv) The claim that God has exalted Jesus

| Acts 2:33-36 | 3:13, 21 | 10:42 | (omitted) |

(v) Call for repentance or offer of forgiveness of sins

| Acts 2:37-40 | 3:19 | 10:43 | 13:38-41 |

The single exception is found in Paul's message of Acts 13, in which there is no explicit mention of the exaltation of Jesus, although very full attention is given to Jesus' resurrection, which, as we have seen, is the initial stage of Jesus' exaltation. Thus the omission of this element does not significantly alter the argument being presented here: there is a distinctive pattern appearing in the early apostolic preaching as recorded in the Book of Acts.

3. Among the five elements present in the apostolic evangelistic messages two common elements are the resurrection and exaltation of Jesus.
In Acts 2, after a full statement of the fact of the resurrection of Jesus, Peter goes on to affirm that Jesus was 'exalted at the right hand of God' (2:33) and that 'God has made him both Lord and Christ' (2:36). In the message of Acts 3, Peter claims that God has 'glorified his servant Jesus' (3:13) after raising Him from the dead (3:15) and that 'heaven must receive' Jesus (a reference to His ascension and exaltation) until the time of His return (3:21). In addressing the household of Cornelius Peter claimed that after His resurrection Jesus 'commanded us to preach to the people and to testify that he is the one appointed by God to be judge of the living and the dead' (10:42). And Paul's message at Pisidian Antioch gave considerable attention to the resurrection of Jesus (13:30-37), the first stage of His exaltation. The conclusion is unavoidable that the apostles in their evangelistic preaching gave strong emphasis to Jesus' resurrection and exaltation along with His atoning death.

APPLICATORY OBSERVATIONS
1) It is an essential part of the 'good news' that God has raised Jesus from the dead and exalted Him to lordship. Without these components the gospel message is incomplete and the

Christian faith is not worth adhering to (1 Cor. 15:12-19). With them the message truly is good news for God has by these events certified His Son's atonement for sin, overcome death for His people and established in principle His reign over all.

2) The pattern of the apostolic preaching arguably should become the pattern of contemporary evangelistic preaching. Although the starting point and emphasis may change for different audiences (as they did in the apostles' preaching), yet the gospel message cannot be biblically presented while ignoring or neglecting any of its essential components.

8

The Apostolic Proclamation of Jesus' Lordship:

The Epistles and Revelation

This chapter will survey the apostolic affirmation of Jesus' lordship as it is found in the letters of the New Testament and the book of Revelation, as well as Paul's descriptions of apostolic preaching.

I. The Pauline Letters

As Paul's common designation of Jesus is 'Lord', and since Paul's affirmations constitute some of the foundational teaching of the New Testament, it is appropriate to begin the survey with his letters.

1. Philippians 2:9-11

The passage in which the exaltation of Jesus is most closely linked with the title 'Lord' is Philippians 2:9-11. This passage and its context, beginning with verse 5, have given rise to a great variety of interpretations.[1] But the full scope of this debate need not concern us now; for as George Eldon Ladd has remarked, 'One fact is clear in all interpretations of this passage: because of his self-emptying and obedience unto death, something new has been bestowed upon him [Jesus] – a new name indicating a new role and status: *kyrios*.'[2] Ladd's remark anticipates the conclusion of our present investigation;

---

1   See R. P. Martin, *Carmen Christi: Philippians 2:5-11 in Recent Interpretation and in the Setting of Early Christian Worship* (Cambridge: Cambridge University Press, 1967), pp. 63-95.

2   Ladd, *Theology of the New Testament*, p. 416; Ladd speaks with some exaggeration, as there is considerable discussion of the nature of 'the name'.

we proceed now to a few pertinent observations on the details of the text.

1) The exaltation of Jesus is represented as something which He experienced in His incarnate state. Jesus' exaltation occurs subsequent to and as a consequence of His self-humbling and obedience unto death (v. 8). The implications of this fact are not always appreciated; if they were, there would be less confusion over the question of how Jesus, if He existed previously in the form of God (v. 6), could now be exalted. Confusion over this point can be found, however, among scholars as diverse in outlook as E. Kasemann[3] and Lewis Sperry Chafer.[4] The answer is that it was not with respect to God the Son, conceived purely as deity, that the exaltation took place, but with respect to Jesus of Nazareth, the God–man, the Son of God incarnate, that this event occurred. Paul himself identifies the subject of the affirmation here as 'Messiah Jesus' (v. 5), the incarnate Son. The entire incarnate existence of Jesus previous to His exaltation had been one of humiliation (vv. 6-8); but now, He who once willingly humbled Himself has been gloriously exalted.

2) The exaltation of Jesus was accomplished in the closest connection with the bestowal on Him of the supreme name (v. 9). Upon His exaltation, Jesus was 'given graciously' (*echaristato*, aorist; often of honorific titles, etc.[5]) by God 'the name which is above every name', a name which we may thus assume (without necessarily looking beyond verse 9) to be expressive of supremacy and of the highest authority. In His exaltation and in the bestowal of the name which He received Jesus was inaugurated into a new and distinct phase of His redemptive career, which is expressed in that supreme name which He was given. He entered into a status that He had not known before *as the God–man*: previously, He was the God–man in humility; now He is the God–man in exaltation – and He is given a name commensurate with His new status.

---

3   See Martin's discussion of Kasemann's view, *Carmen Christi*, p. 238.

4   'It is difficult to understand how authority could be committed to the Son which was not properly His in His own right.' Lewis Sperry Chafer, *Systematic Theology*, 8 vols. (Dallas: Dallas Seminary Press, 1947), 5:274.

5   BDAG, 1078.

3) The name which Jesus received at the time of His exaltation, that name which both constitutes and expresses His exaltation, is the title 'Lord' (kyrios, v. 11). R.P. Martin comments: 'As to the content of the name which is bestowed, there is now general agreement that this is to be understood in terms of *Kyrios*.'[6] There are several reasons for making this identification:

(a) Verse 9 leads us to expect *the* pre-eminent name. 'The repetition of the definite article in verse 9c [*to onoma to hyper pan onoma*, "the name the one above every name"] prepares us for a declaration of the very name of God Himself',[7] which *kyrios* in fact is in common Septuagint and New Testament usage.

(b) This identification fits well with the flow of the passage. J.A. Motyer has noted that the movement in verses 9-11 is from the bestowal of 'the name' in verse 9 straight through to 'the universal confession that "Jesus Christ is Lord" in verse 11.'[8] The passage begins with 'the name' and climaxes with *kyrios*. The identification of the two is natural.

(c) In verses 10-11, where the affinities with Isaiah 45:23 are too strong to ignore (compare with the Septuagint), the exalted Jesus occupies the place assigned to God in the Old Testament text. If divine honor is bestowed on Jesus, as this use of the Isaiah passage implied (a passage which, it should be noted, is strongly monotheistic in tone), then it is not unreasonable that the divine name should also be given to Him – which is exactly what occurs when the name *kyrios* is applied to Jesus (v. 11)[9].

---

6   Martin, *Carmen Christi*, p. 245. Martin lists in a lengthy note on page 245 several interpreters who favor this identification, to which may be added Ladd, *Theology*, p. 339; Foerster, TDNT 3:1088; Peter T. O'Brien, *The Epistle to the Philippians: A Commentary on the Greek Text* (Grand Rapids: Eerdmans, 1991) p. 238.

7   Martin, *Carmen Christi*, p. 245.

8   J. A. Motyer, *Philippian Studies: The Richness of Christ* (Chicago: Inter-Varsity Press, 1966), p. 83.

9   O'Brien argues that it is precisely because *Kyrios* is the divine name that it was given to Jesus, *Philippians*, p. 238.

(d) No other name so admirably as *kyrios* fits the description in verse 9. 'Jesus' was given in infancy, not at the exaltation (and, as J.B. Lightfoot notes, verse 10 reads, 'at the name *of* Jesus', not 'at the name Jesus'[10]). 'Christ' is the title of an office which He exercised well before this exaltation (although it could be used in a heightened sense of a more exalted status, Acts 2:36). Other suggested names are no more suitable than these. Even Lightfoot, who prefers to take 'name' as 'not meaning a definite appellation but denoting office, rank, dignity', must admit that 'if St Paul were referring to any one term, *kyrios* would best explain the reference.'[11] But there is no compelling reason to divorce the office from the appellation, especially when the latter is provided by the passage itself.

4) The bestowal of the name 'Lord' (kyrios) upon Jesus indicates His installation as supreme sovereign of the universe. This is demonstrated by the fact that every knee shall bow and every tongue confess His lordship (vv. 10-11), as well as by the concept and content of the 'name' itself. In biblical usage 'name' is commonly understood as a revelation of the character of the one named;[12] thus 'the name of *Kyrios* involved divine equality, for it authorizes Jesus to act in the capacity of God *vis-a-vis* the world, to receive the rightful obeisance of all created powers and to share the throne of the universe.'[13] The God–man, Christ Jesus, is granted (under the Father) all the rights and prerogatives of God in the governance of the universe, and as verses 10-11 indicate, all due acknowledgment will be made of that fact by those over whom His rule is established. Peter O'Brien has stated it well:

But now, by way of vindication and approval of Jesus' total self-humbling, the Father has magnificently exalted his Son to

---

10　J. B. Lightfoot, *Saint Paul's Epistle to the Philippians* (London: Macmillan, 1891), p. 114. See also Martin, *Carmen Christi*, p. 250.

11　Lightfoot, *Philippians,* p. 113.

12　'Name,' in J. D. Douglas, ed., *The New Bible Dictionary* (Grand Rapids: Eerdmans, 1962), p. 863.

13　Martin, *Carmen Christi* 246. For a discussion of whether it is universal or ecclesiastical lordship to which Jesus attains, see Martin, pp. 249-55.

the highest station and graciously bestowed on him the name above all other names, that is, his own name, Lord (=Yahweh), along with all that gives substance and meaning to the name. In his exalted state Jesus now exercises universal lordship.[14]

5) It is by means of the acknowledgment of the lordship of Jesus that God the Father is glorified (v. 11). This verse serves as an indicator of one of the ultimate purposes of God: that Jesus should be acclaimed as Lord by all the personal beings of the universe, which acclamation will redound to the glory of God the Father Himself.[15] Since this acclamation will, at least on the part of those beings who are hostile to God, be made dutifully rather than willingly, the verb 'confess' (*exomologeo*) should be understood to indicate an acknowledgment of fact rather than necessarily a confession arising from faith.[16] The confession is, for those hostile beings, the recognition of the undeniable fact of their subjection to Jesus as Lord, and stands in contrast to the humble and adoring submission rendered by believers. O'Brien is in agreement with this understanding:

> ... on the last day every knee will bow and every tongue will 'openly declare' that Jesus alone has the right to rule (cf. Rev. 5:13, etc.). For those who, in the here and now, have already bowed the knee to Jesus and confessed him as Lord, as clearly the Philippian Christians had done, the acclamation at his parousia would spring from the heart. Others, however, such as the principalities and powers of Col. 2:15, are not depicted as gladly surrendering to God's grace, but as submitting against their wills to a power they cannot resist.[17]

---

14 O'Brien, *Philippians*, p. 233.

15 O'Brien argues (*Philippians*, pp. 250-51) that it is the fact of Jesus' lordship that is said to redound to the glory of God the Father, not the confession of it.

16 Similar in meaning to James 2:19: 'The demons also believe, and shudder.' See BDAG, p. 351; Martin, *Carmen Christi*, pp. 263-64. Although the company of those so acclaiming Christ will certainly include hostile spirits, it is not necessary to understand it as exclusively so (as do Martin and many others, pp. 258-64). BDAG remarks concerning *epigeion* ("of those on earth") that this class is 'not confined to human beings' (p. 368) implying that it does in fact include them. There is no compelling reason for excluding humans, redeemed or otherwise, from participation in this acknowledgement

17 O'Brien, *Philippians*, p. 250.

While on the one hand the exaltation of Jesus to lordship is already an accomplished fact (note aorists in verse 9: 'exalted ... bestowed'), and on the other hand the universal acknowledgment of that fact is yet future and awaits the powerful and glorious manifestation of His lordship,[18] the present implications of the point now under consideration ought not to be ignored. If it is through the specific confession that 'Jesus is Lord' that God will be glorified at the consummation there is the strong presumption (in the light of the unity of God's redemptive purpose) that the same would hold true for the present age: that it is specifically through the Christian confession (rendered in advance of the consummation) that 'Jesus is Lord' (with the implication of personal submission to that lordship) that God has chosen to bring glory to Himself. There is in the New Testament a consistent pattern of teaching which confirms this supposition, as we shall see later in this study.

APPLICATORY OBSERVATIONS

1) There is an absoluteness and exclusivity and finality to the Christian faith because of the present position of Jesus Christ as Lord of the universe. All human beings, living and dead, great and small, will be judged by Him and will be required to acknowledge His lordship. This applies to founders of alternative philosophies and religious movements as much as to anyone else. Those philosophies and religious movements will be shown in that day to be false, and their leaders and adherents compelled to acknowledge Jesus' lordship. Christians (a) ought to be encouraged by this truth, and (b) have no right to diminish this element of the biblical message but must lovingly and faithfully proclaim it, even in the face of hostility and opposition.

2) There is an urgency to the present need to offer willing acknowledgment of Jesus as Lord. All personal beings shall be required to acknowledge His lordship, either in this life or in the resurrection of the just and the unjust. If the confession

---

18 For a discussion of the time of the universal confession, see Martin, *Carmen Christi*, pp. 266-70. The position adopted here is in agreement with that of Ladd, *Theology*, p. 416; and O'Brien, whose entire discussion is worthwhile (*Philippians*, pp. 238-51).

is made sincerely and willingly in this life, it is unto salvation (Rom. 10:10); if it is compelled in the next, it will be unto condemnation, for it will include no element of trust and love. No one knows when he or she will be taken from this life and the opportunity will be forfeited. 'Behold, now is the favorable time, now is the day of salvation' (2 Cor. 6:2).

2. Romans 1:3-4

This is another passage which contributes significantly to our understanding of Jesus' exaltation and lordship, but concerning the interpretation of which there is considerable diversity of opinion. The major difficulties will be dealt with as we make a few observations on the text.

1) Paul here affirms that the incarnate Son of God was, at a definite point in His career, appointed to a position of power which He had not before occupied.[19] The interpretation of the passage hinges on the meaning of the Greek word *horizo,* translated 'declared' by many English versions (KJV, NASB, NIV, ESV). The consistent meaning of the word in the New Testament, however, is not 'declare' but 'appoint', 'designate', or 'determine'. In other instances of its use in the New Testament *horizo* refers to events foreordained by divine decree (Luke 22:22; Acts 2:23) or to the divine determination of appointed times (Acts 17:26; Heb. 4:7) or to a human decision or determination (Acts 11:29). In none of these cases does it bear the meaning 'declare'. And in two other instances where the object of the action of the verb is a person, in both cases it refers to Christ, and in both cases it clearly means 'appoint', 'ordain', or 'designate'. 'He is the one *appointed* by God to be judge of the living and the dead' (Acts 10:42). 'He will judge the world in righteousness by a man whom he has *appointed*' (Acts 17:31). It is consistent, therefore, with the meaning of the word and with New Testament usage to

---

19 The question, debated by some scholars, of whether we have here a pre-Pauline formula or an original Pauline passage does not materially affect the present discussion; for a treatment of the question, see Douglas J. Moo, *The Epistle to the Romans*, New International Commentary on the New Testament (Grand Rapids: Eerdmans, 1996), pp. 45-46, esp. footnote 31.

translate Romans 1:4: 'Who was *appointed* Son of God in power ...'[20]

The inclination of translators and interpreters to assign to *horizo* the meaning 'declare' in this passage stems from the understandable desire to avoid having Paul (or the early church) appear to espouse an adoptionist Christology[21] (the idea that as a mere human, Jesus was adopted to divine sonship), which would certainly be the case if Jesus were said without further qualification to have been appointed the Son of God. But there is a qualifying element supplied by the passage itself, and when it is properly understood, adoptionism is no longer the necessary alternative. It was not simply to the position of Son of God that Jesus was appointed but (as the translation suggested above indicates) to that of 'Son-of-God-in-power'. As George Ladd notes, 'The key phrase is "with power".'[22] Those two words make the essential distinction: they denote that mediatorial sovereignty with which Jesus was invested at His exaltation. He was the Son of God already; He was appointed the 'Son of God in power' when God raised Him from the dead and exalted Him to His own right hand. The phrase 'in power' is intended to contrast Jesus' present exalted position with His former status of humility and weakness. Furthermore, '"Son in power," Cullman observes, 'is clearly synonymous with *Kyrios*.'[23] We have in this verse an affirmation concerning Jesus' exaltation to lordship. The HCSB seems to catch this sense: Jesus 'was established as the powerful Son of God by the resurrection from the dead'.

This interpretation of Romans 1:4 is adopted by no less an exegete and theologian than John Murray, whose views are set forth most fully in his commentary on Romans and are worthy of extensive quotation and careful attention.

On the meaning of *horizo*, Murray writes: 'There is neither need nor warrant to resort to any other rendering than that

---

20 Moo supports this understanding of the verb *horizo*, *Romans*, pp. 47-48.

21 This tendency is clearly evident in Robert H. Mounce, *The Essential Nature of New Testament Preaching*, pp. 96-97.

22 Ladd, *Theology* 418; see also Moo, *Romans*, pp. 48-49.

23 Cullmann, *Christology*, p. 235.

provided by the other New Testament instances, namely, that Jesus was "appointed" or "constituted" Son of God with power and points therefore to an investiture which had an historical beginning parallel to the historical beginning mentioned in verse 3.'[24]

With regard to the propriety of speaking of the 'appointment' of Jesus to this position of power, Murray notes that it is with respect to the Son of God *incarnate* that the assertion is made, and is altogether proper: 'The apostle is dealing with some particular event in the history of the Son of God incarnate by which he was *instated* in a position of sovereignty and invested with power, an event which in respect of investiture with power surpassed everything that could previously be ascribed to Him in His incarnate state.' The entire passage (vv. 3-4) thus concerns the 'distinction drawn ... between "two successive stages" of the historical process of which the Son of God became the subject' – the incarnation (v. 3) and the exaltation (v. 4).[25]

2) This exaltation of Jesus was accomplished in connection with His resurrection. The instrumentality through which He was appointed Son-of-God-in-power was 'by the resurrection from the dead'. This serves to underline the fact that we are indeed dealing here with 'two successive stages' in the ministry of Jesus – 'before the resurrection' and 'after the resurrection', the former period characterized by humiliation and suffering, the latter by power and glory. The phase of humiliation clearly had its culmination in Jesus' death and burial; the phase of glory just as clearly had its historical origin in His resurrection from the dead, and constituted for Jesus an advance over

---

24 John Murray, *The Epistle to the Romans*, 2 vols. New International Commentary on the New Testament (Grand Rapids: Eerdmans, 1959, 1965), p. 1:9.

25 Murray, *Romans*, 1:10, 7. For other support of the position adopted here, see C. E. B. Cranfield, *A Critical and Exegetical Commentary on the Epistle to the Romans*, 2 vols., International Critical Commentary (Edinburgh: T.& T. Clark, 1975, 1979), 1:61-65; Moo, *Romans*, p. 50; Thomas R. Schreiner, *Romans*, Baker Exegetical Commentary on the New Testament (Grand Rapids: Baker, 1998), pp. 41-45; Marshall, *New Testament Theology*, p. 426. Opposing it is Reymond, *Systematic Theology*, pp. 238-45.

His previous position: the Son of God in evident weakness became, by virtue of His resurrection, the Son of God in manifest power. 'By his resurrection and ascension the Son of God incarnate entered upon a new phase of sovereignty and was endowed with new power correspondent with and unto the exercise of the mediatorial lordship which he executes as head over all things to his body, the church.'[26]

3) It is significant that in connection with the events described in verse 4 Paul applies to Jesus the title 'Lord'. Paul says it is 'Jesus Christ our Lord' who has been thus exalted. And, as Murray reminds us, it is no thoughtless formula that Paul uses here; rather, 'each name has its own peculiar associations and significance ... "Lord" indicates the lordship to which he is exalted at the right hand of the Father in virtue of which he exercises all authority in heaven and in earth.'[27] Moo points out, 'For Paul, "Lord", expressing both Jesus' cosmic majesty and his status as master of the believer, is the single best title to express the true significance of Jesus.'[28] The teaching of this passage thus corresponds closely to what was found in Philippians 2:9-11 and Acts 2:36. The significance of this correspondence was not lost on George Ladd: 'Paul concludes the passage by calling Jesus "our Lord", for His becoming the Son of God in power is precisely parallel to the bestowal of lordship in Philippians 2:9.'[29] And Thomas Schreiner notes how effectively this affirmation fits into the context:

> The lordship of Jesus as Messiah flows naturally from what Paul has just written. He who was born as the seed of David has been exalted by God to reign over all. He is the Lord of all nations, and in his name Paul endeavored to fulfill his missionary call to bring about the obedience of faith among the Gentiles [v. 5].[30]

---

26   Murray, *Romans*, 1:11; see Cullmann, *Christology*, p. 292.

27   Murray, *Romans*, 1:12.

28   Moo, *Romans*, p. 50.

29   Ladd, *Theology*, p. 418.

30   Schreiner, *Romans*, p. 45.

APPLICATORY OBSERVATION

The gospel concerns Jesus' exaltation as much as it does His death. Paul in this context refers to the 'gospel of God' (Rom. 1:1) which concerns God's Son (1:3), and he then goes on to mention Jesus' descent from David (v. 3) and His exaltation (4, assuming the correctness of the interpretation offered above), but with no explicit mention of the redemptive significance of His death in the opening greeting (1:1-7). Since Paul is not shy in this letter about mentioning the redemptive death of Jesus (3:24-25; 4:24-25; 5:6, 8, 10; etc.), we must assume he has envisioned the redemptive significance of the death of Jesus to have been wrapped up in the phrase 'appointed Son of God in power' by 'his resurrection from the dead' (1:4). What constitutes the 'good news' of the gospel in this context, then, is that Jesus, following His death, has been exalted as the powerful Son of God. Paul is not afraid to describe the content of the gospel in such abbreviated terms. Should not the contemporary proclamation of the gospel in our own day thus include the element of Jesus' resurrection and exaltation as well as the (sometimes almost exclusive) mention of His death for sinners? His victory over death and His present position as exalted Lord were important elements of the apostolic message and should be of ours as well.

3. Ephesians 1:20-23

A passage which describes Jesus' exaltation, with special reference to His authority as mediatorial Lord, is Ephesians 1:20-23. While the sentence in which this passage is found begins much earlier than verse 20 (it starts in verse 15, according to the 25th edition of the Nestle-Aland Greek Testament, although the 27th edition begins a new sentence at verse 20 with a relative pronoun), yet it is in verse 20 that Paul begins to expound the doctrine of Jesus' exaltation in a way that is germane to our present discussion. This entire passage (vv. 15-23) is a prayer expressing Paul's desire for the spiritual enlightenment of the Christians to whom he is writing, that they might understand, among other things, the greatness of God's power which is at work in believers (v. 19) – a power comparable to that which God exercised in raising Christ from the dead and exalting Him to his right hand (v. 20). It is in the second half of this comparison, occupying verses 20-23, that Paul treats the matter of the exaltation of Christ; a perusal of the passage yields the following points.

1) The exaltation of Jesus was accomplished in conjunction with His resurrection (v. 20). It is evident that Paul has in view in verses 20-22 a connected series of events ('raised him ... seated him ... put all things under his feet ...') which when taken together constitute the exaltation of Christ and demonstrate the greatness of God's power. The necessary first element in this process is the raising of Jesus from the dead, which, as we have already seen, marked His entrance into the exalted state. Apart from the resurrection, there could be no exaltation; in the resurrection, the exaltation was begun.

2) The exaltation of Jesus involved His installation in a position of supreme authority. After raising Jesus from the dead God 'seated him at his right hand' (v. 20), a phrase which derives from Psalm 110:1 and which is 'a figurative expression for the place of highest honour and authority.[31] For Jesus to be seated at the right hand of God means nothing less than 'participation in dominion',[32] that is, a sharing in the throne and lordship of the Father. As Harold Hoehner has expressed it, this position displays Jesus' 'sovereignty at the present time and indicates his authority over the world and the church.'[33]

Christ's position at the right hand of God is perhaps the most commonly used expression of His exaltation and lordship to be found in the New Testament. It is a favorite of the apostolic church, being found in a wide range of writers and speakers: Peter (Acts 2:33-35; 5:31; 1 Pet. 3:22), Stephen (Acts 7:55-56), Paul (Rom. 8:34; Eph. 1:20; Col. 3:1) and the writer of Hebrews (Heb. 1:3, 13; 8:1; 10:12; 12:2). The expression is also found on the lips of Jesus Himself in all the synoptic Gospels on two occasions: in His question concerning the Davidic sonship of Messiah (Matt. 22:44; Mark 12:36;

---

31 Bruce, *Ephesians*, p. 42. See also BDAG, *dexios*, pp. 217-18; TDNT 2:37-40.

32 Karl Braune in Lange's *Commentary*, vol. 11, 'Ephesians', p. 61.

33 Harold W. Hoehner, *Ephesians: An Exegetical Commentary* (Grand Rapids: Baker Academic, 2002), p. 275.

Luke 20:42), and in His confession before the Sanhedrin (Matt. 26:64; Mark 14:62; Luke 22:69). The pervasive use in the New Testament of this phrase from Psalm 110 is not without significance for our present study, as Cullmann has observed: 'Nothing indicates better than the very frequent citation of this very psalm how vital was the present lordship of Christ in early Christian thought. It is quoted not just in a few isolated places, but throughout the whole New Testament. Almost no other Old Testament passage is cited so often.'[34] The use of this single phrase (occurring some twenty times in the New Testament) constitutes a weighty demonstration that the early church put great emphasis on the exaltation and lordship of Jesus.

3) The lordship which Jesus exercises involves His supremacy (as mediatorial Lord, under God the Father) over all other authority in the universe. This fact is indicated by three elements in verses 21-22a.

(a) His position is said to be 'far above [*hyperano*, referring to rank, power[35]] all rule and authority and power and dominion' (v. 21a). The four categories mentioned here (respectively: *arche, exousia, dynamis, kyriotes*) are commonly understood to represent 'familiar distinctions of spiritual forces',[36] that is, classes of supernatural spirit-beings, whether angelic or demonic.[37] While some interpreters apparently do not regard Paul as viewing these spirit-forces as 'objective realities',[38] Paul's own words elsewhere would seem to indicate otherwise. At the end of Ephesians he writes that 'our struggle is not against flesh and blood, but against the *rulers*, against the *powers*, against the world forces of this darkness, against the spiritual forces of wickedness in

---

34 Cullmann, *Christology*, p. 223.

35 BDAG, 1032.

36 J. Armitage Robinson, *St. Paul's Epistle to the Ephesians* (London: James Clarke & Co., n.d.), p. 41.

37 The meanings suggested by BDAG may be found on pp. 138, 353, 263 and 579 respectively.

38 T. K. Abbott, *A Critical and Exegetical Commentary on the Epistles to the Ephesians and to the Colossians*, International Critical Commentary (Edinburgh: T. & T. Clarke, 1897), pp. 32-33.

the heavenly places' (Eph. 6:12). The first two terms here, 'rulers' and 'powers', are the same as the first two in 1:21. These two categories are also mentioned in Ephesians 3:10, where Paul states that it is part of the eternal purpose of God to make known through the church His manifold wisdom 'to the *rulers* and the *authorities* in the heavenly places'. In these instances Paul certainly seems to regard the spirit-forces as possessing objective reality. In any case, it is true that 'the apostle's purpose in mentioning them ... is to emphasize the exaltation of Christ above them all.'[39]

The importance which the early church attached to Christ's lordship over the spirit-forces has been noted by Cullmann[40] and is indicated in the New Testament by the frequency with which the concept is mentioned. Christ is not only the Creator of these spirit-forces (Col. 1:16), but through His triumph on the cross He has disarmed and displayed those which were hostile to Him (Col. 2:15) so that He is now 'the head over all rule and authority' (Col. 2:10). His exaltation to the right hand of God means that 'angels and authorities and powers' have been subjected to Him (1 Pet. 3:22). Eventually, 'when he has abolished all rule and all authority and power', Christ will 'deliver up the kingdom' to the Father (1 Cor. 15:24). When these references are added to the three already noted in Ephesians, it becomes clear that this theme carried considerable significance for the New Testament writers.

(b) Jesus is also said to have been exalted 'above every name that is named, not only in this age but also in the one to come' (Eph. 1:21b). This very comprehensive statement means that there is no power or authority that will surpass that of Christ, either before the consummation or after. His name is above all others (cf. Phil. 2:9-11). 'Above all that anywhere is, anywhere can be – above all grades of dignity, real

---

39 Robinson, *Ephesians*, p. 41. Hoehner argues (*Ephesians*, pp. 276-80) that the language of the passage indicates that 'these powers most likely are angelic and evil and wish to rob us of our spiritual benefits', and that 'Christ is over these authorities and they will not have the final victory' (p. 280).

40 Cullmann, *Christology*, pp. 223-24.

or imagined, good or evil, present or to come – the mighty power of God has exalted and enthroned the Christ.'[41]

(c) God, in exalting Christ, is said to have 'put all things under his feet' (Eph. 1:22a). This is also a broad and comprehensive statement of the authority possessed by Christ as exalted Lord, indicating (in the words of Westcott) that 'He is invested with universal sovereignty'.[42] A more comprehensive expression than this would be difficult to imagine: 'all things' (*panta*) have been 'put in subjection' (*hypetaxen*, aorist) under (the feet of) Christ. These words attribute to Christ an authority that is universal in scope and absolute in degree. Hoehner agrees: 'The "everything" subjected under his feet would have reference to inanimate things and animate creatures, human and angelic beings. Hence, Christ has been given the right to exercise his control over everything in God's creation ....'[43]

4) The authority of the exalted Christ includes His lordship over the church (vv. 22b-23). Lordship is here defined in terms of headship, not a synonymous but a related concept, which in this context denotes 'superior rank'.[44] Paul's mode of expression here is not as clear as it is in Ephesians 4:15 and 5:23 ('Christ is the head of the church'), which has given rise to diverse interpretations of 1:22b. Some, such as F.F. Bruce, understand the phrase 'head over all things' to mean 'supreme head', and relate it directly to Christ's position as 'supreme head of the church'.[45] Others, for example William Hendriksen, understand the 'all things' of verse 22b to be as comprehensive as the same phrase in 22a, and thus believe that 'Christ is not actually said to be the head of the church, but rather "head over everything to the church".' Christ is given

---

41 Robinson, *Ephesians*, p. 41. 'Jesus as Lord is greater than any other title, whether in heaven or on earth,' Hoehner, *Ephesians*, p. 281.

42 Brooke Foss Westcott, *Saint Paul's Epistle to the Ephesians* (reprint ed., Minneapolis: Klock & Klock Christian Publishers, 1978), p. 27.

43 Hoehner, *Ephesians*, p. 283.

44 BDAG, p. 542

45 Bruce, *Ephesians*, p. 43.

to the church as the One who is Head over all things and '*in its interests* he exercises his infinite power in causing the entire universe with all that is in it to co-operate, whether willingly or unwillingly.'[46] On the basis of the former interpretation, Christ is explicitly said to be the Head of the church; on the basis of the latter (which is probably to be preferred), He is said to be Head over all things, which would then include the church. At any rate, Paul in verse 23 identifies the church as Christ's body, a connection which virtually demands that the headship mentioned in verse 22 be understood to include the church, regardless of whether a larger sphere of authority is also in view. Thus the authority belonging to the exalted Lord Jesus involves in a special sense His lordship or headship over the church as well as His lordship over the universe.[47]

APPLICATORY OBSERVATIONS

1) The fact that Jesus is said to be superior to every demonic being should serve as encouragement to Christian believers in the present. There is no force or foe in the universe that is outside His sovereignty and control, and thus He is not lacking in the authority and power to dispose of events for the benefit of His people. Nothing that is beyond His will and purpose and His capacity to control can befall His people. We can place ultimate confidence in our sovereign Lord.

2) Jesus' present position as exalted Lord guarantees His future and final victory. As Hoehner says, 'In reality Christ is at the right hand of the Father and everything has been subjected under his feet, but the full exercise of that power will not be evident until his return.'[48] At the consummation of all things, Jesus' lordship will be made manifest to all. In the meantime, Christians are to exercise faith and to be faithful, in the confidence that all will be well.

4. Romans 14:9

A further passage to be considered in the present connection is Romans 14:9. In the course of Paul's argument concerning

---

46 William Hendriksen, *Exposition of Ephesians*, New Testament Commentary (Grand Rapids: Baker, 1967), pp. 102-103.

47 Hoehner is in agreement with this conclusion, *Ephesians*, pp. 285-90.

48 Hoehner, *Ephesians*, p. 284.

Christian liberty in the fourteenth chapter of Romans, he makes this assertion: 'For to this end Christ died and lived again, that he might be Lord both of the dead and of the living.' Again, let us make some observations on the text.

1) The death and resurrection of Jesus are said to be connected with regard to their purpose. It was the divine intention that by means of these two events, the death and resurrection of Jesus, that Jesus might become Lord of the dead and the living. The purpose clause with which the sentence begins (*eis touto*, 'for this'[49]) links together in a single purpose the two aspects of Jesus' redemptive work: His death and resurrection (*apethanen kai ezesen*, 'died and lived,' should be so understood[50]). The assertion is that He died and rose again in order that this purpose might be fulfilled.

2) It was specifically in order to attain lordship over the dead and the living that Jesus died and lived again. It is not the noun *kyrios* that is used here to express lordship, but the verb *kyrieuo*, meaning 'to exercise authority or have control, *rule*'.[51] Its subjunctive mood again indicates that this purpose was in view in Jesus' death and resurrection, and its position at the end of the sentence gives added emphasis to the thought. Paul is affirming that it was in order to achieve this concrete purpose, the gaining of lordship or rulership over those persons who are in view, that Jesus suffered the anguish of the cross and was raised in glory by the power of the Father. This is a clear statement of broad scope indicating the divine purpose in the saving work of Christ; that purpose was no less than the establishment of His lordship over those for whom He died and lived again.

3) The 'dead and the living' over whom the lordship of Christ is established must in this context be restricted to those who belong to Christ, that is, Christian believers. While there is not universal agreement on this point the preceding verses certainly seem to demand the restriction of this purpose, in this context, to

---

49   See BDAG, p. 290, 4f.

50   Murray, *Romans*, 2:182-83.

51   BDAG, p. 576.

believers.[52] In this passage Paul is warning against a censorious attitude among Christians on matters of conduct where liberty is permitted. He appeals to the exclusiveness of the master–slave relationship between Christ and the believer in verse 4a (applying the term *kyrios* to Christ) as grounds for His exhortation that believers are not to judge one another. He refers each man's observance or non-observance as unto the Lord (Paul's usual title for Jesus, v. 6). The whole of every Christian's life, and even his death, is not for himself but for the Lord (vv. 7-8), this fact being grounded not in the subjective 'faith which is consciously exercised by the believer' but in the objective 'relation which Christ sustains to him, namely, that of possession.'[53]

While Paul makes these assertions with respect to *every* believer (he envisages no exceptions: '*None of us* lives to himself', v. 7), it is likewise the case that they are made with exclusive reference to believers. It is specifically the living and dying of believers that is in view in verses 7-8; and it is over believers both dead and living (v. 9b; Paul reverses the order to conform to the dying and living – crucifixion and resurrection – of Christ) that Christ establishes His lordship by means of His redemptive work. While it is certainly true that there is a broader and more universal aspect of the lordship of Christ, it must be maintained that such is not in view in this passage. Thus we agree with Murray's conclusion that 'because of the context it would not be feasible to understand this text as having all-inclusive reference.'[54] We may with good warrant understand Paul as saying that it was for the express purpose of establishing His lordship over believers that Christ died and rose again.

4) We must regard the purpose in view in Christ's death and resurrection as finding actual (not potential) fulfillment in all believers. Jesus is in fact Lord over all Christians by virtue of His possession of them. Paul's language demands this conclusion; in its support appeal may be made to much of the same evidence

---

52 The contrary view is held by Ladd, *Theology*, p. 416.

53 Murray, *Romans*, 2:181. Notice the genitive *tou kyriou* ('of the Lord') at the end of v. 8; ESV: 'we are the Lord's'; HCSB: 'we belong to the Lord.'

54 Murray, *Romans*, 2:183.

noted above: (a) In the analogy of verse 4a he speaks of Christ as the Master or Lord (*kyrios*) and the believer as a servant. (b) In verses 7-8a, Paul says that 'none of us' lives or dies unto or for himself, but for the Lord (Jesus). (c) In 8b he says that 'we are the Lord's', indicating the objective relationship of possession and thus the legitimate right of control. Nowhere in these verses does Paul intimate that he is speaking of a special group of Christians who have acknowledged the lordship of Christ as distinct from those who have not; he simply assumes that for every believer Jesus is Lord, both by objective right and by subjective confession.

5) The lordship over believers ascribed to Jesus in Romans 14:9 is a position that was attained by Him through His death and resurrection, and thus differs from that sovereignty which He possesses and exercises by inherent right as God the Son.

It is not merely Jesus' deity which is in view in the ascription to Him of lordship over believers, for He was God apart from His death and resurrection, whereas the lordship attributed to Him here required His redeeming work in order for its accomplishment to be realized. Paul says that it was '*to this end*' that 'Christ died and lived again, that he might be Lord both of the dead and of the living.' As Murray has written, 'The lordship of Christ here dealt with did not belong to Christ by native right as the Son of God; it had to be secured. It is the lordship of redemptive relationship and such did not inhere in the sovereignty that belongs to him in virtue of his creatorhood. It is achieved by mediatorial accomplishment and is the reward of his humiliation.'[55] Likewise Douglas Moo: 'Paul's focus is on that unique exercise of 'kingdom' power and rule that were established only through Christ's death and resurrection and the appropriation of the benefits of those acts by individual persons in faith.'[56] The lordship of Jesus over believers belongs to Him by right of His peculiar possession of them, which was secured by His redemptive work on their behalf.[57]

---

55   Murray, *Romans*, 2:182.

56   Moo, *Romans*, p. 846.

57   On this matter Charles Hodge also writes: 'While the divine nature of Christ is the necessary *condition* of his exaltation, his mediatorial work

APPLICATORY OBSERVATIONS

1) Jesus becomes the personal Lord of believers at the moment of their conversion. Paul's language in this passage allows for no other conclusion than this. Jesus becomes the Lord of believers by right of redemption (He has paid the price for their ransom or deliverance) through His death and resurrection. This is an objective relationship which obtains because the Lord Jesus owns believers from the point of their initial exercise of trust in Him ('we belong to the Lord', 14:8, HCSB). This suggests (a) that acknowledgment of Jesus' lordship is at least implicit in the act of becoming a Christian believer (although we must allow that it may not be explicit and that some genuine believers may not have been properly informed of the fact); and (b) that it is not theoretically possible to 'opt out' of recognition of Jesus' lordship by one who professes faith in Him. It is part and parcel of becoming a Christian that one enters into the objective relationship of 'servant' to his or her 'Lord' (14:4), whether one subjectively recognizes that the relationship exists or not.

2) It follows that this truth should not be omitted from the evangelistic message set forth by Christians. It is misleading to our hearers to omit a significant portion of the apostolic message, and it is derogatory to the honor of Christ for unbelievers to be told that they can enter into salvation on any other terms than 'unconditional surrender' (giving up their right to own themselves=repentance) to the One who will truly own them.

3) It follows also that professing Christians ought to reflect the purpose for which Jesus died and rose again on their behalf: that He might become their Lord. He therefore should control their lives. Any activity or pattern of life which violates His lordship is a denial of His legitimate right of ownership and an affront to His redemptive self-sacrifice to deliver them from sin.

---

is the immediate *ground* of the Theanthropos, God manifested in the flesh, being invested with this universal dominion.' (Emphasis mine.) Hodge, *Commentary on the Epistle to the Ephesians* (reprint ed.; Old Tappan, NJ: Fleming H. Revell, n.d.), p. 83.

5. 1 Corinthians 15:3-8

We began this portion of the study with an examination of the apostolic proclamation recorded in the Book of Acts to gain an appreciation for the message of the primitive Christian community, especially as it related to the lordship of Jesus. Then we proceeded to examine several Pauline passages in which the lordship of Jesus is set forth and defined. These passages, however, were set in the context of Paul's letters to Christian congregations and do not necessarily constitute his evangelistic message. We are not left to guess, however, what was the content of Paul's preaching in an evangelistic context, for he informs us in his letters what his message in fact contained. The content of Paul's evangelistic preaching is set forth in such passages as 1 Corinthians 15:3-8, 2 Corinthians 4:5 and Romans 10:8-10. In all of these, Paul's message is found to include as a prominent element the facts of Jesus' resurrection, exaltation and present lordship.

Paul claimed in 1 Corinthians 15:1-11 that the message which he originally proclaimed in Corinth ('the gospel I preached to you', 15:1b) and which was received by his converts there (15:1c; see Acts 18:1-17) was one which he held and preached in common with the other apostles ('what I also received', v. 3; 'Whether then it was I or they, so we preach [present tense] and so you believed', v. 11). As Paul outlined the message, it had four primary components, each introduced by *hoti* ("that"):

1. 'that Christ died for our sins in accordance with the Scriptures' (15:3b). This indicates that Christ's death was an atoning sacrifice for sin.

2. 'that he was buried' (15:4a). Jesus' burial 'verifies the reality and finality' of His death.[58]

3. 'that he was raised on the third day in accordance with the Scriptures' (15:4b). Paul used the perfect tense of the verb 'was raised', suggesting 'something that has an effect on present reality',[59] which it does, of course,

---

58 David E. Garland, *1 Corinthians*, Baker Exegetical Commentary (Grand Rapids: Baker, 2003), p. 686.

59 Garland, *1 Corinthians*, p. 686.

as the entryway into Jesus' present exalted status (the culmination of which is mentioned in 15:24-25), as achieving victory over death in fact for Himself and in principle for His people (15:54-57), and as the guarantee of His people's resurrection (15:20-23).

4. 'that he appeared to Cephas, then to the twelve...' (15:5). The listing of post-resurrection appearances of Jesus served 'to confirm the tradition's veracity.'[60] Last in the list is Paul himself (v. 8), who saw the risen Christ in His ascended glory (Acts 9:1-9, etc.).

It may be observed that the latter two of these components of the primitive gospel, (3) and (4), involved the initial stage of Jesus' glorification: the resurrection of Jesus and His appearance to His disciples in His transformed state. The fact that Paul was here passing on tradition which he had received (v. 3) and that he claimed that this message was common to all the apostles (v. 11: 'so we preach') indicate, in the words of David Garland, that 'Peter, the Twelve, James, Paul, and all the other apostles are unified on the basic fact of Christ's resurrection and its meaning.' 'Christ's resurrection is the common denominator on which all are in accord. It is non-negotiable and cannot be jettisoned without gutting the Christian faith.'[61] And part of the meaning of Jesus' resurrection was that it represented the initial stage of His exaltation to universal lordship.

6. 2 Corinthians 4:5

Paul in 2 Corinthians 4:5 provides a characterization of the preached message: 'For what we proclaim is not ourselves, but Christ Jesus as Lord, with ourselves as your servants for Jesus' sake.' This comprehensive statement must be taken as co-ordinate with and complementary to such passages as 1 Corinthians 2:2 (where Paul's purpose requires an emphasis on Jesus as the crucified One). It may be observed with regard to 2 Corinthians 4:5 that:

---

60 Garland, *1 Corinthians*, p. 689.

61 Garland, *1 Corinthians*, pp. 689, 695.

1) Paul here provides a broad characterization of his preaching. This is indicated by Paul's use of the first person plural verb ('we proclaim', certainly referring to Paul's preaching, and perhaps indicating that of the broader company of Paul and his companions or even of the apostolic company). Furthermore, the verb is in the present tense, suggesting Paul's continuing or customary activity.

2) Paul's language indicates that his message had definite and authoritative content. Paul uses the Greek word *kerusso*, whose basic meaning is 'to proclaim aloud' (originally as a herald), specifically 'of proclamation that is divine in origin',[62] thus suggesting the authoritative and reliable transmission of a message which one has received and is not at liberty to alter.

3) The content of Paul's message concerned the lordship of Jesus the Messiah. Paul stated that the content of his proclamation was *Iesoun Christon kyrion*, 'Jesus Christ as Lord', that is, Jesus Christ as the exalted Savior and Sovereign of the universe. 'In his [Paul's] gospel the glory is of Christ, and accordingly the burden of its proclamation is Christ Jesus *as Lord* (*Kyrios*), for the Lordship of Christ is central and altogether indispensable to the evangelical message.'[63] In this verse we have it from Paul himself that 'the heart of the apostolic kerygma is the proclamation of the Lordship of Jesus.'[64] This emphasis stands not in opposition to the preaching of Christ crucified (1 Cor. 2:2), but as complementary to it: it is Jesus in His identity as the crucified One who has now been exalted as Lord, and He is so proclaimed by the apostolic message.

7. Romans 10:8-10

Another passage that is germane to our discussion is Romans 10:8-10, where Paul brings together two elements: the proclamation and the confession of Jesus' lordship. We will give attention now to the first of these (and later in this

---

62   BDAG, pp. 543-54; see also Verbrugge, NIDNTT-A, pp. 304-6.

63   Philip Edgcumbe Hughes, *Paul's Second Epistle to the Corinthians*, New International Commentary on the New Testament (Grand Rapids: Eerdmans, 1962), p. 131.

64   Ladd, *Theology*, p. 339.

study to the content and meaning of the confession which the apostolic preaching intended to elicit).

In Romans 10:6-8 Paul is drawing support for the doctrine of justification by faith from Deuteronomy 30:12-14. In verse 8 he identifies the 'word' of Deuteronomy 30:14 with the 'word of faith which we are preaching', namely, 'if you confess with your mouth that Jesus is Lord and believe in your heart that God raised him from the dead, you will be saved' (v. 9). These verses reveal two important facts about the apostolic *kerygma* (message).

1) Among the preachers of the gospel there was essentially one common message. Paul again uses the first person plural of *kerusso* ("we proclaim', v. 8), indicating that it is not merely his own personal message that he is describing but one that was commonly accepted and proclaimed by a broader community. Verse 9 is thus 'a concise summary of the "word of faith" that was everywhere proclaimed by the apostles and the missionary church. Since Paul assumes his readers' knowledge of this "word of faith", we may infer that it is both common to all the apostles and pre-Pauline in origin.'[65]

2) The lordship of Jesus was integral to the message. Verse 9 is a description not only of the confession elicited but of the message proclaimed. The confession that 'Jesus is Lord' is 'not only related to the proclamation but is actually a part of the kerygma.'[66] It is only natural that the confession which the gospel seeks should itself be found as a vital element in the church's preaching. 'The essentials of the gospel which the church proclaimed were closely related to the *homologia* [confession] to which the Christian community adhered'[67] and which it sought from its converts.

APPLICATORY OBSERVATIONS

1) The earliest Christian preaching included the elements of Jesus' resurrection and lordship along with the fact of His death and its significance. There is perhaps a tendency among modern evangelicals to emphasize the latter and de-emphasize the

---

65 Mounce, *Essential Nature of New Testament Preaching*, p. 94.

66 Vernon H. Neufeld, *The Earliest Christian Confessions* (Grand Rapids: Eerdmans, 1963), pp. 62-63.

67 Neufeld, *Earliest Christian Confessions*, p. 24.

former. However, in order for our proclamation to be faithful to the New Testament pattern, all of this must be included.

2) That Jesus' lordship was such an essential and integral part of the apostolic message suggests that it was intended to elicit a practical response: that of acknowledgment of and submission to His lordship. This response should be sought, therefore, not only in the hearers of our evangelistic message, but also to an increasing degree in the lives of those who already profess to be disciples of Jesus.

II. The Non-Pauline Letters and Revelation

1. Letter to the Hebrews
The non-Pauline corpus of letters in the New Testament (in the canonical order) opens with a powerful affirmation of the threefold messianic function of Jesus in Hebrews 1:1-4, with a subsequent special emphasis on His present lordship (1:5-14). This opening paragraph affirms:

1) The Prophetic Function of Messiah: Jesus is the definitive revelation of God (1:1-2a). The author writes of God as having 'spoken to us by his Son,' in both continuity and contrast with God's having spoken through the prophets. The continuity is found in the fact that the Old Testament events, institutions, and prophets had forecast the messianic age. The contrast is that whereas God had formerly spoken through the merely human instrumentality of prophets, He has now in 'these last days' (indicating the messianic age) spoken 'in Son' – with no definite article or possessive pronoun in Greek, emphasizing the quality of God's giving His final word by means of His own Son, Jesus the Messiah.[68]

2) The Priestly Function of Messiah: Jesus accomplished purification for sins on behalf of His people (1:3c). Only the briefest expression is used here for what much of the rest of the letter is devoted to, namely, Jesus' accomplishment of 'making purification for sins' by means of His death (see 7:27; 9:11-14, etc.)

---

68 Philip Edgcumbe Hughes suggests that the Greek 'aorist tense, used both of God's speaking by the prophets (*lalesas*) and also of his speaking by Christ (*elalesen*), indicates that God has finished speaking in both cases,' *A Commentary on the Epistle to the Hebrews* (Grand Rapids: Eerdmans, 1977), p. 37.

3) The Kingly Function of Messiah: Jesus has been installed as co-regent of the universe (1:3d-4). Hughes observes three points of significance in the phrase 'he sat down at the right hand of the majesty on High' (v. 3): First, Jesus' being seated 'signifies the completion of the work of purification'. Second, His location 'at the right hand' of God 'indicates that his is the place of highest honor, that he is not merely on a seat but on a throne, and that he is not just "sitting" but ruling'. Third, Jesus' 'session, moreover, is "on high": his exaltation, which started with his resurrection from the grave and continued with his ascension into heaven, is completed by his session.... He who humbled himself for our sakes is now supremely honored.'[69]

The explicit undertone of all this is that God has accomplished these three messianic achievements through the person of His incarnate Son (v. 2), who is now exalted to a status which is higher than that of the angels (1:4-14). Furthermore, these attainments are achieved in the interest of fulfilling the divine aim for humankind and of redeeming a people from the thrall of sin and of death (2:1-18).

Much of the rest of the letter is devoted to a treatment of the high priesthood of Jesus, first mentioned in 2:17 and carrying the argument of the letter from 3:1 through 10:39. Jesus' resurrection, ascension, and exaltation are explicitly mentioned or constantly assumed. Thus, Jesus' resurrection and lordship are mentioned in 13:20, referring to God 'who *brought again* [or 'up', HCSB] *from the dead* our *Lord* Jesus.' Jesus' ascension is mentioned in 4:14 ('we have a great high priest who has *passed through the heavens*, Jesus, the Son of God') and is presupposed and His exaltation explicitly mentioned in 7:26 ('For it was indeed fitting that we should have such a high priest, holy, innocent, unstained, separated from sinners, and *exalted above the heavens*'). His exaltation is explicitly referred to in 2:9 ('we see him ... *crowned with glory and honor*', alluding to Psalm 8:5). Jesus' ascension is assumed and His exalted status referred to in those passages which speak of His presence at the right hand of God (besides 1:4,

---

69   Hughes, *Hebrews*, p. 47.

these are 8:1; 10:12; 12:2) a phrase derived from Psalm 110:1. This enthronement theme from Psalm 110 is also implicit in the citations of the Melchizedek reference of Psalm 110:4 (Heb. 5:6; 6:20; 7:15-17, 21), for it is in Psalm 110:1 that the original reference to Messiah's exaltation to God's right hand occurs. As Donald Guthrie observes, 'Without assuming the ascension and exaltation of Jesus, the writer would not have been so ready to apply Psalm 110 to him.'[70] It is no exaggeration to say that the Letter to the Hebrews is full of the exaltation of Jesus.

2. Letter of James

The Letter of James is not known for an emphasis on Christology, yet it is not without allusions to Jesus' exaltation. Thus in James 2:1 Jesus Christ is referred to as 'our *Lord*', a title amplified by the following phrase, 'the [Lord] *of glory*,' suggesting Jesus' present exalted status. The letter opens with a greeting from 'James, a servant of God and of the *Lord* Jesus Christ' (1:1), the latter phrase occurring without the personal possessive pronoun, suggesting the objective reality of Jesus' lordship. James in 5:7 urges readers to 'Be patient, therefore, brothers, until the coming the *Lord*', and then reminds them that 'the coming of the *Lord* is at hand' (5:8). These must be references to the *parousia* (coming) of Jesus in His second advent, an event which presupposes His resurrection, ascension and exaltation, with all that those events imply.

3. Letters of Peter and Jude

The First Letter of Peter refers to Jesus as '*Lord*' in 1:3, and urges readers, 'in your hearts regard *Christ the Lord* as holy' (3:15; HCSB: 'set apart the Messiah as Lord in your hearts') Furthermore, there are explicit references to His resurrection and exaltation: God '*raised him from the dead* and *gave him glory*' (1 Pet. 1:21). In the course of his argument the writer refers to 'the resurrection of Jesus Christ, *who has gone into heaven* and is *at the right hand of God*, with angels, authorities, and powers having been *subjected to him*' (3:21-22), a clear and full statement of His exaltation.

---

70   Donald Guthrie, *New Testament Theology*, p. 397.

In 2 Peter, the title 'Lord' is a favorite of the author, applying it to Jesus in 1:2, 8, 11, 14, 16; 2:20; 3:2, 18, besides many other uses of 'Lord' where it may be difficult to determine whether the author is referring to Jesus or God the Father.

The same is true of the Letter of Jude, where in the span of twenty-five verses the author applies the title 'Lord' to Jesus four times (Jude 4, 17, 21, 25).

4. Letters of John and Revelation

The distinctive idiom of the Johannine letters finds the author neither referring to Jesus as 'Lord', nor as explicitly mentioning Jesus' resurrection and exaltation. The observation of Donald Guthrie is undoubtedly true: 'Christ can bring eternal life [an emphasis of 1 John] to people only if he has first overcome death by his resurrection. John takes this for granted to such an extent that he sees no need to mention it.'[71]

The term 'Lord' is applied to Jesus five times in the Book of Revelation. In 11:8 He is referred to as 'Lord' of the two witnesses who are killed. In 17:14 and 19:16 He is described as '*Lord* of lords', indicating His supremacy over any others who are termed 'lord'. And in 22:20-21 He is twice addressed or referred to as the '*Lord* Jesus'.

More impressive than these usages, however, is the total picture of Jesus presented in the entire book. Guthrie is correct in stating that Revelation is 'a book centering on the risen Christ' and 'the whole book centres on the ascended Lord'.[72] Jesus' resurrection and supremacy are emphasized in 1:5, where He is termed 'the *firstborn of the dead*, and the *ruler* of kings on earth.' The doxology of 1:5-6 says, 'to him be glory and *dominion* forever and ever.' The opening vision portrays Jesus in His glorified majesty (1:12-20). The letters to the churches of chapters 2 and 3 present him as Lord of the churches, the one who commands, comforts, encourages and judges them. The heavenly scene of chapters 4 and 5 portrays Jesus as the 'Lamb', slain yet risen from the dead, who is worthy to control the future destiny of the earth by taking the scroll and breaking

---

71 Guthrie, *New Testament Theology*, p. 389.

72 Guthrie, *New Testament Theology*, pp. 389, 398.

its seals, thus initiating the action of the rest of the book. The Lamb is worshipped and pronounced worthy alongside of God in the doxologies of 5:9-10, 11-12, and 13-14. He shares in the dominion of God, for 'The kingdom of the world has become the *kingdom* of our Lord and *of his Christ*, and he shall reign for ever and ever' (11:15). His triumphant return issues in the defeat of God's enemies followed by a thousand-year reign and the final judgment (19:11–20:15). A more complete picture of the Messiah's supreme exaltation could hardly be imagined.

APPLICATORY OBSERVATIONS

1) Jesus the Messiah's threefold work is a unity. The opening verses of Hebrews move seamlessly through His prophetic, priestly, and kingly functions. Since His work is a unity, so must the reception of His person and work implicitly acknowledge that unity: Jesus' lordship as king cannot be separated from His priestly work in offering Himself as an atoning sacrifice for sin. He must be embraced whole or not at all. His saving work cannot be divorced from His current ruling position. That is, He must be received in faith as both Lord and Savior.

2) Teaching about Jesus' exaltation pervades the New Testament. Even the later or 'lesser' writings consistently call Him 'Lord', explicitly refer to His resurrection and ascension, or presuppose His exaltation as the basis for the teaching presented. There is no legitimate way to escape the fact or implications of Jesus' lordship throughout the entire New Testament. And it could be argued that a professing Christian should not even desire to do so.

9

The Confession of Jesus as Lord:

Its Meaning and Significance

'If you *confess* with your mouth that *Jesus is Lord* and believe in your heart that God raised him from the dead, you will be saved. For with the heart one believes and is justified, and with the mouth one *confesses* and is saved' (Romans 10:9-10).

'Therefore God has highly exalted him and bestowed on him the name that is above every name, so that at the name of Jesus every knee should bow, in heaven and on earth and under the earth, and every tongue *confess* that *Jesus Christ is Lord*, to the glory of God the Father' (Philippians 2:9-11).

'*For us* there is one God, the Father, from whom are all things and for whom we exist, and *one Lord, Jesus Christ*, through whom are all things and through whom we exist' (1 Corinthians 8:6).

'No one speaking in the Spirit of God ever says "Jesus is accursed!" and no one can *say* "*Jesus is Lord*" except in the Holy Spirit' (1 Corinthians 12:3).

All four of these passages express what became the predominant Christian confession early in the New Testament era, namely, the confession 'Jesus is Lord'. Not only does this confession occur in these passages which emphasize its singular character as *the* Christian confession, but it also occurs numerous times in a variant form in the phrase 'our Lord', a designation of Jesus which was so widely used that it became the distinctive and universally recognized Christian confession, known and acknowledged by all believers.[1] This chapter will first examine the meaning of the terminology of 'confession' in the New

---

1   The phrase 'our Lord' will be treated in a later section of this chapter.

Testament and will then deal with the specific confession 'Jesus is Lord'.

I. The Significance of the 'Confession' Terminology in the New Testament

The language of 'confess' and 'confession' is scattered throughout the New Testament and concerning its meaning there is little dispute.

1. The basic meaning of 'to confess' is 'to make an acknowledgment'.

Two related Greek words are translated 'confess' in the passages quoted above. The verb *homologeo*, translated 'confess' in Romans 10:9, and its noun form *homologia*, are both compounds of *homos*, 'the same, similar', and *lego*, 'say'. Hence *homologeo* means 'say the same thing', that is, agree in one's statements; *homologia* means 'agreement, consent'.[2] The verb is used in the New Testament to refer to a promise to do something, either on the part of man (Matt. 14:7) or of God (Acts 7:17). It is used of the act of publicly acknowledging someone, on the part of both Jesus and His disciples (Matt. 10:32), or affirming the lack of a personal relationship (Matt. 7:23). The word can be used to describe the acknowledgment of a fact (John 1:20; Heb. 11:13), or the confessing of one's sins (1 John 1:9). In at least one instance the verb seems to refer to the act of praising God (Heb. 13:15). It can also refer to the act of acknowledging or confessing Jesus as the Messiah (John 9:22; 1 John 2:23, cf. v. 22) or that the Son has come in the flesh (1 John 4:2). It can thus express an act of faith, as in acknowledging or confessing that 'Jesus is Lord', as in Romans 10:9. In this latter context it may be observed that while believing is performed with the heart (10:10), confession is made with the mouth (10:9, 10).[3]

The second verb translated 'confess', used in Philippians 2:11, is simply a compound of the previous verb, *exomologeo*. Like *homologeo*, it can also be used of confessing one's sins (Matt 3:6;

---

2   NIDNTT-A, p. 410. See also TDNT, 5:200.

3   Mounce, *Expository Dictionary*, pp. 5-6; Verbrugge, NIDNTT-A, pp. 410-11; BDAG, pp. 708-709.

Mark 1:5; Acts 19:18; James 5:16), and it can refer to an agreement to perform some action (Luke 22:6). Likewise, it is used of giving praise to God (Matt. 11:25; Luke 10:21; Rom. 15:9). In Philippians 2:11 and Romans 14:11 the verb refers to confessing or acknowledging Jesus' lordship or God's supremacy (or giving praise to God; both are allusions to or quotations of Isa. 45:23).[4]

The noun *homologia*, meaning 'confession', is used six times in the New Testament, half of which are in Hebrews. A distinction may perhaps be drawn between confession as an 'expression of allegiance as an action, *professing, confessing*', as in 2 Corinthians 9:13, where the Corinthians' professing of the gospel of Christ results in their submission to its demands; and confession as a 'statement of allegiance, as content of an action, *confession, acknowledgment that one makes*.'[5] The latter sense seems to be the meaning in Hebrews 3:1 (confession of Jesus as High Priest), 10:23 (confession of the Christian hope or confident expectation with regard to the future) and 4:14 (confession of Jesus as High Priest and Son of God). The other two uses are in 1 Timothy 6:12, 13, where Timothy and Jesus are said to have made 'the good confession' (of the truth?).

In summary, then, the general basic meaning of the word group seems to be that of 'making an acknowledgment', whether of fact, of one's sins, of the reality that God is worthy of praise or of the content of Christian proclamation and belief, specifically that 'Jesus is Lord' or other elements of Christian truth.

By the time of the New Testament era, the verb *homologeo* could bear the meaning 'to make solemn statements of faith' or 'to confess something in faith'.[6] It is used in this sense in Romans 10:9-10 and several other places in the New Testament (John 9:22; 1 John 4:2, 15; etc.). Vernon Neufeld, following his study of the word, concludes that in such instances it has the significance of personal acceptance and acknowledgment of

---

4   Mounce, *Expository Dictionary*, pp. 131-32; Verbrugge, NIDNTT-A, pp. 410-11; BDAG, p. 351.

5   BDAG, p. 709.

6   TDNT, 5:209.

a truth adhered to by the entire community of believers. 'The *homologia* represented the agreement or consensus in which the Christian community was united, that core of essential conviction and belief to which Christians subscribed and openly testified.'[7] And the central truth in which the Christian community was united was the lordship of Jesus Christ.

2. Early in the New Testament era, the predominant Christian confession became 'Jesus is Lord'.

There is a considerable body of opinion that 'Jesus is Lord' may have been the earliest Christian confession of faith. Thus Robert Mounce argues that 'Jesus is Lord' was the 'earliest single-clause Christological confession of primitive Christianity.'[8] James D. G. Dunn states, '"Jesus is Lord" may be the earliest Christian confession that we have.'[9]

Neufeld argues, however, that 'Jesus is the Christ [=Messiah]' was the chronologically prior confession, for 'historically and logically the question of Jesus' messiahship preceded the question of his lordship or his sonship'; in his view, the confession that 'Jesus is Lord' was a slightly later development, 'and the faith expressed by this confession was essentially identical with the post-resurrection understanding of the Christ-formula: it was *Jesus*, the person who lived and died in the course of history, who is *Lord* of the Christian and of the church by virtue of his resurrection from the dead.'[10]

Marshall, in his essay 'Jesus as Lord: The Development of the Concept', plausibly presents a possible course of development

---

7   Neufeld, *Earliest Christian Confessions*, p. 20; his study of the word is found in pp. 13-20.

8   Mounce, *Essential Nature*, p. 94.

9   James D. G. Dunn, *Christianity in the Making*, vol. 2: *Beginning from Jerusalem* (Grand Rapids: Eerdmans, 2009), p. 106

10   Neufeld, *Earliest Christian Confessions*, pp. 140-44, citations from pp. 142, 143. Messiahship was most relevant within a Jewish context, and is found as an issue in Jesus' earthly ministry (John 1:41; 4:29; Matt. 16:16, etc.) Of course, lordship appears to be closely related to an exalted state of messiahship (Acts 2:36), so the two concepts are not entirely discontinuous, and this latter text shows that they existed side-by-side, even within the Jewish context; perhaps they even developed simultaneously.

of the concept of Jesus' lordship in the early church which begins with Jesus' own teaching (including His handling of Psalm 110:1). This teaching was reinforced and made tangible by His resurrection, and was developed in further reflection by the earliest disciples. This led directly to what Marshall calls 'the earliest Christian confession' (by which he means 'Jesus is Lord'), to the further concept of 'the personal relationship of the believer to Jesus as his Lord', then to the twin convictions that Jesus must have been Lord before His resurrection and that He will return as Lord.[11]

Whatever the course of development, it is correct to say that 'Jesus is Lord' soon became the prevailing form of Christian confession. By the time of Paul it was predominant. As Neufeld observes, 'The evidence clearly indicates that the basic *homologia* in the Pauline Epistles is the simple formula *kyrios iesous* [Jesus is Lord]'; and he goes on to point out: 'The *homologia* itself was in all likelihood received by Paul from the primitive church.'[12] In other words, this confession probably did not originate with Paul; it was received by him as a confession commonly known and used in the church, and his use of it therefore reflects an early and broad theological tradition.

APPLICATORY OBSERVATIONS

1) Becoming a Christian involves making a public acknowledgment of certain realities concerning Jesus of Nazareth. In the early Christian community these realities included His messiahship, His resurrection and His lordship. This suggests that a certain minimum of knowledge about Jesus is necessary to believing in Him. The communication of the gospel cannot occur apart from the conveying of historical and theological information concerning Jesus, and likewise, intelligent faith in Him cannot occur apart from such knowledge.

---

11 Marshall, 'Jesus as Lord: The Development of the Concept,' *Jesus the Saviour*, pp. 197-210, esp. pp. 203-9, citations from p. 207.

12 Neufeld, *Earliest Christian Confessions*, pp. 51, 56; see also Cranfield, *Romans*, 2:527.

2) Historical and theological knowledge by itself, however, is inadequate. It must be accompanied by a personal attachment to Jesus and reliance upon His person and work, an attachment and reliance which are willing to risk public identification with Him. Thus in John 12:42-43, we are told that some of the Jewish authorities 'believed' in Jesus but were unwilling to 'confess it' out of fear of the Pharisees. John gives as the explanation that they 'loved the glory that comes from man more than the glory that comes from God.' We must conclude that a genuine faith is willing to 'confess' Jesus, and that it is questionable whether these people did actually possess such a faith, for Romans 10:10 says, 'with the mouth one confesses and is saved' (an obvious exception is the compelled confession of Phil. 2:11, which on the part of some will simply be an acknowledgment of the reality of Jesus' lordship; for them it will be a hostile confession, offered under compulsion). The same is still true today. One test of the genuineness of faith is the willingness to confess it before men.

II. The Meaning of the Confession 'Jesus is Lord'

The biblical evidence suggests that the confession 'Jesus is Lord' (Rom. 10:9; 1 Cor. 12:3; Phil. 2:11) is quite broad in scope and involves four related but distinguishable elements which are explicit or implicit in the confession.

1. It involves the acknowledgment of Jesus' position as exalted Lord.

As Neufeld notes, 'The *homologia* [confession] was the confession of Jesus with specific reference to his person or work, and was therefore Christological in character.'[13] Thus a fundamental theme of apostolic preaching – the resurrection and lordship of Jesus – finds a natural and prominent place in the Christian confession. And it should be noted, as Murray states, 'how far-reaching are the implications' of this confession. It explicitly affirms the exaltation of Jesus and implies all that preceded the exaltation; the whole redemptive work of Christ is in view in this single statement. 'The confession "Jesus as

---

13   Neufeld, *Earliest Christian Confessions*, p. 20.

Lord" or "Jesus is Lord" refers to the lordship which Jesus exercises in virtue of his exaltation.... This lordship presupposes the incarnation, death, and resurrection of Christ and consists in his investiture with universal dominion.'[14]

By means of this confession, the Christian convert affirms 'an article of faith, namely, that by virtue of his death and resurrection, Jesus has been exalted to a place of sovereignty over all men,'[15] that is, the exalted Jesus is God's personal agent in the exercise of God's government of the world and of the universe. As already noted, the lordship of Jesus does not stand in opposition to His atoning work, but is the culmination and fulfillment of it, as well as His personal vindication. Thus all the basic facts of the gospel story are implicit in the single brief confession, 'Jesus is Lord.'[16]

2. This confession involves the acknowledgment of the rightful authority of Jesus Christ over the believer.

The believer in Jesus Christ, by his confession that 'Jesus is Lord', is expressing his abandonment *in principle* of the assertion of personal autonomy. He is recognizing the right of the exalted Jesus to rule over his life. This is implied by (a) the basic meaning of the title 'Lord' (see Appendix 1); (b) by the position of Jesus as the exalted Sovereign; and (c) by Jesus' legal possession of the believer (1 Cor. 6:19-20; see the later section on the basis of Jesus' lordship over the believer); and it is indicated in the New Testament by the nearly universal Christian designation of Jesus as 'our Lord' (see the later section on the corporate nature of this confession). The broad purpose of God is to bring all things under the authority of

---

14 Murray, *Romans*, 2:55.

15 Ladd, *Theology*, p. 416.

16 While this is the necessary factual data which the confession acknowledges, the confession cannot be reduced to factual data alone, as Everett F. Harrison attempts to do in his work on Romans in *The Expositor's Bible Commentary* (Grand Rapids: Zondervan, 1976-), 10:112. Harrison's approach results in a mere intellectualism or 'historical faith' (an acknowledgement of factual data, not necessarily arising from spiritual regeneration and not involving personal trust). On 'historical faith', see Hoeksema, *Reformed Dogmatics*, (Grand Rapids: Reformed Free Publishing Association, 1966), p. 491.

Christ (Ps. 2; 1 Cor. 15:25-28; Phil. 2:9-11); the Christian is one who willingly enters the sphere of that acknowledged authority when he confesses Jesus as Lord. This confession, says Ladd, 'reflects the personal experience of the confessor. He confesses Jesus as Lord because he has received Jesus Christ as *his* Lord (Col. 2:6). He has entered into a new relationship in which he acknowledges the absolute sovereignty and mastery of the exalted Jesus over his life'.[17] This is not to claim, of course, that the believer will henceforth perfectly obey the Lord Jesus (for he will not), but it is to insist that the believer acknowledges at least *implicitly* and *in principle* that Jesus possesses the legitimate authority to rule over him and to require his submission and obedience. Thus this confession involves no intrusion of the works of fallen human beings into the 'justification of the ungodly' (Rom. 4:5) but simply expresses the recognition that the Creator possesses rightful authority over human beings, an authority which the Christian convert confesses he had formerly rebelled against, but which he now acknowledges as making legitimate claims upon himself or herself personally. In this sense, the sincere offering of this confession is tantamount to repentance, a topic which will be treated later in this chapter.

3. This confession implies or acknowledges the deity of Jesus Christ.

While the apostolic preaching found in Acts did not demand acknowledgment of the deity of Jesus in order for hearers to be saved, yet the deity of Jesus is an implication of the New Testament terminology relating to Jesus' lordship. Cranfield argues persuasively that the Septuagint (the Greek translation of the Old Testament) usage of *kyrios* as God's name should play an important part in understanding the designation of Jesus as *kyrios*. 'The use of *kyrios* more than six thousand times in the LXX to represent the Tetragrammaton [God's personal

---

17 Ladd, *Theology*, p. 415. Charles Hodge's comment is also worth noting: 'This confession, therefore, includes in it an acknowledgement of Christ's universal sovereignty, and a sincere recognition of his authority over us.' *A Commentary on Romans* (reprint ed., London: Banner of Truth Trust, 1972), p. 341.

name YHWH, rendered "Yahweh" or "Jehovah"] must surely be regarded as of decisive importance here.' After summarizing several substantial lines of reasoning he concludes that 'the confession that Jesus is Lord meant the acknowledgement that Jesus shares the name and the nature, the holiness, the authority, power, majesty and eternity of the one and only true God.'[18]

Neufeld points out, as others also have done, that 'in at least three passages [Paul] applies to Jesus Old Testament references which refer to God'[19] (Rom. 10:13 [Joel 2:32], 1 Cor. 2:16 [Isa. 40:13], and Phil. 2:11 [Isa. 45:23]), Old Testament passages which Paul elsewhere applies to God (Isa. 40:13 in Rom. 11:34; Isa. 45:23 in Rom. 14:11). Dunn comments: 'The most striking aspect of the attribution to Jesus of rule "at God's right hand" is the way scriptural texts which spoke of God as "Lord" began to be used of Jesus', and he traces this feature back to the pre-Pauline church, found as early as Peter's speech in Acts 2.[20] It has therefore come to be widely recognized that possession of divinity is an implication of the title 'Lord' as applied to Jesus.[21] And although the early Christian preaching as found in Acts may not have explicitly insisted on acknowledgment of this reality (since the Christology of the early Messianic community was

---

18 Cranfield, *Romans*, 2:529.

19 Neufeld, *Earliest Christian Confessions*, p. 57.

20 Dunn, *Beginning from Jerusalem*, p. 220.

21 'Implicit in the recognition of the Lordship of Jesus is the acknowledgement of his essential divinity.' Ladd, *Theology*, p. 341. Moo suggests that the confession of 'Jesus as Lord carried with it significant overtones, for it would inevitably associate Jesus as Lord closely with God, the "Lord",' *Romans*, p. 658 n. 58. See also TDNT, 3:1089; Cullmann, *Christology*, pp. 234-35; N. T. Wright, *The Resurrection of the Son of God* (Minneapolis: Fortress, 2003), pp. 571-78. Dunn suggests the likely development of this implication from the early application of Psalm 110:1 to Jesus; *Beginning from Jerusalem*, pp. 220-21. See also I. H. Marshall, *Jesus the Saviour*, pp. 207-9; Larry W. Hurtado, 'Lord,' in Gerald F. Hawthorne, et al., ed., *Dictionary of Paul and His Letters* (Downers Grove, IL: InterVarsity, 1993), pp. 560-69, throughout; and F. F. Bruce, *Jesus: Lord and Savior* (Downers Grove, IL: InterVarsity, 1986), pp. 196-205.

not yet fully developed), it was nevertheless an implication of the title 'Lord' as applied to Jesus, and in later centuries the Christian church came to regard the acknowledgment of Jesus' deity as necessary for a consistently biblical Christian faith.

4. This confession involves personal trust in Jesus Christ.
It should not need to be said that the utterance of the confession 'Jesus is Lord' must be more than just an empty ritual or the expression of an arid intellectualism; Paul regards it as reflecting the sincere conviction, humble trust and submissive attitude of the believer's mind and heart. The 'confessing' of Romans 10:9-10 assumes the prior act of 'believing' mentioned in these same verses; and together they are such confessing and believing as result in 'righteousness' and 'salvation' (v. 10). Nor is there any disjunction between the two. The lordship of Jesus (which is confessed, v. 9a) is intimately connected with His resurrection (which is believed, v. 9b), as we have already seen. 'The content of the confession and the content of the belief are differently formulated, but in Paul's thought they amount to the same thing. He does not mean to imply that the mouth is to confess anything other than that which the heart believes.'[22]

All of which is to say that this confession is a confession of *faith*, a faith by which one enters into a personal relationship with Jesus Christ the Lord. Neufeld observes: 'The *homologia* [confession] was the admission and acknowledgment of the individual's loyalty to Jesus Christ, and as such represented a personal testimony of his faith.'[23] Since confession implies believing, and since the title 'Lord' implied the whole of Jesus' work, then to confess Him as Lord is to trust Him and receive Him in the fullness of who He is and what He has done. It means to believe in Him as the Son of God, the crucified Savior and exalted Lord. It means to appropriate to oneself the benefits of all His redeeming work, past, present and future. It means to take upon oneself the responsibilities which are entailed in personal submission to the Sovereign of the universe and the Agent of the government of God.

---

22 Cranfield, *Romans*, 2:527.

23 Neufeld, *Earliest Christian Confessions*, p. 20.

APPLICATORY OBSERVATION

The confession of Jesus' lordship involves the subjective recognition of an objective reality. If the New Testament is true as it stands, then it is an objective fact that Jesus has been exalted to the supreme position of 'Lord' as proclaimed in the Christian message. For a person to confess that 'Jesus is Lord' is to acknowledge the truth of that claim and to recognize that *it has personal implications for himself or herself.* Once the objective fact of Jesus' lordship is granted, then the conclusion is inescapable that *He deserves to be my Lord.* This involves a complete reorientation of human thinking, a reorientation in which one surrenders the claim to personal autonomy which characterizes the human race in its fallenness. Thus there occurs a reversal of the attitude of rebellion against God and of the human assertion of personal autonomy, which, of course, is a primary goal of God in the gospel and in the redemption it proclaims. If the mission of Jesus is to 'save his people from their sins' (Matt. 1:21), then the elimination of this primal root of all sin – the assertion of personal autonomy or independence from God – must be included in that salvation. It could not be otherwise.

III. The Basis of the Confession 'Jesus is Lord'

It has been argued that the confession of Jesus as Lord involves the acknowledgement of the rightful authority of Jesus Christ over the confessor. This authority or lordship of Jesus over the individual believer may be regarded as grounded in two realities: creation and redemption.

1. Creation: The ultimate ground of God's lordship over humans, and of the human acknowledgment of it, is God's rightful authority over His creatures by virtue of His creation of them.

God holds a rightful claim upon every individual human by virtue of His creation of the world and all that is in it. The cattle on a thousand hills are his, and every beast of the forest: 'the world is Mine, and all it contains' (Ps. 50:10, 12; see also Ps. 104:24; 24:1; 89:11). Every human being belongs to God by right of creation and owes to his Creator love and service, obedience and submission (Mark 12:28-34; the great commandment can by legitimate extension be applied to all men). Specifically, in terms of the concepts with which this study began, humans are obligated to recognize God's lordship in the three areas of human existence: epistemological lordship (over human knowing), metaphysical lordship (over human nature) and ethical lordship (over human willing and behavior). Ever since the resurrection and exaltation of Jesus God exercises His authority over men through Jesus the Lord, and for people to confess His lordship is to recognize God's legitimate authority as Creator.

2. Redemption: The ground of God's lordship over Christian believers is Jesus' rightful ownership of and authority over Christians by virtue of His redemption of them.

The line of argumentation involving the New Testament concept of redemption runs from (a) the reality that Jesus purchased or redeemed or ransomed a people for God's own possession (b) through the idea that Christian believers therefore no longer exercise ownership over themselves (c) to the conclusion that Christians are now slaves or bondservants of God through the Lord Jesus. The biblical evidence may conveniently be set forth under these three headings.

1) The New Testament portrays Jesus' priestly work for His people as a purchasing, redeeming or ransoming of them through His death. The New Testament is replete with language which speaks of Jesus as ransoming, purchasing or redeeming His people. For example: 'The Son of Man came not to be served but to serve, and to give his life as a *ransom* for many' (Matt. 20:28; Mark 10:45); 'You were *bought* with a price' (1 Cor. 6:20); 'Christ *redeemed* us from the curse of the law by becoming a curse for us' (Gal. 3:13).

New Testament scholar Leon Morris, in his classic study of this terminology, has demonstrated that such language refers to the securing of release or freedom through the payment of a price.[24] There are essentially three Greek word-groups which are used to express this idea.

---

24   Leon Morris, *The Apostolic Preaching of the Cross*, pp. 11-64.

(i) The *lutron* word-group. The basic word means 'ransom' or 'ransom price', that is, the price paid to secure release. This is the term Jesus used in Matthew 20:28 (also Mark 10:45) to describe the effect of His giving of His life. From this noun are derived the verb *lutroo*, 'to release by paying a ransom, to redeem', used in Titus 2:14 and 1 Peter 1:18; the noun *lutrosis*, 'a ransoming, redemption', Hebrews 9:12; the compound noun *apolutrosis*, meaning 'release effected by payment of ransom, redemption, deliverance', used ten times in the New Testament, as in Romans 3:24 to refer to 'the *redemption* that is in Christ Jesus'; and the further compound noun *antilutron*, 'a ransom', used only in 1 Timothy 2:6.[25]

(ii) The *agorazo* word-group. This verb means 'to buy in the market, purchase', in the common sense of ordinary commercial transactions, as in Matthew 13:44 and 46, but is used six times metaphorically of spiritual purchase by Christ's death, as in 1 Corinthians 6:20 (quoted above); 7:23; 2 Peter 2:1; Revelation 5:9; 14:3, 4. The compound form *exagorazo*, 'to redeem, ransom', is used in a spiritual sense in Galatians 3:13 (quoted above) and 4:5.[26]

(iii) The verb *peripoieo*. The literal meaning of this verb is 'to make to remain over, preserve', with the resultant sense of 'to get or gain for oneself, get possession of'.[27] It is used of Christ's death in Acts 20:28, which speaks of 'the church of God, which he *obtained* with his own blood'. Morris points out that 'This verb seems to have about it a flavour of personal possession.'[28]

2) Redemption establishes God's ownership of Christian believers. As the last-quoted text indicates (Acts 20:28), because Jesus by means of His redemptive work on behalf of His people has purchased them, the result is that they no longer belong to themselves, but to Him (or to God). 'Do you not know,'

---

25 Definitions quoted are from G. Abbott-Smith, *A Manual Greek Lexicon of the New Testament* (Edinburgh, UK: T & T Clark, 1994), pp. 273, 52-53, 42.

26 Abbott-Smith, *Manual Greek Lexicon*, pp. 7, 158.

27 Abbott-Smith, *Manual Greek Lexicon*, pp. 356-57.

28 Morris, *Apostolic Preaching*, p. 60.

Paul writes to the Christians at Corinth, '*You are not your own*, for you were *bought* with a price. So glorify God in your body' (1 Cor. 6:19, 20). The basis of the ethical obligation here is the fact of the divine redemption and ownership of believers. The word translated 'bought' is *agorazo* (mentioned above) meaning here 'buy, acquire as property'.[29] It is used in a similar sense with reference to believers in 1 Corinthians 7:23 and Revelation 5:9. We have already noted Acts 20:28, where a different verb is used, a passage which, as Morris has been quoted, has 'a flavour of personal possession'. Jesus' possession of believers is also affirmed in Romans 14:8, another passage we have already examined: 'Whether we live or whether we die, *we are the Lord's.*' All of this does more than suggest – it affirms – that the Christian's person and life are no longer his own possession, but now belong to the one who has bought him, the Lord Jesus. That this is the teaching of Scripture is affirmed by the Heidelberg Catechism (1563): 'QUESTION 34. Why callest thou him [Jesus Christ] *our Lord?* ANSWER. Because, not with silver or gold, but with his precious blood, he has redeemed and purchased us, body and soul, from sin and from all the power of the devil, to be his own.'[30]

3) The New Testament uses the language of 'slave' to describe the new relationship with God brought about by redemption through the death of Christ. Morris draws the obvious conclusion from the New Testament language of redemption, which the biblical writers also draw, that 'it is clear that those so purchased are in a special relationship to God, and it is this which determines their conduct.' He goes on to observe that 'this thought is to be found in many passages which do not make explicit use of the redemption or purchase terminology, as for example when Christians are said to be "slaves" of God or of Christ' – and 'we are His slaves because we were bought by Him.'[31]

There are passages which indicate that this spiritual enslavement to Christ or God is the status of all professing

---

29   BDAG, p. 14.

30   Philip Schaff, *The Creeds of Christendom*, 6th ed. (Grand Rapids: Baker, 1985 [1931]), 3:318.

31   Morris, *Apostolic Preaching*, p. 55.

Christian believers. In 1 Corinthians 7:22-23, for example, Paul argues that Christians who are not currently slaves of human owners should not become slaves, because they are Christ's slaves: 'he who was free when called is a *slave of Christ*. You were *bought* with a price; do not become slaves of men.' Likewise, when recalling the conversion of the Roman Christians, Paul reminds them, 'now that you have been set free from sin and have become *slaves of God*, the fruit you get leads to sanctification and its end, eternal life' (Rom. 6:22). This entire passage is full of such language (Rom. 6:15-23).

The New Testament word commonly translated 'slave', *doulos*, represents one who 'owed his master exclusive and absolute obedience'. This term and the related verbs, *douleuo* and *douloo*, describe the new condition into which believers have been freed by Christ, a freedom from domination by sin but one in which they are bound as slaves to the Lord Jesus. Thus believers, 'having been set free from sin, have become *slaves of righteousness*' (Rom. 6:18). Thus, 'our manumission from bondage of a supposed independence [autonomy] does not lead to a new independence. Rather, the one manumitted is set free for "the obedience that comes from faith" (1:5), which he or she offers to the Lord Jesus Christ as a slave (12:11; 14:18; Col. 3:24; cf. Rom. 7:6; 1 Thess. 1:9).'[32]

The New Testament language of redemption and slavery indicates that the Christian is redeemed by Christ, not for a life of self-determining and autonomous freedom, but for a life of slavery to God and to righteousness. Paul could state it to earthly slaves in this way: 'You are *serving* [as a slave] the *Lord Christ*' (Col. 3:24).

APPLICATORY OBSERVATIONS

1) Redemption by Christ simply frees people to render to God that honor which is due Him as Creator: to respect, trust and love Him to the point of obedience. It is a lifestyle that is not worthy of praise or reward, nor should it be a ground of pride: 'When you have done all that you were commanded, say, "We are unworthy servants; we have only done what was our

---

32 Verbrugge, NIDNTT-A, pp. 152, 153.

duty"' (Luke 17:10). Redemption frees us for the first time to begin to be what humans were intended to be: personal beings who honor the lordship of God.

2) The New Testament concepts of bondage and freedom ultimately refer to spiritual and moral bondage and freedom. Jesus said, 'Truly, truly, I say to you, everyone who practices sin is a slave to sin' (John 8:34). Thus He could also say, 'So if the Son sets you free, you are free indeed' (8:36). The reference here is to a pattern of life dominated by sin – literally, everyone 'doing' or 'practicing' sin (a participle in the present tense, indicating an ongoing activity) – in contrast to a life freed from domination by sin. That is true freedom, and that is what is involved in redemption by the Lord Jesus.

3) Ownership of the Christian by God through the Lord Christ ought to be a governing reality in the life of every believer. Christians are those who no longer claim autonomous rights over their own lives as people of the world do; the Christian has acknowledged that the right to command his allegiance and obedience belongs to God.

IV. The Centrality of the Confession 'Jesus is Lord'

The argument thus far has maintained that 'Jesus is Lord' became the predominant Christian confession of faith very early in the movement's history. At this point, we will undertake a review of the presentation of this confession in passages already mentioned and in other important passages where it occurs in order to demonstrate that the New Testament identifies the confession 'Jesus is Lord' as the characteristic and distinctive Christian confession, central to what Christians in the New Testament era believed, affirmed, and were committed to. It represented the heart of Christian conviction and identity.

1. Romans 10:9. In Romans 10:9 the confession 'Jesus is Lord' is identified as the characteristic and distinctive Christian confession. It was by means of this confession that genuine Christian faith was expressed, resulting in justification; it was by means of this confession that a person presumptively entered into the possession of salvation ('is justified', 'is saved', v. 10). Thus Moo could say, commenting on this passage,

'The acclamation of Jesus as Lord is a very early and very central element of Christian confession.'[33] Likewise I. Howard Marshall: 'This verse shows that the decisive mark of being a Christian was public confession of Jesus as Lord ...'[34] And the confession must be seen as antedating Paul and as having wide circulation and acceptance among the Christian communities of the Mediterranean world. For as J. D. G. Dunn observes, 'Rom. 10:9 clearly expresses a long-established summary of the agreed response to inquirers (Romans was sent to a church Paul had never visited), as confirmed by the even more impressive array of parallels'; Dunn goes on to list many of the passages considered in this current study.[35]

2. Philippians 2:9-11. We have already examined Philippians 2:9-11 with its affirmation of the universal confession of Jesus' lordship at the consummation. It is worth noting again, however, that at the consummation of all things, when God's victory over hostile forces will be made complete and manifest, the one reality which all personal beings will be compelled to acknowledge is the fact that *'Jesus Christ is Lord'*. This truth must therefore be central to the divine purpose as well as to Christian truth claims and to Christian confession and identity.

3. 1 Corinthians 12:3. A third passage in which this confession is used in its straightforward and basic form, 'Jesus is Lord', is 1 Corinthians 12:3: 'Therefore I want you to understand that no one speaking in the Spirit of God ever says, "Jesus is accursed!" and no one can say, *"Jesus is Lord"* except in the Holy Spirit.'

While some scholars such as Neufeld and Cullmann[36] suggest that the context here may be that of state persecution in which some professing Christians yielded to the pressure to

---

33 Moo, *Romans*, p. 658.

34 I. Howard Marshall, *Jesus the Saviour: Studies in New Testament Theology* (Downers Grove, IL: InterVarsity, 1990), p. 197.

35 Dunn, *Beginning from Jerusalem*, p. 106 n. 211.

36 Neufeld, *Earliest Christian Confessions*, p. 63; Cullmann, *Christology*, pp. 218-20.

curse Jesus and then claimed the guidance of the Holy Spirit in doing so, it would seem that David Garland has offered a more plausible interpretation.[37] Following Garland's approach, the following points may be made.

a) *Paul in this passage is concerned to correct a misconception about what makes a 'spiritual' person.* Responding to questions raised by the Corinthians in a letter to Paul (see 7:1), Paul seeks to discuss 'spiritual things' (12:1), the term used by the Corinthians but utilized by Paul in a deliberately ambiguous way (it could refer to either spiritual persons or spiritual gifts). Paul is concerned to overturn the notion, apparently held by some at Corinth, that because they exercised certain spiritual gifts ('conspicuous speech gifts'), they constituted a spiritual elite. 'Paul's purpose is to identify who qualifies as spiritual.'[38]

b) *Paul is concerned to point out that every Christian experiences the working of the Holy Spirit and is therefore spiritual.* In opposition to the assumptions of the 'spiritual elite' at Corinth, Paul sought to demonstrate that every Christian believer is 'spiritual'.

c) *Specifically, Paul affirms that the Holy Spirit produces the conversion and profession of faith of every Christian believer.* Every Christian is to be regarded as 'spiritual' because he or she is the object of the working of the Spirit. Specifically, the Holy Spirit is at work in the conversion and the confessing of Christian faith on the part of every believer.

d) *Paul utilizes the standard Christian confession, 'Jesus is Lord', as the distinctive point of identity of the Christian.* As the demonstration of the spirituality of every believer, Paul

---

37 Garland, *1 Corinthians*, pp. 558-73, introduces this section of the letter (chs. 12–14) and discusses the opening paragraph (12:1-3), setting forth his view over against the alternatives. Garland understands the statement 'Jesus is anathema [cursed by God]' to reflect the unbelieving Jewish attitude toward Jesus, the claimed Messiah (pp. 570-71). It would seem that a proper appreciation of the use of the confession 'Jesus is Lord' in this context is difficult to attain apart from an awareness of the purpose of these chapters of the letter and of this introductory paragraph.

38 Garland, *1 Corinthians*, pp. 573, 572.

points out that no one can genuinely offer the confession 'Jesus is Lord' unless he is enabled to do so by the Holy Spirit (the Greek preposition *en* should probably be understood in the instrumental sense of 'by', as in HCSB: 'by the Holy Spirit'). Thus Paul begins his argument in this section of the letter 'by making clear that *all* who make the saving confession "Jesus is Lord" (Rom. 10:9) are led by the Spirit and qualify as spiritual ones.'[39] Again, 'This saving confession, made by every single Christian, can be made only under the inspiration of the Spirit. It means that turning from their past blindness is made possible only by the reception of the Spirit.'[40] The point of particular interest for the current study is that Paul chose this confession, 'Jesus is Lord', as the distinctive point of identity for every Christian. It is this which Paul fastened upon when he wanted to emphasize the working of the Holy Spirit in every believer, in opposition to the elitism of some members of the Corinthian congregation. This confession, therefore, is what set the Christian believer apart from the surrounding society and what set the Christian community apart from every other group in society. Paul assumed that every member of the Christian community at Corinth personally identified with this confession and would know what Paul meant in referring to it. It is by means of this confession, and the necessity of the working of the Holy Spirit in order to offer it sincerely, that Paul 'argues here that all who confess Jesus as Lord are spiritual.'[41]

Garland has some further comments about the meaning of the confession 'Jesus is Lord' which harmonize well with the conclusions being reached in the current study:

> This confession is not some spontaneous, ecstatic utterance that anyone could blurt out. It affirms the majesty of Jesus as the one raised from the dead to become the universal Lord above all other so-called lords (8:6). It declares absolute

---

39   Garland, *1 Corinthians*, p. 570.

40   Garland, *1 Corinthians*, p. 572.

41   Garland, *1 Corinthians*, p. 572.

allegiance to him and accepts his absolute authority over every aspect of life.[42]

Even though Garland's overall reconstruction of the context of Paul's use of the confession 'Jesus is Lord' in 1 Corinthians 12:3 seems quite plausible, it must be acknowledged that the life situation in view here cannot be determined with certainty. What is clear is that, as stated by Ladd, in this verse 'the importance of this confession in the Pauline churches is vividly set forth.'[43]

4. 1 Corinthians 8:5-6. A contrast between Christianity and paganism is in view in 1 Corinthians 8:5-6,[44] and thus Paul directs attention to the distinctive elements of Christian faith as set forth in what some scholars believe is a creedal formula. In this passage Paul acknowledged that in the surrounding society there were indeed many so-called gods and lords (v. 5), but for Christians 'there is one God, the Father, from whom are all things and for whom we exist, and *one Lord, Jesus Christ*, through whom are all things, and through whom we exist' (v. 6). When the question of the essential distinction between Christianity and paganism arose, the Christian faith was distinguished by its confession of one God, the Father, and one Lord, Jesus Christ. Surely such a confession must be expected to define the heart of the Christian faith; and at its heart is found the acknowledgment of the lordship of Jesus.[45]

5. Ephesians 4:4-6. There are other New Testament passages which give indication of being creed-like formulas or confessions. In support of his call to maintain unity among believers (Eph. 4:3) Paul in Ephesians 4:4-6 mentions seven

---

42 Garland, *1 Corinthians*, p. 572.

43 Ladd, *Theology*, p. 415.

44 See Neufeld, *Earliest Christian Confessions*, p. 65; Oscar Cullmann, *The Earliest Christian Confessions*, trans. J. K. S. Reid (London: Lutterworth Press, 1949), p. 32.

45 Note the observation by Garland: Paul in this section 'begins his argument by defining the nature of the people of God, who believe in one God and one Lord and who live in the midst of a pagan society where there are many gods and lords.' *1 Corinthians*, pp. 375-76.

elements which do in fact establish unity among Christians. 'There is one body and one Spirit ... one hope ... *one Lord*, one faith, one baptism ... one God and Father of all ....' As Harold Hoehner observes, 'The word *kyrios* [lord] logically refers to Christ since Paul has just discussed the Holy Spirit in verse 4 and will discuss the Father in the next verse. Christ is the "one Lord" who provided redemption (1:7), hope (1:12), and headship over the church (1:22-23).'[46] Whether this passage is or is not a creedal formula inherited by Paul (Hoehner thinks not, pp. 513-14) it is significant that reference is made to the one and only Redeemer, the exalted Jesus, by means of the terminology of 'one Lord', a form of expression which assumes that Paul's readers would be able readily to identify that 'one Lord' as Jesus Himself. Thus in a passage defining the distinctive unitive elements of the Christian faith, Paul refers to the central figure of that faith by the simple term 'Lord', suggesting that such terminology had come to occupy a central role within the Christian community as a means of referring to Jesus.

6. *Romans 1:3-4.* Some writers regard Romans 1:3-4 as a pre-Pauline confession or kerygmatic formula.[47] As already noted, it designates the exalted Jesus as 'Lord' and as the 'Son of God in power'. Again, whether or not it is a formula received by Paul, it indicates the centrality of the identity of the exalted Jesus as 'Lord', for Paul was writing to a Christian community which he had not founded and which he had never visited, yet which he expected to recognize and affirm what he said about 'the gospel of God' (Rom. 1:1) and about Jesus' place in that gospel as the one who is now 'the powerful Son of God' (HCSB) and 'our Lord' (2-4).

7. *Romans 4:24-25.* Mounce believes that Romans 4:24-25 may also fall into the category of an early confession or kerygmatic formula.[48] This passage describes Christians as

---

46 Hoehner, *Ephesians*, p. 516.

47 Mounce, *Essential Nature of New Testament Preaching*, pp. 95-98; Neufeld, *Earliest Christian Confessions*, p. 51; Dunn, *Beginning from Jerusalem*, pp.105-06.

48 Mounce, *Essential Nature of New Testament Preaching*, pp. 98-99;

those 'who believe in him who raised from the dead *Jesus our Lord*, who was delivered up for our trespasses and raised for our justification.' Both the death and resurrection of Jesus are mentioned, and He is designated 'Lord'. Once again Jesus is identified in a simple formulaic statement as 'Lord'. Such passages may or may not be confessional in nature; some would appear to be so. In any case, they lend corroborating support to the view that the lordship of Jesus was central to early Christianity.

8. *Colossians 2:6.* This passage does not give evidence of being a formula or early confession yet it shows how central was the acknowledgment of Jesus' identity as 'Lord' in early Christianity. Paul exhorts: 'Therefore, as you have *received Christ Jesus the Lord*, so walk in him'. P. T. O'Brien observes, '*Received* is a technical term meaning to "receive a tradition" and here indicates that they had welcomed both the person and the authoritative teaching about him.'[49] Paul expected that his readers would recognize and affirm that at their conversion they had acknowledged and received Jesus 'as Lord' (NIV) and he exhorted them so to live. The centrality of the identity of Jesus as Lord is simply assumed, which speaks eloquently of its central place in the thinking and confession of the earliest Christian communities.

APPLICATORY OBSERVATION

The widespread and various use of the confession 'Jesus is Lord' in the New Testament indicates that this claim (with all it implies), maintained within the confines of a committed monotheism, was the distinctive and distinguishing feature of Christian faith in the first century. This suggests that it might be a salutary development if Christians were to become thus known again in our own day, which like the first century is an era of religious pluralism and relativism. If all Christians were to become known as people who acknowledge and live

---

see also Neufeld, *Earliest Christian Confessions*, p. 51. Dunn refers to this passage along with others as 'semi-credal assertions or liturgical responses,' *Beginning from Jerusalem*, pp. 106-07.

49   Peter T. O'Brien, 'Colossians' in *New Bible Commentary*, 4th ed., D. A. Carson et al., eds. (Downers Grove, IL: IVP Academic, 1994), p. 1269.

consistently with the claim that 'Jesus is Lord', it would bear a powerful testimony to a watching world.

V. The Corporate Nature of the Confession: 'Our Lord'

There is a phenomenon in the New Testament which is often overlooked (it seems) but which convincingly demonstrates that the confession 'Jesus is Lord' was not only central to the New Testament faith, but also that it was universally recognized and used among the churches and that it involved personal acknowledgement of the authority of Jesus Christ over believers. This phenomenon is the pervasive use in the New Testament of the simple phrase 'our Lord' in reference to Jesus.

1. Features of the use of the phrase 'our Lord'

This phrase is typically used at the beginning of an epistle in the opening greeting (e.g. Rom 1:4) or at the conclusion (Rom. 16:20), but may be found anywhere in between (Rom. 4:24; 5:1, 11, 21; 6:23; 7:25; 8:39; 15:6, 30; 16:18). The common Greek form of the phrase, through the use of the definite article, is somewhat more expressive than the typical English translation. A baldly literal rendering would read something like 'Jesus Christ the Lord of us' (Rom. 1:4) or 'the Lord of us Jesus Christ' (Rom. 5:1). The Greek form emphasizes the peculiar identity of Jesus as *the* (one and only) Lord of Christian believers, drawing attention to the exclusiveness of that relationship.

1) The terminology 'our Lord' was used by a wide range of New Testament writers. The writers of the New Testament literature commonly used the term 'our Lord' in combination with various names and titles to refer to Jesus: (i) Paul, in various combinations (according to Ladd, 'our Lord Jesus Christ', twenty-eight times; 'our Lord Jesus', nine times; 'Jesus Christ our Lord', three times[50]); (ii) the writer of Hebrews (7:14; 13:20); (iii) James (2:1); (iv) Peter (1 Peter 1:3; 2 Peter 1:2, 8, 11, 14, 16; 3:18); (v) Jude (Jude 4, 17, 21, 25); (vi) Luke,

---

50   Ladd, *Theology*, pp. 415-16. Cf. also Rom. 16:18, 'our Lord Christ.'

in Acts (15:26; 20:21). Furthermore, a variant form of the phrase, with the singular pronoun ('my Lord') is found in Philippians 3:8 and in Thomas' confession in John 20:28 ('My Lord and my God'), which Cullmann regards as the climax of the book.[51]

Thus it is evident that the phrase 'our Lord' was used as a common means of referring to Jesus within the Christian community, and it was so used multiple times by the various writers of the New Testament (it occurs in every New Testament book from the Gospel of John onward except for Philemon, the Epistles of John, and Revelation). It would be difficult to find in the New Testament a more universally used designation of Jesus than 'our Lord'.

2) The use of the terminology 'our Lord' was widespread over a broad geographical area. By determining the provenance of the writers and addressees of the various New Testament writings in which the phrase 'our Lord' is used it is possible to sketch the extent of the geographical area in which this title of Jesus was known and used. The utilization of this phrase is by this means seen to have been widespread geographically, including the regions of Palestine, Syria, the provinces of Asia Minor, Macedonia, Achaia, Italy and Crete – that is, everywhere that Christianity had spread.

3) The phrase 'our Lord' was used early in Palestinian Christianity. That the common designation 'our Lord' was furthermore used early in the life of the young church is demonstrated by the occurrence of the Aramaic phrase *marana tha* in 1 Corinthians 16:22 (written by Paul in approximately A.D. 55). This phrase means 'Our Lord, come', and because of its occurrence in the Aramaic language it must be regarded as having had its origin in the Palestinian church. Thus it appears that 'our Lord' was used as a designation of Jesus from a very early (pre-Pauline) stage of the church's history. Dunn argues that the use of this Aramaic form here 'presumably indicates that the title [*mar*=Lord] became quickly fixed in the Aramaic-speaking

---

51 Cullmann, *Christology*, p. 232. It should be noted that this confession occurs after the resurrection and that it distinguishes between Jesus' identity as 'Lord' and as 'God'.

communities of Palestine.'[52] Likewise Moo, who claims that this Aramaic phrase 'in particular, points to an early date for this confession since it preserves the Aramaic that was spoken by the first Jewish Christians.'[53] It is also worthy of note that Paul used this Aramaic phrase, without translation and within the span of a generation after Jesus' death and resurrection, in a letter written to a Greek-speaking congregation located in the Greek city of Corinth. This suggests the wide dissemination of this particular phrase in its original form at a very early stage of the Christian movement's history. It may therefore be concluded that the confession of Jesus' lordship stems from the very earliest phase of the development of the Christian movement. This conclusion is consonant with the early proclamation of Jesus' lordship in Acts 2:33-36.

2. Implications of the use of the phrase 'our Lord'
The implications of this phrase for our current investigation are at least four.

1) It indicates the personal relationship that exists between Jesus Christ and all Christian believers. When, instead of the simple article with 'Lord' to designate Jesus ('the Lord Jesus Christ', etc.), 'there is joined with the title *kyrios* a personal pronoun in the genitive [*hemon*, "our" etc.], there is expressed ... the sense of his ownership of those who acknowledge him and of their consciousness of being his property, the sense of personal commitment and allegiance, of trust and confidence.'[54] It is significant that in the New Testament professing Christians are never urged to make (subsequent to conversion) an initial acknowledgement of Jesus' lordship, nor is any distinction drawn between those who have done so and those who have not; rather, as the phrase 'our Lord' demonstrates, it is simply assumed (as a fact lying at the basis of the Christian faith) that

---

52 Dunn, *Beginning from Jerusalem*, p. 217. For a discussion of this term and its significance, see Cullmann, *Christology*, pp. 208-15; Ladd, *Theology*, pp. 340-41; C. F. D. Moule, *The Origin of Christology* (Cambridge University Press, 1977), pp. 35-46; Garland, *1 Corinthians*, pp. 773-75; Hurtado, 'Lord,', pp. 562-63, and *Lord Jesus Christ*, p. 110.

53 Moo, *Romans*, p. 658 n. 58.

54 Cranfield, *Romans*, 2:529.

every believer already stands in relation to Jesus as a subject to his Lord. So transparent is this phenomenon in the New Testament that Dunn can write: 'That baptism in the name of Jesus carried with it a commitment to Jesus as Lord and to a pattern of living which accorded with that lordship – to what Paul describes as a slave-like obedience to righteousness (Rom. 6:15-22) – should be obvious.'[55] Similarly, Hurtado notes that 'in these expressions the fundamental force of the term kyrios denoting the superior or "master" seems primary. Jesus is the "master" of Christians, to whom in turn they are his followers, his subjects bound to obey him.'[56] It simply was naturally expected that every Christian was in sympathy with the expression 'our Lord'.

2) Particular instances of the use of this phrase indicate that there was no disjunction between the Christian's relationship to Jesus as Lord and his relationship to Jesus as Savior. In 2 Peter there are four instances of the combination 'Lord and Savior' in referring to Jesus. Two passages, 2 Peter 1:11 and 3:18 speak of *'our Lord and Savior* Jesus Christ'. The phrase also occurs in 2:20, with some ancient manuscripts including the personal pronoun ('our') and some omitting it. It also is found in 3:2 with just the definite article. In all of these cases, however, it is apparent that Peter regards all Christians as sustaining this dual relationship to Jesus – that of relating to Him as their Lord *and* Savior (in fact, 'Lord' always occurs first) – and that He expects nothing less than instant recognition of this designation and wholehearted assent to its content.

3) This phrase expresses that commitment by which the Christian community was identified. To be a Christian meant to be counted among those who confessed Jesus as 'our Lord'. In fact, Dunn argues that, 'Self-identification by reference not only to Jesus, but to *Jesus as Lord*, constituted a massive step in the basic self-understanding of the early disciple groups ....'[57] Indeed, it could plausibly be argued that the very essence of Christian identity in early Christianity quickly came to be

---

55 Dunn, *Beginning from Jerusalem*, p. 108.

56 Hurtado, 'Lord', p. 566.

57 Dunn, *Beginning from Jerusalem*, p. 16; emphasis added.

found in this reality: Christians were those who acknowledged Jesus as Lord, and who corporately referred to Him as 'our Lord'.

4) This phrase expresses that commitment by which the Christian community was united. Not only did this confession identify the church, it also united it. The confessor became a part of that great company of Christian believers throughout the Roman Empire which maintained this common allegiance. One's relationship to Jesus as Lord 'is not alone personal and individualistic; it is a relationship enjoyed by the church as a whole.... In confessing Jesus as Lord, the confessor joins a fellowship of those who have acknowledged his Lordship.'[58] This was *the* confession common to all Christians. This is what identified them and bound them together; for all could say, 'Jesus is [our] Lord'. This is especially borne out in a text like 1 Corinthians 1:2: 'To the church of God that is in Corinth, to those sanctified in Christ Jesus, called to be saints *together with all those who in every place call upon the name of our Lord Jesus Christ, both their Lord and ours.*'[59] The New Testament writers could send their epistles across the empire, refer to Jesus as 'our Lord', and do so in the confidence that their readers would be in absolute sympathy with that expression. It pervades the New Testament as the identifying and unifying confession of the Christian community.

APPLICATORY OBSERVATIONS

1) When a person becomes a Christian by confessing Jesus as Lord and placing his trust in Him, he does so not merely as a solitary individual but automatically joins the world-wide company of 'all those who in every place' exercise the same faith. This fact should counter the individualism that seems to prevail in some forms of modern Christianity. Christian believers are as indissolubly bound to one another as they are to Christ. Their association with one another in this community

---

58   Ladd, *Theology*, pp. 415-16.

59   Note the comment by Garland, 'The confession binds them to the one Lord (8:5-6) and to all other believers. It also severs them from those who insist that Caesar is the world's lord,' *1 Corinthians*, p. 29.

of faith should reflect the love which Jesus called for among His disciples (John 13:34-35).

2) It is the existence of such a community of love, with each member acknowledging the lordship of Christ over them all, that justifies and necessitates the corporate disciplinary action which the New Testament calls for in congregations (Rom. 16:17-18; 1 Cor. 5:1-13; 2 Thess. 3:6-15). It is ultimately an exercise of love to call one another to consistent submission to Jesus' lordship and by this means as well to maintain the purity and testimony of the church.

VI. Repentance and the Lordship of Jesus

A related question involves the issue of repentance: What is the relationship between repentance and confessing Jesus' lordship? The heart of the matter may be expressed as follows: 'Confessing Jesus as Lord is virtually the practical equivalent of repentance, and conversely, repentance implies acknowledgment of God's (or Jesus') lordship'.

Sometimes the New Testament presents the appropriate human response to the gospel in terms of both repentance and faith, as when Paul summarized his ministry in Ephesus as one of 'testifying both to Jews and to Greeks of repentance toward God and of faith in our Lord Jesus Christ' (Acts 20:21). At other times faith alone is explicitly mentioned, as in Paul's response to the question of the jailer at Philippi concerning the way of salvation: 'Believe in the Lord Jesus, and you will be saved, you and your household' (Acts 16:31). And sometimes it is repentance alone which is called for, as in Paul's message to the Athenians: 'God ... commands all people everywhere to repent' (Acts 17:30). These facts should alert us to the reality that, in the biblical view of things, while faith and repentance are distinguishable and perform different functions, yet they are not two distinct and separable acts but two aspects of the single act of casting oneself upon God's mercy in Christ. In discussing the question of the priority of faith or repentance, John Murray seems to have struck the biblical note in suggesting their interpenetrating nature: 'The faith that is unto salvation is a penitent faith and the repentance that is unto life is a believing repentance.' Again, 'It is impossible to disentangle faith and repentance. Saving faith is permeated with repentance and repentance is permeated with faith.'[60] Theologian Louis Berkhof concurs: 'true repentance never exists except in conjunction with faith, while, on the other hand, wherever there is true faith, there is also real repentance.... the two cannot be separated; they are simply complementary parts of the same process.'[61] That is, saving faith in Christ is accompanied by the attitude of repentance, and gospel repentance is accompanied by reliance upon Christ alone for one's acceptance before God. This is why one or the other alone can be put forth in the New Testament as the required human response to the gospel; each implies the other. Thus repentance and faith are distinguishable but inseparable elements of the human act of conversion or turning to God through Jesus Christ. It is the contention of this study that 'confessing Jesus as Lord' involves both trusting in Jesus' saving death on the cross (faith) and acknowledgment of His right to rule one's life as risen Lord (repentance). Attention here is drawn particularly to the element of repentance as it is expressed in this basic New Testament confession.

1. Repentance involves acknowledging God's right to rule one's life.

Repentance by its very nature involves the recognition that God, as Creator of the universe and of the human race, possesses the right to command human obedience. This recognition seems to be expressed in David's confession in Psalm 51, 'so that *you may be justified* in your words and *blameless* in your judgment' (Ps. 51:4b). He acknowledged that God possessed the right and authority to judge him for his sins because God possessed the right to rule his life. J. A. Alexander, in commenting on Paul's phrase in Acts 20:21 expressing the tenor of Paul's preaching at Ephesus, 'repentance toward God', says that repentance 'is that change of heart and life which every

---

60 John Murray, *Redemption Accomplished and Applied* (Grand Rapids: Eerdmans, 1955), p. 113.

61 Louis Berkhof, *Systematic Theology* (Edinburgh: Banner of Truth, 1958), p. 487.

sinner owes to God as his rightful sovereign.'[62] As the human person's 'rightful sovereign', God possesses the right to rule, the authority to command obedience and to exact a penalty when such obedience is not forthcoming.

2. Repentance involves acknowledging one's rebellion against God's rule.

The language of repentance in the New Testament includes the verb *metanoeo*, meaning 'change one's mind', the noun *metanoia*, referring to a 'change of mind', and occasionally the verbs *epistrepho*, meaning 'turn', and *metamelomai*, 'change one's mind, repent'. The first two of these terms, as used in the New Testament, 'denote a radical, moral turn of the whole person from sin and to God.'[63]

Biblical repentance implies the awareness that one has been engaged in rebellion against God. This rebellion manifests itself in an attitude of hostility toward God's rule, God's right to command obedience. Such rebellion is essentially an assertion of personal autonomy. This attitude of rebellion in turn expresses itself in active violation of God's commands which are intended to govern human life and behavior. This attitude and these acts of disobedience are what the Bible terms 'sin' and 'sins', respectively. The act of repentance necessarily involves the personal recognition that one has participated in such rebellion against God and His rule, even if the matter is not so formulated in one's mind. Such recognition is perhaps to be found in King David's confession in Psalm 51, which, although it is the expression of an already converted heart, presents an accurate portrayal of repentance, which includes the element of awareness of violating God's law. David said: '*I know my transgressions*, and my sin is ever before me. *Against you, you only, have I sinned* and done what is evil in your sight' (Ps. 51:3-4a). Here David acknowledged his rebellion against God and his violations of God's law.

---

62 Alexander, *Acts*, 2:244.

63 Mounce, *Expository Dictionary*, p. 580; see also Verbrugge, NIDNTT-A, p. 367.

3. Repentance involves renunciation of personal autonomy.
At the heart of repentance is the renunciation of personal autonomy on the part of the human agent. This means the giving up – the abandonment *in principle* – of one's assertion of that autonomy which constitutes the essence of sin. This is an essential component of the human response to the gospel because of the nature of the salvation that is effected by Messiah Jesus: 'he will save his people *from their sins*' (Matt. 1:21). As Murray observes, 'if faith is directed to salvation from sin, there must be hatred of sin and the desire to be saved from it. Such hatred of sin involves repentance which essentially consists in turning from sin unto God.'[64] A faith that is not accompanied by repentance is a disingenuous faith, for it is not sincere in its desire to be delivered from sin; it lacks integrity, for it involves asking forgiveness of something which one does not recognize as wrong and for which one does not acknowledge that a just penalty is due and continues to be due as long as one continues in the offense. It would be similar to the case of a rebel against his rightful monarch asking forgiveness of his rebellion while persisting in his rebellious activities; he wants pardon only because he might have to face disastrous consequences, not because he recognizes that his rebellion is wrong. Psalm 145:18 says, 'The LORD is near all who call out to Him, all who call out to him with integrity' (HCSB). To seek God's forgiveness while persisting in the determination to continue in rebellion against Him is not to call out to Him with integrity. It is a sham which ought not to be accorded recognition as genuine faith. A biblical expression of such repentance may again be found in Psalm 51 when David says, '*Create in me a clean heart*, O God, and *renew a right spirit within me*' (Ps. 51:10). David recognized that his sins of adultery and murder were an assertion of personal autonomy resulting in his violation of God's law. He desired that God would renew in himself that spirit of recognizing God's rightful rule over his life which would result in his renunciation of the assertion of personal autonomy and in his obedience to God.

---

64 Murray, *Redemption Accomplished and Applied*, p. 113.

The necessity and nature of repentance have been well described by the British writer C. S. Lewis. First, the nature of repentance:

> Now what was the sort of 'hole' man had got himself into? He had tried to set up on his own, to behave as if he belonged to himself. In other words, fallen man is not simply an imperfect creature who needs improvement: he is a rebel who must lay down his arms. Laying down your arms, surrendering, saying you are sorry, realising that you have been on the wrong track and getting ready to start life over again from the ground floor – that is the only way out of a 'hole'. This process of surrender – this movement full speed astern – is what Christians call repentance.

And on the necessity of repentance:

> Remember, this repentance, this willing submission to humiliation and a kind of death, is *not* something God demands of you *before* He will take you back and which He could let you off if He chose: it is simply a description of *what going back to Him is like*. If you ask God to take you back without it, you are really asking Him to let you go back without going back. It cannot happen.[65]

In other words, failure or refusal to repent is to maintain one's stance of autonomy and rebellion over against God; a psychology of sincere request for forgiveness cannot coexist with such a stance, for the two attitudes are in contradiction to each other. In William Shakespeare's play *Hamlet*, King Claudius (who had had Hamlet's father, the previous king, killed) is led to ask: 'May one be pardon'd and retain the offense?' (Act III, Scene III) – that is, can someone be forgiven a sin while not repenting of it? The implied answer is, 'No, such a thing is not possible.'

John Murray has written some words which are well worth pondering:

> Repentance consists essentially in change of heart and mind and will. The change of heart and mind and will principally respects four things: it is a change of mind respecting

---

65   C. S. Lewis, *Mere Christianity*. p. 49 (emphasis added).

God, respecting ourselves, respecting sin, and respecting righteousness. Apart from regeneration our thought of God, of ourselves, of sin, and of righteousness is radically perverted. Regeneration changes our hearts and minds; it radically renews them. Hence there is a radical change in our thinking and feeling.... It is very important to observe that the faith which is unto salvation is the faith which is accompanied by that change of thought and attitude.[66]

4. Repentance involves acknowledging Jesus for who He is as God's appointed agent for the exercise of God's rule over humans.

In the New Testament repentance is sometimes explicitly connected with acknowledging the exalted Jesus as the specific agent through whom God's rule is now exercised. A text such as Acts 17:30-31 is quite pointed in calling for repentance in view of the exaltation of Jesus. Paul said at Athens, 'The times of ignorance God overlooked, but now *he commands all people everywhere to repent*, because he has fixed a day on which *he will judge the world in righteousness by a man whom he has appointed*; and of this he has given assurance to all by raising him from the dead.' The ground of the call for repentance is the fact that God has raised His appointed representative – Jesus – from the dead and installed Him as that agent and standard by whom God will judge the human race according to the criterion of righteousness. In other words, the installation of the risen Jesus as Lord serves as the basis of His serving as judge of the human race and as the basis of the universal call for repentance. A similar affirmation was made earlier by Peter: '[Jesus] commanded us to preach to the people and to testify that he is the one appointed by God to be judge of the living and the dead' (Acts 10:42), in the light of which fact Peter declared that 'everyone who believes in him' – the now exalted Jesus who will be judge of all people – 'receives forgiveness of sins through his name' (10:43). Once again the exalted position of Jesus as Lord and future Judge of all undergirds the

---

66 Murray, *Redemption Accomplished and Applied*, p. 114. See the similar summary by Reymond, *Systematic Theology*, p. 725.

call to trust in Him (with repentance implied in the seeking of forgiveness) as the agent of divine forgiveness.

Other New Testament texts, some from the mouth of Jesus Himself, testify to His exalted status and the necessity of being rightly related to Him. Near the beginning of His public ministry, Jesus portrayed Himself as the 'gatekeeper' of the eschatological kingdom of heaven. At the final judgment ('On that day'), upon hearing from those who called Him 'Lord' but did not live out the demands of that title, Jesus said, 'then will I declare to them, "I never knew you; depart from me, you workers of lawlessness"' (Matt. 7:23). At the end of His earthly teaching ministry, Jesus described the final judgment featuring the 'Son of Man' (Jesus Himself) sitting 'on his glorious throne', exercising judgment over 'all the nations' (Matt. 25:31-32). Acting as 'the King' (25:34, 40), He will pronounce the verdict of blessedness or condemnation upon those brought before Him (25:33-46) on the grounds of their treatment of 'my brothers' (25:40), identified elsewhere as those who (through repentance and faith) 'do the will of my Father in heaven' (i.e., Jesus' disciples; Matt. 12:50).

5. Repentance involves no human merit or 'work of law' but is a change of attitude toward God's lordship.

It must be emphasized that repentance is not a 'work' of the law that earns merit before God. Indeed, repentance is represented in the New Testament as a gift of God's grace for which no human credit can be claimed (Acts 5:31; 11:18; 2 Tim. 2:25). Repentance is simply a definitive change of mind or attitude which recognizes the legitimacy of God's lordship and which accepts it as the determining authority for the conduct of one's life. It constitutes an acknowledgment *in principle* of God's rights as Creator and Sovereign of the human race. A standard theological dictionary maintains that repentance (or 'conversion', another possible translation of the term) 'embraces the whole walk of the new man who is *claimed by the divine lordship*. It carries with it the founding of a new personal relation of man to God, i.e., of *pistis* [faith]. It awakens joyous obedience for a life according to God's will.'[67]

---

67 TDNT, 4:1003, emphasis added.

Notice that, in this account of the meaning of the terminology, repentance and faith are joined together in a single movement called 'conversion', the standard form in which the matter is presented in many systematic theologies.[68]

APPLICATORY OBSERVATIONS

1) Regarding the anatomy of conversion, perhaps it should be recognized that not all the elements of repentance mentioned above are necessarily *consciously* present in any given instance; perhaps, indeed, in few cases are they all present in a conscious way, for conversion is a very personal experience and may differ from person to person. However, on the basis of biblical teaching there is probably warrant to say that these elements are *implicit* in turning from sin to God in the movement known as conversion. It may be that only later, in the outworking of conversion in the Christian life, that these elements are recognized and become explicit in the Christian consciousness.

2) The call for repentance must be a part of the gospel proclamation. People who are in rebellion against the God of the Bible must not be allowed to think that they can continue in their self-willed rebellion and yet be forgiven. They must be informed that God requires them to abandon their rebellion and acknowledge His right to rule their lives. It is only when this attitude prevails that they are able to exercise genuine faith in the Lord Jesus.

3) Repentance must be a continuing component of the Christian life. Martin Luther said that the Christian walk is simply one long repentance: 'Our Lord and Master Jesus Christ, in saying "Repent ye, etc.", meant the whole life of the faithful to be an act of repentance.'[69] This is indeed the case (Jesus calls on churches and individuals within them to repent in Revelation 2:5, 16; 3:3, 19). While Christians are those who in principle have acknowledged God's lordship, nevertheless they continue to commit individual sins and are obligated to repent when those sins are brought to their

---

68 For example Reymond, *Systematic Theology*, pp. 721-36.

69 Martin Luther, 'The Ninety-Five Theses, 1517', in Henry Bettenson, ed., *Document of the Christian Church*, 2nd ed. (London: Oxford University Press, 1963), p. 186, thesis 1.

attention. The intimacy of their fellowship with God depends on it (1 John 1:8-10).

VII. Justification and the Lordship of Jesus

A perplexing issue that has led to much confusion in recent decades is that of the relationship between justification and good works in the life of the Christian. The issue is germane to the present study because good works (obedience to Christ) should result from the acknowledgment of Jesus' lordship, yet according to the traditional Reformed doctrine of justification such good works should not be allowed to enter into the ground of the believer's justification before God. Unfortunately, positions adopted in several recent controversies (which ideologically may be connected to one another) have resulted in just such a stance: the theoretical admittance of the works of fallen human beings as a ground of their acceptance before God, that is, their justification.

Perhaps the most widely publicized proponent of such a stance has been N. T. Wright, one of the acknowledged leaders of a movement in New Testament interpretation known as 'the New Perspective on Paul'. In many places, but notably in his popularly-written book, *What Saint Paul Really Said*,[70] Wright has advocated a revised doctrine of justification which views the final justification of believers as based on their entire lives, and thus on their own works and not simply on the basis of faith in Christ's finished work. Wright's thoroughgoing revision of the doctrine of justification is broadly based, resting on the pillars of the New Perspective, and may be summarized in the following propositions:

1. The Judaism of the first century did not exhibit self-righteous legalism (pp. 18-20).

2. God's righteousness is His covenant faithfulness (pp. 100-11).

3. The gospel is not about how to 'get saved' (pp. 90, 133).

4. Justification is not the gospel (pp. 125-26, 132).

5. Justification is not how one becomes a Christian (pp. 119, 125).

---

70   N. T. Wright, *What Saint Paul Really Said: Was Paul of Tarsus the Real Founder of Christianity?* (Grand Rapids: Eerdmans, 1997).

6. The Jewish error which Paul battled was national exclusivism (not legalism), embodied in ethnic boundary markers (circumcision, dietary laws, Sabbath observance; p. 132).

7. The imputation of God's righteousness in justification makes no sense (pp. 98-99).

8. Future (final) justification is based on the whole life lived (p. 129).

On the one hand, Wright is to be commended for emphasizing the resurrection and exaltation of Jesus and the resulting New Testament confession that 'Jesus is Lord' as occupying a central place in apostolic preaching and biblical faith (pp. 45-61). Yet on the other hand, his restructuring of the doctrine of justification seems to run counter to both biblical and Reformation teaching.

It is not the purpose of the present study to offer a detailed response to Wright. In brief, however, it seems that Wright's teaching (and that of others whose positions are coordinate with his) may be addressed on two levels: first, the narrow question of the nature and ground of justification, and second, the broader question of how the works of believers relate to the final judgment.

With reference to the former of these, the narrower matter of the nature and ground of justification, it may be argued that Wright has violated a basic principle that informed the stance of the sixteenth century Reformers: the works of fallen human beings must not be permitted to serve as the ground of human acceptance before God.[71] The integrity of justification through faith alone cannot be maintained if this principle is abandoned, as Wright seems to have done. To allow even works that are generated by faith and produced in the believer by the Holy Spirit to enter into the ground of justification before God is to allow the works of fallen human beings to occupy a place which the New Testament does not permit: as the basis of acceptance of

---

71 See, among the Lutheran confessions, the Augsburg Confession (1530), Art. IV; Formula of Concord (1576), Art. III; and among Reformed confessions, the Belgic Confession (1561), Art. XXII; Heidelberg Catechism (1563), Q. 12-21; Second Helvetic Confession (1566), Ch. XV; Canons of Dort (1619), Second Head; Westminster Confession (1647), Ch. XI; Second London Confession (1677, 1689), Ch. XI.

unholy sinners before a holy God. No amount of reworking the views of Judaism in the first century (which the New Perspective seeks to do) or recasting of Paul's thought can legitimately be utilized to overturn this basic principle: 'by works of the law no human being will be justified in his sight, since through the law comes the knowledge of sin' (Rom. 3:20). That Paul here means moral law as well as ceremonial is clear from the context (3:9-19), where Paul has rehearsed in Old Testament citations the moral corruption of the human race, 'both Jews and Greeks' (3:9), as well as from his reference to 'sin' in verse 20.[72] New Testament scholar I. Howard Marshall concurs that in this question 'the issue is the theological one of the grounds for justification', that 'the element of achievement (merit) cannot be eliminated' from the matter, and that Paul's thought when he deals with justification operates in this sphere (not that of ethnic boundary markers). He concludes, 'The traditional understanding is accordingly essentially right and the "new perspective" must be regarded as flawed.'[73] Wright's view endangers not only the historic Reformed doctrine of justification through faith alone but also the basis of the believer's confidence of acceptance before God and therefore his assurance of salvation. It constitutes, in essence, a return to the Roman Catholic view of justification, expressed in the Council of Trent, with which the Reformers were unwilling to compromise.[74]

---

72 For a treatment of Rom. 3:20 (where Paul cites Ps. 143:2) with specific reference to this question see Andrew Hassler, 'Ethnocentric Legalism and the Justification of the Individual: Rethinking Some New Perspective Assumptions', *Journal of the Evangelical Theological Society* 54.2 (June 2011), pp. 311-27, esp. pp. 319-25

73 Marshall's discussion in found in *New Testament Theology*, pp. 445-48; citations from pp. 447-48.

74 John Piper, *The Future of Justification: A Response to N. T. Wright* (Wheaton, IL: Crossway, 2007) has provided a traditionalist response to Wright's views on justification, although perhaps some of Piper's positions need to be qualified in ways suggested by Michael F. Bird, 'What Is There between Minneapolis and St. Andrews? A Third Way in the Piper–Wright Debate,' *Journal of the Evangelical Theological Society*, pp. 54.2 (June 2011), pp. 299-309 (e.g., it is likely that union with Christ provides the mechanism for both the justification [with the corollary of imputation] and the sanctification of the believer; see the next point below). Piper treats many aspects of the doctrine which cannot be dealt with here.

Regarding the second matter, that of the relationship of works to final justification (which Wright seems to regard as a separate matter from present justification) and the final judgment, the situation has been helpfully clarified by Dane Ortlund in his 'taxonomy of ways in which scholars reconcile justification by faith and judgment according to works in Paul'.[75] Ortlund sets forth fourteen categories of ways in which scholars have sought to deal with the conjoining of these two concepts in Paul's thought. These fourteen are arranged in four broader patterns: (1) they are irreconcilable; (2) reconcilable if justification is given interpretive authority; (3) reconcilable if judgment/obedience is given interpretive authority; and (4) reconcilable if both justification and judgment emerge from a more fundamental reality. In Ortlund's reckoning, exponents of the New Perspective (E. P. Sanders, J. D. G. Dunn, N. T. Wright) fall within pattern number (3) above, in which the judgment/obedience motif is given interpretive authority or priority over the justification motif, and accordingly human moral deeds are allowed to enter into the determination of one's final acquittal (a number of recent professing evangelical authors have adopted a similar position).[76]

The category which Ortlund favors is the one that seems most likely to resolve the issue. It falls within pattern number (4), with both justification and judgment emerging from a more fundamental reality, namely, the union of the believer with Christ, 'a union from which fruit organically and inevitably grows.'[77] Ortlund provides two helpful observations

---

For the historic Roman Catholic doctrine, see Philip Schaff, *Creeds of Christendom*, 2:110-18, esp. Canons IX (112), XI (112-13), XXIV (115). For a rather comprehensive overview and critique of Wright's view of justification, with considerable biblical–theological interaction, and a similar conclusion that Wright's view has affinities with medieval and Roman Catholic views, see Mark Seifrid, 'The Near Word of Christ and the Distant Vision of N. T. Wright', *Journal of the Evangelical Theological Society*, pp. 54.2 (June 2011), pp. 279-97.

75 Dane C. Ortlund, 'Justified by Faith, Judged according to Works: Another Look at a Pauline Paradox,' *Journal of the Evangelical Theological Society* 52/2 (June 2009), pp. 323-39, citation from p. 323.

76 Ortlund, pp. 327-28.

77 Ortlund, p. 329.

on what he calls 'neglected factors'. First, that Paul uses different Greek propositions when talking about these two different situations. 'Paul consistently uses *dia* or *ek* when relating faith to justification (Rom. 3:22, 25; 5:1; Gal. 2:16; cf. Eph. 2:8; Col. 2:12) and *kata* when relating works to judgment (Rom. 2:6; 2 Cor. 11:15; cf. Rom. 2:2; 2 Tim. 4:14). Justification is *through/by/from* faith; judgment is *according to* works.' The significance of this feature is explained by Ortlund:

> This distinction points us toward understanding justification by faith as denoting contingency or instrumentality and judgment according to works as denoting congruence or correspondence. Paul understands salvation to be through (*dia*) faith, and in accordance with (*kata*) a life of obedience and fruit. Faith is a means, works a manner. Justification is *contingent upon* faith; judgment is *congruent with* obedience.[78]

This means that the final judgment will be appropriate to the person's life as lived (and the lives of believers will be qualitatively different from the lives of unbelievers), yet whatever good works may be present in the believer's life do not constitute the ground or basis of justification.

Ortlund's second observation relates to the contrast set up by Paul in Romans 2:13, a passage appealed to by proponents of a revised view of justification. He observes properly that 'the contrast of Rom 2:13 is not [between] human action and faith but [between] human action and mere hearing."[79] Mere possession and hearing of the law is what the Jews seemed to rely on, but Paul goes on to show in 2:17-29 that they certainly did not 'do' what the law required. Paul's argument is negative, emphasizing 'doing' over against 'hearing', and he does not seem to envision anyone actually being justified by his own 'doing' of the law (see 3:9-20); that falls outside the purview of his thought in the current argument.

Ortlund goes on to summarize his position in four propositions in a way that seems to do justice to the tensions found in biblical teaching with respect to both justification and judgment:

---

78   Ortlund, p. 332; emphasis in the original.

79   Ortlund, p. 333.

1. Justification is not a two-staged event (as the revisers want to make it) but 'the single eschatological event of a declaration of forensic acquittal and right standing proleptically brought into the present and grasped by grace-fueled faith in Christ's work.'

2. 'Our understanding of NT faith must avoid the twin pitfalls of mere mental assent, on one side, and synergism on the other.... [I]f the faith that renounces one's own moral resume is organically bound up with the movement of the will by which one casts oneself on God in Christ for all things (*fiducia* [trust]), justification is protected from all human contribution [in contrast to New Perspective revisionism] while faith is protected from unbiblical reductionisms to the merely cerebral [in contrast to the anti-lordship position].'

3. 'Paul taught a real judgment that applies to believers and unbelievers alike and is according to, not on the basis of, obedience.' Believers will experience 'degrees of reward', but they 'have nothing to fear on Judgment Day – every shortcoming is covered by Christ's sacrifice (Rom. 8:31-34; cf. James 2:13).'

4. '[O]bedience is not merely evidential but is rather built into the very fabric of salvation itself, yet without contributing to justification. Justification and judgment are linked not so much in cause-and-effect or linear progression as they are organically unified. This organic bond is *union with Christ*, in which one is not only declared righteous ... but also indwelt by the Spirit. Justification and obedience both sprout from the seed of union with Christ.'

'Union with Christ inaugurates not merely external reformation but internal transformation.... [T]here has been ignited, even now in this diseased world, an inevitable new direction (2 Cor 5:17).'[80]

In other words, union with Christ through faith produces justification on the basis of His righteousness alone while at the same producing willing acknowledgment of His lordship and consequent submission to that lordship.

---

80 Ortlund, pp. 336-39; emphasis added. Ortlund's entire essay is well thought out and is worthy of careful attention.

By means of this understanding the two are kept in balance and within biblical parameters.

10

Objections Considered

The interpretation of the confession 'Jesus is Lord' which is set forth here, as well as the estimate of its place in New Testament faith, has been disputed by such respected and well-known evangelical scholars as Everett F. Harrison and Charles C. Ryrie. In the original incarnation of the thesis of the present study,[1] the opposing arguments of Harrison and Ryrie were the only ones to be dealt with. Harrison's objections to this view were found in an article in *Eternity* magazine, while Ryrie's were set forth in chapter 17 of *Balancing the Christian Life*. Both Harrison's article and Ryrie's chapter are entitled 'Must Christ Be Lord to Be Savior?' and both answer the question in the negative.[2]

Since that time, a rather acrimonious debate broke out in print between, on the one hand, John F. MacArthur, Jr., and on the other, Zane Hodges and Charles Ryrie, prompted by the 1988 publication of MacArthur's book, *The Gospel According to Jesus* (Grand Rapids: Zondervan, 1988, 1994). Ryrie responded with *So Great Salvation* (Wheaton, IL: Victor, 1989) and Hodges with *Absolutely Free!* (Grand Rapids: Zondervan, 1989). MacArthur replied with *Faith Works: The Gospel According to the Apostles* (Dallas: Word, 1993) and a revised and expanded edition of *The Gospel According to Jesus* (1994). Other studies of the issue have appeared as well, and

---

1   T. Alan Chrisope, *Jesus Is Lord: A Study in the Unity of Confessing Jesus as Lord and Saviour in the New Testament* (Welwyn, Hertfordshire, England: Evangelical Press, 1982.

2   Everett F. Harrison, 'Must Christ Be Lord To Be Savior? No,' *Eternity* Sept. 1959: 14+; Charles Caldwell Ryrie, *Balancing the Christian Life* (Chicago: Moody Press, 1969), pp. 169-81.

Hodges was instrumental in founding the Grace Evangelical Society to propagate his viewpoint.

The present study will not report in detail on what was said in the intensified controversy which was initiated over twenty years ago, nor will it follow later exchanges on the issue. The goal of the current study is to provide a biblical rationale for the New Testament use of the confession 'Jesus is Lord'. Little that MacArthur's theological opponents said relates directly to this question; in this limited sense, it is doubtful that they have added much to the discussion.[3] At those points where their arguments intersect with the concerns of the present study they will be considered along with those objections offered in the earlier literature. It is likely that objections arising from other sources will not be significantly different than those already raised by these men.

I. A Fundamental Defect

It may be pointed out immediately that virtually all the objections urged by these men suffer from a single basic defect: they confuse the Christian's *practice* of the lordship of Christ with the Christian's *acknowledgement in principle* of the lordship of Christ. To require the actual practical observance of the lordship of Jesus as essential for justification would be indeed to add something to biblical 'faith' and to make human works-righteousness the ground of salvation. But that is not the biblical position, nor is it the position advocated here. Rather, it is maintained that the New Testament requires the Christian convert's acknowledgement at least by implication and *in principle* that 'Jesus is Lord', that is, the abandonment of the claim to personal autonomy over against God; the practical implications of that principle are to be worked out after conversion, within the maturing process of the Christian life.

II. Major Objections

The major objections to the view herein set forth are three: (i) to require acknowledgement of the lordship of Jesus is to make

---

3   Hodges' *Absolutely Free!* ignores two of the passages which contain the confession, 1 Corinthians 12:3 and Philippians 2:11, and for Romans 10:9 he offers an entirely untenable interpretation, pp. 195-99.

human works-righteousness the ground of salvation; (ii) there are instances of known believers who were not fully committed to the lordship of Jesus; (iii) to require this acknowledgement leaves no room for the 'carnal Christian'. There are also some miscellaneous objections, most of which can be treated more briefly.

Objection 1: Requiring acknowledgment of Jesus' lordship makes human works and righteousness the ground of man's salvation.

Harrison argues that this view 'involves the introduction of a subtle form of legalism'; it 'brings works in by the side door'.[4] Ryrie regularly speaks of the requirement of this confession as demanding something 'in addition to faith' or 'along with faith' as necessary for salvation.[5] Hodges' entire argument is based on this contention.[6]

There are two basic flaws in this objection. They are (i) as mentioned above, the failure to distinguish between the principle and the practice of the lordship of Jesus, and (ii) an unbiblical view of the nature of saving faith. These two matters are closely related, but we will attempt to deal with them separately.

(1) In the first place, by failing to distinguish between the *principle* and the *practice* of the lordship of Jesus, Harrison and Ryrie *confuse a change of attitude* (the convert's acknowledgment in principle of Jesus' rightful lordship or authority over Him) *with the results of that change of attitude* (the practical observance of Jesus' lordship in the Christian life). The Bible indeed denies that fallen man's works can gain him right standing with God. Man's justification before God is based on the righteousness of Christ alone, imputed to humans through faith alone (Rom. 3:21-24; Gal. 2:16; 3:6-14; Phil. 3:9). But the Bible also teaches that because of the natural man's enmity against God (Rom. 8:7; Col. 1:21; etc.), there must be a change of mind, a change of attitude, in order for humans to enter into a positive relationship with God (it would seem to be a psychological necessity on the

---

4 Harrison, 'Must Christ Be Lord?', p. 16.

5 Ryrie, *Balancing*, pp. 169-70.

6 Hodges, *Absolutely Free!* throughout.

human side). This change of attitude the New Testament calls 'repentance' (*metanoia*, 'a change of mind', 'repentance, turning about, conversion'[7]) and it involves a reformation of the natural man's thinking – his thinking about God and self, about sin and righteousness, about Christ and salvation. At its most fundamental level repentance recognizes the right of God the Creator to rule over man the creature; this constitutes an absolute reversal of the natural man's way of thinking (which denies God's right so to rule), a renunciation of the assertion of personal autonomy. Repentance is a mental act (just as faith is a mental act) or state of mind, compelled by the evident facts, which involves no less than a reorientation of man's worldview, with the result that God rather than man is recognized as occupying the center of the moral universe.[8] And this change of orientation, it is suggested, is an integral component of the confession 'Jesus is Lord'. It is instructive to note the conjunction in Acts of the announcement of Jesus' lordship and the preaching of repentance, a connection which would appear to closely relate the two (compare Acts 2:33-36 and v. 38; 3:19 and vv. 20-21; 5:31; 10:36 and 11:18; 17:30 and v. 31).

It was stated previously that the confession of Jesus' lordship means (among other things) the acknowledgement of the rightful authority of Jesus Christ over the believer (i.e., the confessor). This acknowledgement is no works-righteousness. It does not fall into the category of a human 'work' at all; it is a non-meritorious change of mind and attitude, a simple recognition of plain truth which furthermore is wrought by God Himself (1 Cor. 12:3). That is not to say that it has no moral or practical implications. This change of attitude should (and will, in the truly converted person) issue in practical obedience to Jesus; but in itself it is simply the recognition of the divinely given authority of Jesus Christ to rule over humans as exalted Lord and Agent of God's rule, the personal acknowledgement of oneself as properly under that authority

---

7   BDAG, p. 640. See the earlier section on repentance in the current study.

8   See John Murray's perceptive treatment of 'faith,' much of which can also apply to repentance, in *Collected Writings*, 2:235-41.

and as possessing no right to claim personal autonomy. If we may quote Ladd's comment again, the Christian convert, by means of this confession, 'has entered into a new relationship in which he acknowledges the absolute sovereignty and mastery of the exalted Jesus over his life.'[9]

Admittedly, many people have become Christians without making this acknowledgment explicit, or perhaps without even understanding it or its implications. The relinquishing of one's claimed right to rule his or her own life may have been a subconscious or unexpressed or merely assumed element in the exercise of Christian faith, and it is part of the purpose of the educational process in the church to inform converts of the implications of their action. Yet it must be regarded as a biblical requirement that there be found in the convert's thinking at least the *implicit* acknowledgment of Jesus' (or God's) rightful authority over himself; the New Testament teaching can mean no less than this. In other words, no one can be truly converted while *rejecting* the lordship of Jesus Christ and consciously resolving to retain personal autonomy. Such an approach would be to actively continue in one's rebellion against God, make it psychologically impossible to sincerely seek forgiveness of one's act(s) of rebellion and to deny the meaning of 'conversion' (which means a turning to God from one's 'wickedness' and 'unrighteous thoughts', Isaiah 55:6-9).

(2) In the second place, the objection we are now considering manifests *a faulty view of the nature of 'saving faith'*, biblically understood. 'Faith' or 'believing' in the Bible rarely means the mere acknowledgement of historical fact[10] but includes

---

9 Ladd, *Theology*, p. 415.

10 One of the instances of this use of *pisteuo* ('I believe') is in James 2:19, a verse which supports the point being made here. It is emphatically *not* a justifying 'faith' which the demons exercise. Hodges (*Absolutely Free!* throughout) seeks to limit faith to intellectual assent only, without the concomitant element of trust, traditionally included in the definition of faith (knowledge, assent, trust), although he is at times inconsistent in this. For a critique, see Kim Riddlebarger, 'What Is Faith?' in Michael Horton, ed., *Christ the Lord: The Reformation and Lordship Salvation* (Grand Rapids: Baker, 1992), pp. 81-105. For a demonstration of the biblical validity of the threefold analysis of faith see Reymond, *Systematic Theology*, pp. 726-29.

as well the embracing of the God who stands behind those facts, and is accompanied by the change of mind described above. In other words, faith implies repentance and personal trust.[11] It is not a matter of faith *plus* repentance; rather, faith *demands* and *implies* repentance. This is demonstrated by the regularity with which *metanoeo* ('to repent') and *metanoia* ('repentance') occur in Acts, sometimes standing alone to express the appropriate human response to the gospel (Acts 2:38; 3:19; 5:31; 8:22; 11:18; 17:30; 20:21, significant as Paul's own summary of his three-year ministry at Ephesus; 26:20). J. Behm correctly observes that 'according to Acts the heart of the apostolic mission is the message of *metanoia*,' a *metanoia* that is to be rendered particularly in the light of Jesus' exaltation to lordship.[12]

Repentance occurs earlier in the New Testament preaching as well. It is the predominant note in the preaching of John the Baptist, where it has clear moral implications (Matt. 3:2, 8; Luke 3:10-14; etc.).[13] Repentance is also the hallmark of Jesus' proclamation, as recorded by Mark: 'The time is fulfilled, and the kingdom of God is at hand; repent and believe in the

---

11 Hodges rejects the understanding of repentance presented here, portraying it as an unwarranted addition to faith and as necessary only for fellowship or 'harmonious relations' with God (*Absolutely Free!* pp. 145-46). In response to the latter point, it is heartily acknowledged here that repentance is indeed required for fellowship or 'harmonious' terms with God. But if salvation (in biblical terms) is not properly said to usher one into fellowship or harmonious terms with God, what is that more advanced condition which does? Salvation is defined in precisely such terms, e.g., in 1 Corinthians 1:9: 'God is faithful, by whom you were called into the fellowship of his Son, Jesus Christ our Lord.' In Paul, divine calling is always effectual, and it brings believers into fellowship with Jesus the risen and exalted Messiah, 'our Lord'. See also Romans 5:1: 'Therefore, since we have been justified by faith, we have peace ['harmonious relations'] with God through our Lord Jesus Christ.'

12 TDNT, 4:1003. Mounce's outline of the *kerygma* also notes the conjunction of the preaching of repentance and the lordship of Jesus; *Essential Nature*, p. 77.

13 John's preaching of *metanoia* 'implies a change from within. This change must be demonstrated in the totality of a corresponding life (Matt. 3:8), a life of love and righteousness, in accordance with the will of God (Luke 3:10-14).' TDNT, 4: 1001.

gospel' (Mark 1:15; the parallel in Matthew 4:17 mentions only repentance). The whole of Jesus' ministry is characterized by the demand for repentance, expressed in the strongest terms.[14]

It will not do to regard repentance as possessing a peculiar dispensational or 'kingdom' application relevant only to Jews,[15] nor can it be reduced to the mere acknowledgement of Jesus' deity.[16] It is required by God of all men (Acts 17:30), has definite moral implications (Acts 26:20), and is an integral part of the preaching of the gospel (Acts 20:21) and of the believing response which God seeks (Acts 2:38). As expressed in the oft-quoted statement of John Murray, 'The faith that is unto salvation is a penitent faith and the repentance that is unto life is a believing repentance.... It is impossible to disentangle faith and repentance.'[17] We conclude that 'saving faith' is invariably accompanied by a change of attitude known as 'repentance', a change which involves the abandonment before God of the claim to personal autonomy and which is roughly equivalent to acknowledging in principle (particularly after Jesus' resurrection and exaltation, at which point He became the agent for the exercise of God's lordship) the rightful authority (or lordship) of Jesus Christ over oneself.

APPLICATORY OBSERVATIONS

1) What is called for in the demand for repentance is not a change of behavior which counts toward one's justification before God, but rather a change of attitude (which, if genuine, will result in a change of behavior) toward God's rightful

---

14 'The whole proclamation of Jesus, with its categorical demands for the sake of God's kingdom (the Sermon on the Mount, the sayings about discipleship) is a proclamation of *metanoia* even when the term is not used.' TDNT, 4: 1002.

15 As Lewis Sperry Chafer attempts to do with some passages, *Systematic Theology*, 3:375-76. It is worthy of note that in Acts the kingdom of God, as well as repentance, continues to be preached, even to Gentiles (Acts 8:12; 19:8; 20:25; 28:31). For a helpful treatment of the kingdom, see Ladd, *Theology*, pp. 34-210.

16 As Ryrie attempts to do, *Balancing*, pp. 175-76.

17 Murray, *Redemption Accomplished and Applied* 113. Chafer acknowledges this, *Systematic Theology*, 3:373-75.

lordship over one's life. Without the recognition of God's rightful lordship there could be no conviction of sin and no sense of the need of forgiveness. Without these there is no possibility of sincerely seeking forgiveness from God, but only a self-centered seeking after 'heaven' – i.e. deliverance from condemnation and hell – when one dies. And without forgiveness, there is no salvation (in biblical terms).

2) Indeed, in the evangelistic preaching recorded in Acts there can be found no pattern or instance of apostolic presentation of the gospel in terms of 'going to heaven when one dies'. This may seem a shocking claim to many evangelicals who engage in evangelism in just such terms, but it is indeed the case: in these precise terms, not even a single such instance can be adduced from the book of Acts (not that reception of the gospel does not *result* in 'going to heaven' when one dies; it is just not *presented* to unbelievers in such terms, a feature which changes the motivation for conversion over against modern evangelical practice). The emphasis in apostolic preaching is rather on humans' present relationship with God and the corresponding need for repentance, forgiveness, and acknowledgment of Jesus as the agent of God's rule (there are at least two references to Jesus as the agent of God's judgment [10:42; 17:31], which may imply the desirability of avoiding condemnation, but it is left implicit). The overriding concern is the need for sinful humans to become right with a holy God and in the process to recognize His lordship. All of this suggests the need for a rather severe revision of the evangelistic message and methods utilized by many evangelical Christians who claim to be guided by the Bible. It prompts the question, Why should our evangelistic practices differ so sharply from those of the apostles?

(This claim should not be confused with N. T. Wright's claim that the gospel is not a message about 'how to get saved'. The gospel emphatically is a message about how to be saved; the claim here is that the salvation into which one enters involves a present relationship with God in which one acknowledges God's rule through Jesus Christ. The point is that the apostolic message emphasized this, and not what happens to a person at death.)

Objection 2: There are instances in the Bible of known Christians (or Old Testament believers) who were not always submissive to the lordship of Christ, thus demonstrating that such submission is not essential to one's salvation.

Ryrie adduces the examples of Peter (in Acts 10:14), Barnabas (Acts 15:39), the Ephesian converts who formerly practiced magic (Acts 19:18-19), and Lot (in Genesis) as exhibiting various degrees of being unyielded to the lordship of Christ.[18] Harrison also mentions Peter (Matt. 16:22; Acts 10:14), adding that Peter 'certainly was not making Christ Lord on these occasions'.[19]

(1) In the first place, it may be noted that the Bible never uses language such as Harrison does here. The Christian is not said to 'make Christ Lord', nor is he ever urged to do so in the New Testament. Rather, God has made Jesus Lord (Acts 2:36), and those who hear the gospel are called upon to acknowledge His lordship. The language of 'making Jesus Lord' may have originated in evangelical pietism to express a post-conversion experience, but it is not to be found in the New Testament or in mainstream Reformation theology. Within the context that we are considering in the present study the very term is objectionable. The lordship of Jesus is an objective fact which people are called on to acknowledge, and they have no part in 'making' Him Lord.[20]

(2) In the second place, the New Testament never expresses the expectation that the Christian's submission to the lordship of Jesus will in fact be perfect. Full submission and obedience are certainly desirable, and are the goal that is set before Christians, but the New Testament throughout recognizes that the believer will continue to sin and to need forgiveness (e.g., the Lord's prayer, Matt. 6:12; 1 John 1:8–2:2). This objection thus constitutes another instance of confusing the Christian's acknowledgement *in principle* of the lordship of Jesus with the *practical* observance of that lordship. The confession that

---

18 Ryrie, *Balancing*, pp. 170-73; *So Great Salvation*, pp. 111-12.

19 Harrison, 'Must Christ Be Lord', p. 16.

20 Hodges acknowledges this; *Absolutely Free!*, pp. 170-71.

'Jesus is Lord' involves acknowledging His rightful sovereignty over the believer; it is not a declaration that the Christian will render perfect submission from that point forward. Never is it pretended, in Scripture or in a biblical Christian theology, that the believer will always render absolute and perfect obedience to his Lord, and the confession makes no such claim. Rather, the confession constitutes an acknowledgement that the believer *owes* allegiance and obedience to Jesus the Lord; but it is growth in the Christian life that leads the believer into greater and greater degrees of holiness and practical submission to the Lord Jesus.

This objection, expressed in its simplest form, is that Christians sin. The fact is readily granted (although Ryrie's examples are not particularly persuasive).[21] But an instance of sin, or even a prolonged period of backsliding, does not, in biblical terms, constitute a rejection or invalidation of the principle of Christ's lordship over the believer; it simply constitutes disobedience to one's Lord. The relationship of the believer to Jesus Christ as a subject/servant to his Lord is an objective one; it is a reality that does not change. The subject/servant may be more or less obedient to his Lord, but his obedience or disobedience is always rendered in relation to the one who is his Lord.

Ryrie's use of this argument is not only faulty, but it can also be used against his own position. In the last chapter of his book he expounds his own view of 'The Balanced Christian Life'.[22] At the heart of true spirituality (he believes) is an experience he calls 'dedication', in which the believer makes a 'complete, crisis commitment of self for all the years of one's life'.[23] The question then arises, 'What is the situation when a Christian who has "dedicated" himself to Christ

---

21 For a brief treatment of Ryrie's examples, see David C. Needham, *Birthright: Christian, Do You Know Who You Are?* (Portland, OR: Multnomah Press, 1979), p. 178. Needham's entire chapter, 'A New Master: The Lordship of Christ is Central' (pp. 167-84), is worthy of attention.

22 Ryrie, *Balancing*, pp. 182-91.

23 Ryrie, *Balancing*, p. 186. Ryrie's 'dedication' is based largely on his interpretation of Romans 12:1. For a different understanding of this verse, see Cranfield, *Romans*, 2:598, especially note 4.

falls into sin?' Is he to be regarded as no longer (or perhaps never) 'dedicated'? Ryrie would appear not to think so, for he considers the period after 'dedication' to be one of growth and gradual maturation, not one of perfection (and he has also defined 'dedication' as a lifetime commitment).[24] Yet he inconsistently argues that the confession 'Jesus is [my] Lord' is rendered invalid if the confessor later falls into sin. He does not appear willing to recognize the fact (in this case) that the practical implementation of the rightful claims of the Lord Jesus is a gradual and growing process. Ryrie's objection is as applicable to his own position as to that which he opposes; it must be regarded as valid for both or as valid for neither. It seems that the latter is the case.

Related to this objection is another, offered by Harrison, to the effect that requiring the confession of Jesus' lordship 'rules out the necessity for large portions of the practical teaching of the epistles.'[25] In other words, if Christians are already submitted to the lordship of Christ, why should they be further urged to submit? At the risk of becoming repetitious, it must once again be said that this objection confuses the *principle* and the *practice* of the lordship of Jesus. The practical exhortations of the New Testament do not urge Christians to make an initial acknowledgment of Jesus' lordship; it is assumed that they have already done so. Rather, Christians are urged to render practical daily obedience to Jesus who is their Lord. Indeed, it is precisely on the basis of Jesus' acknowledged lordship over believers that obedience is enjoined: 'Therefore, as you received Christ Jesus the Lord [NIV: "as Lord"], so walk in him' (Col. 2:6). The practical portions of the New Testament show believers how the lordship of Jesus is to be manifested in daily life. The exhortations are part of the means that God uses to bring them into increasing conformity to their profession. Harrison's objection is thus seen to be without substance.

---

24 Ryrie, *Balancing*, p. 187.
25 Harrison, 'Must Christ Be Lord', p. 16.

Objection 3: Requiring of converts the confession that 'Jesus is Lord' leaves no room for the 'carnal Christian'. Ryrie asks, 'If only committed people are saved people, then where is there room for carnal Christians?'[26] A proper response to this objection must be made on two levels.

(1) In the first place, if the objection suggests that the confession 'Jesus is Lord' demands perfection of the believer in order for him to be regarded as truly a Christian, then the objection is not valid. The confession of Jesus' lordship does not promote a form of perfectionism. We have already noted this above. The acknowledgement of the principle of Jesus' lordship is not rendered invalid by the Christian's failure to achieve absolute submission and total obedience to the Lord Jesus. Growth in submission and obedience is the task of a lifetime, and is the result of the process known as 'progressive sanctification'.[27]

(2) But in the second place, if this objection intends to say that requiring the acknowledgement of the principle of Jesus' sovereignty over the believer allows no room for what is popularly known as the 'carnal Christian' – a professing Christian who shows no practical evidence of conversion – then the objection is correct. The biblical view of conversion and the practical implications of confessing Jesus' lordship are incompatible with the commonly held theory of the 'carnal Christian'.

The New Testament speaks of the Christian as one who has made a definite break with the ruling power of sin, as one who has experienced a radical God-ward reorientation of his life. One of the most compelling scriptural passages to set forth this view of the believer is Romans 6. Paul in this chapter describes the Christian as one who has experienced a radical break with the dominion of sin. 'Our old self,' Paul says, 'was crucified with him ... so that we would no longer be enslaved to sin' (Rom. 6:6). Just as Christ died to sin once for all and is now alive unto God, so should the believer regard himself, by virtue of his union with Christ in His death and resurrection (6:8-11).

---

26 Ryrie, *Balancing*, p. 170.

27 See Murray, *Collected Writings*, 2:294-304; Reymond, *Systematic Theology*, pp. 767-81.

The practical exhortation of verses 12-13 is based on this truth; the Christian is called upon to live in accordance with what he is in fact. This is further emphasized by verse 14, which says that 'sin will have no dominion over you, since you are not under law, but under grace.' It is instructive to note that the word translated 'have dominion over' is *kyrieuo,* a verb of the *kyrios* word-group meaning generally 'to be lord/master of', and in this context, 'be master of, dominate'.[28] The force of Paul's statement is that sin will in fact no longer be 'lord' or 'master' of the Christian; its dominion has been broken. The Christian has exchanged one 'lord' (sin) for another (Christ). This understanding of the chapter is confirmed by verses 15-23, in which believers are described by means of a series of contrasts between their old life and their new. Christians once were 'slaves of sin' (v. 17) but have become 'slaves of righteousness' (v. 18). They have been 'set free from [the slavery of] sin and have become slaves of God' (v. 22). These terms describe a definite and permanent change of masters in the Christian's life, a change which theologians call 'definitive sanctification'.[29]

The same sharply drawn portrait of the Christian is found in the First Epistle of John. 'Whoever says, "I know him" but does not keep his commandments is a liar, and the truth is not in him' (1 John 2:4). This black-and-white picture of the believer characterizes the whole Epistle (see 1:6; 2:9; 3:6-10; 4:8, 20; 5:18), and speaks not of the Christian's sinlessness (cf. 1:8–2:2) but of a definite break with the ruling power of sin in his life.

This biblical view of the Christian contrasts sharply with the theory of the 'carnal Christian'. This term, as commonly used,

---

28 BDAG, p. 576.

29 For the interpretation of Romans 6, see Murray, *Romans,* and D. M. Lloyd-Jones, *Romans: An Exposition of Chapter 6* (London: Banner of Truth, 1972). See also Murray's chapter, 'The Dynamic of the Biblical Ethic', in *Principles of Conduct: Aspects of Biblical Ethics* (Eerdmans, 1957), pp. 202-28, where he identifies the dynamic as 'union with Christ in the virtue of his death and the power of his resurrection', p. 203; Murray, 'Definitive Sanctification' and 'The Agency of Definitive Sanctification' in *Collected Writings,* 2:277-84 and 285-93 respectively; and Reymond, *Systematic Theology,* pp. 756-59.

describes a professing Christian who shows little or no evidence of having been truly converted; he approaches the state of being totally and permanently carnal (meaning unspiritual, unsanctified).[30] The term 'carnal' derives from the King James Version's rendering of 1 Corinthians 3:1-3, where it translates *sarkinos* (v. 1) and *sarkikos* (v. 3). The current standard Greek lexicon suggests that strictly speaking, *sarkikos* means 'belonging to the *sarx* [flesh]', or 'fleshly', as the opposite of 'spiritual', while *sarkinos* means 'consisting/composed of flesh', or 'fleshy', but that this distinction does not always seem to be observed in the New Testament. Nevertheless, it suggests that *sarkinos* in 3:1 means 'belonging to the physical realm, *material, physical, human, fleshly*' especially 'in contrast to the non-physical', as here, where it is contrasted with 'spiritual' in v. 1. *Sarkikos* means 'pert[aining] to being human at a disappointing level of behavior or characteristics, *(merely) human*', in verse 3 referring to 'immature Christians'.[31]

This passage is often appealed to in support of the 'carnal Christian' theory, but it should be noted that Paul is here dealing with a single particular sin of the Corinthian church (divisiveness), and on that basis calls them 'carnal'. There is certainly no ground here, nor elsewhere in the New Testament, for regarding as a genuine Christian believer one who is in a constant and total state of carnality. Yet that is what is often demanded by the 'carnal Christian' theory. One widely used booklet describes the 'carnal' Christian as manifesting the following qualities: controlled by self, discouragement, self-seeking, doubt, a critical spirit, defeat, wrong doctrine, frustration, aimlessness, envy, worry, jealousy, impure thoughts, a legalistic life, a poor prayer life and a fruitless witness for Christ.[32] The question might arise in the minds of some readers of the New Testament, 'Where is there any biblical basis for considering such a person a Christian at all?' This list is strikingly

---

30 Ryrie acknowledges that all Christians will bear fruit (*So Great Salvation*, pp. 32, 45-46, 59) and that carnality in a true Christian must be limited (p. 32).

31 BDAG, p. 914.

32 'Have You Made The Wonderful Discovery of the Spirit-Filled Life?' (Campus Crusade for Christ, 1966), p. 7.

similar in some of its elements to Paul's catalogue of 'the deeds of the flesh' in Galatians 5:19-21, concerning which he says that 'those who do such things will not inherit the kingdom of God'. There indeed seems to be little room in the New Testament for the 'carnal Christian' as popularly depicted. Rather, for the Christian, the New Testament teaches, the dominion of sin has been replaced by the lordship of Christ.[33]

APPLICATORY OBSERVATIONS

1) When a person is regenerated by the Spirit of God, he is genuinely changed. The great Welsh preacher Martyn Lloyd-Jones called it 'a new disposition'.[34] As stated by Robert Reymond: 'It is not simply *positional* holiness that is envisioned by definitive sanctification: it is a real *existential* breach with the reign and mastery of sin, which breach is created by the Christian's actual spiritual union with Christ in his death and resurrection, and which is as decisive and definite as are Christ's death and resurrection.'[35] That change will show itself in a transformed outlook and pattern of life.

2) A professing Christian who manifests no 'fruit of the Spirit' (Gal. 5:22-23) and no evidence of the effects of regeneration should take no comfort in the doctrine of the 'carnal Christian'. Such a person may need to start over again with God, going back to the very beginning, back to the foundational aspects of the human response to the gospel: repentance and faith. The humbling of oneself before God in this way may be uncomfortable, but it is preferable to eternal loss.

Objection 4: Apostolic preaching in Acts does not support this position.

Harrison argues that 'this position is unsupported by the examples of gospel preaching in the book of Acts.'[36] For support

---

33 For a more detailed study of the 'carnal Christian' theory, see Ernest C. Reisinger, *What Should We Think of 'The Carnal Christian'?* (Edinburgh: Banner of Truth, n.d.).

34 This is the title of Lloyd-Jones' chapter on regeneration in *Great Doctrines of the Bible*, vol. 2, *God the Holy Spirit*, 3 vols. in one (Wheaton, IL: Crossway, 2003), pp. 74-83.

35 Reymond, *Systematic Theology*, pp. 757-58, italics his.

36 Harrison, 'Must Christ Be Lord?', p. 14.

of this assertion he appeals to Acts 2:38, which contains a call to repentance (following immediately upon the announcement of Jesus' exaltation and lordship, Acts 2:32-36). Clearly, this passage does not support Harrison's position; rather, it refutes it. Admittedly, Acts does not contain the specific language that Harrison demands, that is, that people be 'pressed to acknowledge Jesus Christ as their personal Lord in order to be saved', but that is simply because the apostles speak in different terms than those of Harrison's formula. They proclaim the death, exaltation and lordship of Jesus and call for repentance and faith (see the earlier section on the apostolic proclamation in Acts). In different terms, Acts affirms what Harrison denies.

Objection 5: Requiring confession of Jesus' Lordship endangers the ground of assurance of salvation.

Harrison argues that 'the ground of assurance of salvation is endangered if surrender to Christ's lordship is a part of that ground.'[37] As Harrison pursues this argument it becomes clear that he regards perfect and constant obedience to be the criterion of 'surrender to Christ's lordship', a standard to which no Christian will attain. This once again manifests confusion between the *principle* and the *practice* of Christ's lordship, and what has already been said on this matter applies here as well.

It should be noted, however, that while the ground of the believer's *justification* before God is the righteousness of Christ, the *assurance* of his salvation is confirmed in part by his own practical holiness. In this respect Harrison is objecting to something which is thoroughly biblical.

The New Testament would have us understand that as the believer proceeds in the walk of the Christian life under the authority of his or her newly acknowledged Lord, a transformation of lifestyle should become evident. The believer will live out the reality of his regeneration, repentance and faith in a new conformity to the teaching and example of the Lord Jesus and the commands of Scripture. A renewed pattern of life will begin to manifest itself. This transformation provides one of the elements of personal assurance of salvation.

---

37   Harrison, 'Must Christ Be Lord?', p. 16.

Assurance of salvation has been be likened to a three-legged stool.[38] The three legs together hold up the stool; if any one of them is missing or weak then the stool will fall. Likewise, when the three bases of assurance are present, then the individual has sound reason to believe that he has been graced by God with the gift of salvation and everlasting life. But if any of the three is absent or doubtful, then the subjective assurance of salvation may be lacking or may be falsely based. The three bases of assurance are the testimony of Scripture, the testimony of the Holy Spirit, and the testimony of a transformed lifestyle.

1) Assurance is based on the testimony of Scripture. The first ground of assurance is the Word of God. The Bible ministers assurance in at least three ways: (i) in its explanation of the way of salvation and its general assertions regarding the state of those who exercise trust in Jesus Christ; (ii) in its teaching concerning the nature of salvation; (iii) and in its affirmations that God will bring to its appropriate consummation that salvation in which His people participate by grace. These will be taken up in turn.

(i) The Bible states, for example, that all those who believe in Jesus will not perish but will have eternal life (John 3:16), or that anyone who believes in the Lord Jesus will be saved (Acts 16:31), or that 'everyone who calls on the name of the Lord will be saved' (Rom. 10:13). The person who exercises such faith or who thus calls upon the name of the Lord may therefore have the confidence, because God's Word is true and God is faithful, that he has been the recipient of the gift of salvation. The New Testament encourages the confidence that the believer enjoys the gift of salvation as a present possession. 'I write these things to you who believe in the name of the Son of God that you may *know* that you have eternal life' (1 John 5:13; see also 2:12-14, etc.)

(ii) The Bible describes in some detail the nature of the salvation into which one enters upon exercising repentant trust in Jesus Christ. It is a salvation that is planned and

---

38 This image is suggested by Thomas R. Schreiner and Ardel B. Caneday, *The Race Set Before Us: A Biblical Theology of Perseverance and Assurance* (Downers Grove, IL: InterVarsity, 2001), pp. 276-305.

insured by God's purpose in eternity and effected by His grace and power in time, and is thus ultimately dependent upon God's action, not man's. The scope of this biblical teaching is so broad that here one can only be referred to a full treatment of the doctrine of salvation in a dependable systematic theology.[39]

(iii) The Bible contains assurances that God will bring His people into the final consummation of that redemption which they enjoy in Jesus Christ. Thus Paul affirms to the Philippian believers, 'I am sure of this, that he who began a good work in you *will bring it to completion* at the day of Jesus Christ' (Phil. 1:6). And John asserts, 'Beloved, we are God's children now, and what we will be has not yet appeared; but we know that when he appears *we will be like him*, because we shall see him as he is' (1 John 3:2). The believer can be assured that if God has indeed begun a saving work in him, He will bring it to its completion.

2) Assurance is based on the testimony of the Holy Spirit. The testimony of the Holy Spirit may be understood as encompassing two distinct elements.

(i) Passages such as Romans 8:15 and Galatians 4:6 teach that the indwelling Holy Spirit leads the believer to respond to God with filial consciousness and childlike confidence: 'For you did not receive the spirit of slavery to fall back into fear, but you have received the Spirit of adoption as sons, by whom we cry, "Abba! Father!"' (Rom. 8:15); 'And because you are sons, God has sent the Spirit of his Son into our hearts, crying, "Abba! Father!"' (Gal. 4:6). Such passages seem to affirm that the Holy Spirit prompts the human spirit in believers to call out naturally to God as their spiritual and heavenly Father. As a result, they approach God in the confidence that He will hear and respond appropriately as the loving Father who has redeemed and adopted them through Jesus the Messiah.

---

39 Such as, e.g., from a traditional Reformed viewpoint, Robert Reymond, *Systematic Theology*, chapters 13, 18, and 19; and from a Reformed but Baptistic stance, Wayne Grudem, *Systematic Theology*, chapters 32 through 43.

(ii) John Murray argues that the next verse in Romans 8 (8:16) may be understood to refer to a further testimony by the Holy Spirit directly *to* the human spirit: 'The Spirit himself bears witness with our spirit that we are children of God.' If Murray is correct, this would be a direct subjective testimony that persuades the believer of his filial relationship.[40] It is something that cannot be objectified, but it is a reality nonetheless.

3) Assurance is affirmed by the testimony of a transformed lifestyle. There are many passages which indicate that the consequence of regeneration, repentance and faith is a trans-formed lifestyle, and further, that Christians may take assurance from observing such a transformation within themselves and in their behavior: 'And by this we know that we have come to know him, if we keep his commandments' (1 John 2:3); 'We know that we have passed out of death into life, because we love the brothers' (1 John 3:14).

Schreiner and Caneday argue that assurance of salvation cannot be *grounded* on this aspect of Christian experience but that this aspect does provide a *confirming* element of assurance, and that without it there is no basis for being complacent about one's salvation. 'There is no warrant for assurance if sin is dominant in our lives.'[41] Further support for this position is found in those passages which describe certain types of continuing sinful behavior as inconsistent with inheriting the kingdom of God (1 Cor. 6:9-11; Gal. 5:19-21).

This component of assurance is tantamount to following a pattern of life which is predominantly consistent with the confession of Jesus as Lord. Such a transformed life cannot form the primary basis of assurance, but without it one's confession is open to question.

---

40 Murray, *Collected Writings*, 2:272-73.

41 Schreiner and Caneday, *The Race Set Before Us*, p. 311. They specifically counter the arguments of Hodges (pp. 285, 287, 288, 293) and Ryrie (p. 309).

Objection 6: Confessing Jesus as Lord involves only acknowledging His deity.

Ryrie attempts to demonstrate that *kyrios* when applied to Jesus simply means 'God', and that to confess Jesus as Lord is only to acknowledge His deity.[42] This position cannot be sustained by the evidence. The implication of legitimate authority inheres in the word *kyrios* (see Appendix 1) and it is so used both in the Septuagint and throughout the New Testament. Ryrie's approach ignores Jesus' mediatorial lordship (that He is the divinely-appointed agent of God's rule as the God-Man, not merely as God), and is refuted by a single sentence in the New Testament: Thomas' confession of Jesus as 'my Lord and my God' (John 20:28), in which 'Lord' must clearly mean something other than simply 'God'.

Objection 7: Requiring the confession of Jesus as Lord confuses salvation and discipleship.

Ryrie charges that to require the confession of Jesus' lordship confuses salvation with discipleship.[43] But Ryrie's treatment of the gospel passages dealing with discipleship is unconvincing; while the concepts of discipleship and salvation may be distinguished, Jesus never intended to separate the two. Ryrie thus fails to grasp the true meaning of Jesus' teaching in such passages as Luke 14:25-35. Jesus here affirms that in coming to Him one enters a life of discipleship, a life in which Jesus' legitimate and absolute claim on the convert and his possessions must be acknowledged. In light of this fact, Jesus says, it is best for the would-be follower to count the cost. 'There could be no following,' as John Stott puts it, 'without a forsaking, a renunciation (in principle if not in literal fact)

---

42 Ryrie, *Balancing*, pp. 173-76; *So Great Salvation*, pp. 72-73. In the latter place (pp. 71-73), Ryrie quotes Harrison with approval concerning the distinction between Christ's 'objective lordship' and 'subjective lordship'. The distinction may be granted and yet both could be present in Romans 10:9: Jesus' objective lordship is a fact not to be avoided, indeed, but in 'confessing' Him as Lord the convert offers a subjective acknowledgment of that fact and of Jesus' rightful lordship (authority) over himself as a result.

43 Ryrie, *Balancing*, pp. 178-79.

of competing loyalties, of family relationships, of personal ambitions, of material possessions.'[44] There is no indication in Jesus' teaching that He intended to separate discipleship from the salvation He offered.

Furthermore, Ryrie's position is positively refuted by such a passage as Matthew 11:28-30. Here Jesus invites His hearers both to 'come to me' and to 'take my yoke upon you and learn of Me', with the promise of 'rest' connected with both these elements, binding them into an indivisible unity. The verb translated 'learn' is *manthano* (related to *mathetes*, 'learner' or 'disciple', or 'adherent'[45]), and the aorist imperative 'indicates the decisive step of *becoming* a disciple, of *entering* His school, of *acknowledging* Him as our Teacher and Lord'. There is found in this passage, Stott rightly says, 'the true balance of the gospel. Jesus offers us both rest and a yoke.'[46]

Also, the usage of the term *mathetes* ('disciple') in Acts is decisively against Ryrie's position. The term is used of Jesus' followers after His death, resurrection and ascension (when they obviously could not literally and physically 'follow' Him) throughout Acts (in the plural: 6:1, 2, 7; 9:19; 11:26, 29; 13:52; 15:10; 21:16a; of individuals: 9:10; 16:1; 21:16b). In such cases, 'disciple' is used 'almost exclusively to denote the members of the new community of believers ..., so that it almost=*Christian*.'[47] In other words, 'disciple' is used in Acts virtually as a synonym for 'Christian'. Especially telling is the usage in Acts 11:26: 'And in Antioch the *disciples* were first called *Christians*.' There is no indication here or anywhere in Acts that the term was applied to a smaller subset of the Christian community who had taken a further step of entering into discipleship in contrast to those Christians who had not. All Christians were simply called 'disciples'.

---

44 Stott, 'Must Christ Be Lord?', p. 18. See also the section on discipleship in Kenneth L. Gentry, *Lord of the Saved: Getting to the Heart of the Lordship Debate* (Phillipsburg, NJ: Presbyterian & Reformed, 1992), pp. 67-83.

45 BDAG, p. 609.

46 Stott, 'Must Christ Be Lord?', pp. 17, 18.

47 BDAG, p. 610.

Applicatory Observations

1) There is such a thing as false assurance. The claim that one has entered into salvation or has been 'saved' should not rest merely upon a single past experience, but should be supported by present realities in one's life and consciousness. Wayne Grudem offers some helpful questions to assist in determining whether a person may legitimately possess assurance of salvation:

> Do I have a present trust in Christ for salvation?
>
> Is there evidence of a regenerating work of the Holy Spirit in my heart?
>
> Do I see a long-term pattern of growth in my Christian life?

Grudem works out these questions in greater detail than can be given here, but they lead the professing Christian on the right track to gaining genuine and warranted assurance.[48]

2) The salvation that the Lord Jesus brings to humans demands discipleship to Himself. To accept His salvation while rejecting His claims upon those who do so is not an option that is given to humans. Jesus must be received in the fullness of His person and work, as Prophet, Priest and King, as the one who is currently Lord of the universe, the personal Agent of God's rule and God's kingdom. He cannot be divided and received as anything less.

---

48   Grudem, *Systematic Theology*, pp. 803-6.

PART FOUR

THE IMPLICATIONS
OF JESUS' LORDSHIP

11

The Practical Significance of the Confession of Jesus as Lord

The truth of the lordship of Jesus Christ – and the New Testament pattern of confessing Jesus as Lord – being a wide-ranging truth of manifold implications, has a multitude of specific applications. A few of these may be considered here.

I. Application to Non-Christians
Those who are not believers in Jesus Christ need to be aware that the lordship of Jesus Christ has immediate application to themselves.

1. The Historical Reality
The eminent British New Testament scholar C. F. D. Moule has argued that there are certain historical phenomena which manifest themselves in the New Testament for which there is no viable historical explanation apart from the assumption that the accounts of events (and of their significance) presented in the New Testament are true.[1] One of these is the resurrection of Jesus as the impetus for the existence of the Christian community (the 'church', which Moule calls 'the sect of the Nazarenes', that is, the continuing community of the disciples of Jesus). 'From the very first,' Moule writes, 'the conviction that Jesus had been raised from death has been that by which their very existence has stood or fallen. There was no other motive to account for them, to explain them.'[2] Moule reviews

---

1   C. F. D. Moule, *The Phenomenon of the New Testament: An Inquiry into the Implications of Certain Features of the New Testament* (London: SCM Press, 1967).

2   Moule, *Phenomenon*, p. 11.

various alternative explanations and finds them inadequate.[3] And he observes that the resurrection of Jesus was not just a bringing back to life of a random individual. 'It is not simply a restoration to the old life, but a raising, *an exaltation*. Nor is it the raising of just anybody, but of *the one who Jesus was*.'[4] Furthermore, it is observable that the sole reason for the existence of the Christian community was to bear witness to Jesus' resurrection and exaltation. 'Their sole function is to bear witness to what they claim as an event – the raising of Jesus from among the dead.'[5] No other features of the New Testament or the early disciple community (moral exhortation, social warmth and cohesion) provide an adequate explanation. '[T]he elements in the New Testament which a non-Christian would not share are precisely the ones which account for the Church's existence. They are those which relate to and depend on the Christian estimate of Jesus as crucified and raised from among the dead, and of man's relationship to God through him.'[6] The undoubted historical reality of the rise of the Christian faith, its community, and its literature presents a historical development that is without explanation apart from the resurrection of Jesus the Messiah.

2. The Theological Reality

Moule recognizes that this event of the resurrection and exaltation of Jesus cannot be accounted for by the normal categories of human history. 'Equally clear is the fact that what the Christians alleged of Jesus is something which cannot be confined within historical terms. It transcends history; but for all that, it is rooted in history.'[7] The historical reality leads one to conclude that a power from outside human history exercised itself within human history – the power of the God of the Bible, raising the Son of God from the dead. This momentous event points to a theological reality which transcends our

---

3   Moule, *Phenomenon*, pp. 6-10.

4   Moule, *Phenomenon*, p. 14, emphasis added.

5   Moule, *Phenomenon*, p. 14.

6   Moule, *Phenomenon*, p. 15.

7   Moule, *Phenomenon*, p. 20.

current earthly existence, yet such a conclusion is not a blind faith but an intelligent belief. As Moule observes, 'The creed [the affirmation of belief, e. g. "Jesus is Lord", or the so-called Apostles' Creed] is not a series of assertions made in a vacuum, but a summary of value-judgments reached on the basis of eye-witness testimony to an event.'[8] That is, the Christian evaluation of Jesus as Messiah, Son of God, and exalted Lord is based on the historical data provided by the New Testament itself.

3. The Personal Reality
The unavoidable conclusion of the historical and theological realities is that the current exalted status of Jesus the Messiah impinges upon every individual human existence. The exalted status of Jesus constitutes a call for every person who is made aware of it to acknowledge Jesus' position as the agent of God's rule, to abandon his rebellion against that rule and his assertion of personal autonomy, and to receive the forgiveness which God has made possible and holds forth to humans through the crucified and exalted Lord Jesus. The only alternative is to continue in willful rebellion against the Creator of the universe and to consign oneself to the everlasting perpetuation of that rebellion and to the eternal condemnation pronounced by a holy and just God. The choice is that stark.

II. Application to Evangelical Christianity
It is profitable also for us to consider some of the practical implications of the biblical pattern of proclaiming and confessing Jesus Christ as Lord for the Christian tradition known as evangelicalism. Evangelicals constitute that trans-denominational, trans-national tradition which emphasizes the authority of the Bible, the centrality of the divine person and redeeming work of Jesus Christ, the need for personal conversion through faith in Christ and the importance of spreading the good news about Jesus' death and resurrection. (This is not to deny the legitimate implications of Jesus' lordship for other Christian traditions or bodies; it just

---

8   Moule, *Phenomenon*, p. 79.

happens to be the case that evangelicalism is that tradition to which the present writer belongs, with which he is most familiar, and which seems to him to be desperately in need of the applications mentioned here.)

1. Evangelical Christians must evaluate and adjust the message and methods of their evangelism in light of the lordship of Jesus Christ.

The immediately clear and obvious implication is that modern evangelicals, as professed heirs of the apostolic tradition, are obligated to adhere as closely as possible to that biblical pattern of proclamation and confession which has been handed down to them. In practical terms, this suggests that we ourselves must confess Jesus as Lord, that we must proclaim to the world that Jesus is Lord and that we must seek from those whom we evangelize the acknowledgment that Jesus is Lord. But it is evident that such is not the uniform conviction or practice within present-day evangelicalism. There is widespread confusion regarding the nature and content of the gospel, and equally widespread deviation from the pattern of preaching and evangelism found in the New Testament. The present writer wishes to address this situation by posing some questions concerning the practical results of such deviation and then by suggesting some positive ways in which the biblical pattern may be restored.

1) Possible consequences of ignoring the lordship of Jesus in preaching and evangelism. That modern evangelicalism has to a considerable degree failed to reflect the biblical pattern as set forth in the present study needs no elaborate demonstration; the view advocated by Harrison, Ryrie and Hodges is very popular. But could there not be some serious practical consequences of such a failure? The following questions suggest perhaps some of the weightier of these consequences.

(a) By ignoring the lordship of Jesus in preaching and evangelism, *are we not fostering a superficial and man-centered form of evangelism which could result in false conversions and in a false sense of assurance among those who are so 'converted'?* This is by far the most serious and disturbing question to be raised here, but it is one which must be faced. If we fail to communicate the necessity of confessing Jesus as Lord at the time of conversion, we are in effect telling our hearers that it is not necessary for them to relinquish their claim to personal autonomy which constitutes the essence of the human condition in sin. We are offering them forgiveness while at the same time implicitly granting them permission to continue in that attitude and activity of rebellion against God which make forgiveness necessary. This approach is incongruous with the message of the gospel and the work of Jesus the Messiah, the purpose of both of which is not merely to bring people into deliverance from condemnation (the penalty of sin) but also deliverance from the attitude (rebellion: 'I want to do what I want to do') and the behavior (actions which manifest that rebellion) of sin (Matt. 1:21 and Rom. 6:14 mean little if they do not include these). God intends through the gospel to bring humans under His kingdom or government, to experience both its blessings (forgiveness, right standing with God, ability to love God) and its demands (righteousness, whole-hearted self-abandonment to God). This is what lies behind the consistent New Testament pattern of preaching the kingdom of God and the need for repentance. To omit these elements of the message is to dilute it beyond recognition. But dilute it is what many evangelicals have done.

If we dilute or alter the biblical message, then it is inevitable that the gospel will be proclaimed erroneously. And if proclaimed erroneously, could it not be received erroneously? By ignoring or eliminating the biblical emphasis on the lordship of Jesus and the necessity for confessing that lordship, could we not be deluding those who hear our message by (i) offering to them a salvation which is radically different from the biblical concept (which involves man's right attitude toward God as well as his formal standing before God), and by (ii) offering to them salvation on terms other than those on which God Himself offers it: repentance (renouncing one's claims to autonomy; acknowledgment of God's right to command obedience) and faith (reliance on Christ alone for one's right standing with God), not a so-called 'faith' which is isolated from repentance, biblically understood? And what of those who receive our message? Could we not be deceiving them into thinking that they have fulfilled the biblical conditions of salvation (if such a term can properly be used) and that they are secure in Christ, when in fact they have not and are not? And are not such people in a worse spiritual condition after such 'believing' than they were before, because they think they are right with God when they are not?

There are indications that such questions are not inappropriate. In the September 1977 issue of *Eternity* C. Peter Wagner published the results of a survey taken in the aftermath of the 'Here's Life America' evangelistic campaign sponsored by Campus Crusade for Christ in 1976. In the six metropolitan areas where the survey was conducted, the 178 participating churches reported 26,535 gospel presentations and 4,106 'decisions for Christ', of which 525 joined follow-up Bible studies and 125 became church members.[9] In other words, 3 per cent of the 'converts' joined Christian churches. When judged on the basis of Wagner's premise that evangelistic results should be reflected in church growth, and even allowing for various extenuating factors, this is a dismal record. What became of the rest? What is their spiritual condition? It would appear that something is drastically wrong here. Is it not worth considering the possibility that the problem may be as much one of faulty theology as it is one of faulty methodology?

More recently, Iain Murray observes the high rate of failure among respondents at Billy Graham evangelistic crusades:

> Further, what are individuals to think who obey the instruction to come to the front and who experience no spiritual change? In fact the BGEA is well aware that many respond to the 'public invitation' who in reality never become Christians. 'I've always thought that in any group that comes forward,' Graham says, 'a fourth of them will be there in five years from now.'[10]

---

9   C. Peter Wagner, 'Who Found It?' *Eternity*, September 1977, p. 16.

10   Iain H. Murray, *Evangelicalism Divided: A Record of Crucial Change in the Years 1950 to 2000* (Edinburgh: Banner of Truth, 2000), p. 53.

In other words, only twenty-five percent of those who respond publicly will continue in their adherence to the Christian faith. What is the condition of the three-quarters who fall away?

In the present writer's own denominational fellowship, the Southern Baptist Convention, recent observers have pointed out the disparity between the claimed sixteen million members of convention churches and the fact that roughly sixty percent to two-thirds of these are nowhere to be seen on a typical Sunday morning.[11] Even allowing for normal absenteeism and bloated church membership rosters, this is an extremely high rate of attrition. Could it be that the missing 'members' are victims of faulty evangelism? The question bears thoughtful consideration.

(b) By minimizing the lordship of Jesus in preaching and evangelism, and thus at the point of conversion, *are we not fostering a faulty view of sin and of the necessity for sanctification on the part of Christians?* The Bible describes the Christian as one who has experienced a definitive break with the ruling power of sin (see the earlier response to Objection 3 in the previous chapter). To eliminate the necessity for acknowledging the lordship of Jesus in the Christian's life is to deny this truth. Not only could this denial lead to a faulty understanding of the Christian life in general, but could it not also serve to obliterate the primary observable distinction between Christians and non-Christians – which is that the Christian is one who has given himself to live in obedience to the Lord Jesus? What is there that visibly distinguishes the believer from the unbeliever, apart from the Christian's relinquishing his or her personal autonomy and acknowledging in one's daily practical life the lordship of Jesus Christ? But a faulty message gives the impression that acknowledging Jesus' lordship and entering a life of discipleship are optional features of the Christian life that may be added later according to one's personal desire.

---

11 Tom Ascol, 'Bureaucracy, Reformation and the Southern Baptist Convention', *The Founders Journal*, Issue 63 (Winter 2006), pp. 1-5, especially p. 3.

It may be instructive in this regard to consider again the matter of the 'carnal Christian'. It is difficult to avoid the suspicion that there is more than a casual connection between the 'carnal Christian' theory and the faulty evangelism illustrated above. Could it be, as John Sanderson suggests, that 'the permanently carnal Christian is a figment of the imagination, invented to accommodate a certain doctrinal view-point'?[12] Invented, perhaps, to explain 'converts' who show no sign of being converted at all? Would it not be more biblical to acknowledge the basic truth, as expressed again by Sanderson, that 'one may (and we all do) have carnal moments, but the Christian must have meaningful character growth, or else he is not a Christian'?[13]

(c) By relegating the acknowledgement of Jesus' lordship to a later point in the Christian life, *are we not encouraging Christians to seek an unbiblical 'second blessing' or crisis experience of God's grace or of commitment to Him?* Whether a second experience (after conversion) be called 'making Jesus Lord of one's life', or 'becoming a disciple', or 'dedication', or 'entering the victorious life', or being 'baptized with the Spirit' – or something else – there is no encouragement in the New Testament to seek such a secondary experience. Therefore, is it not an essentially unscriptural experience that is being encouraged and sought, and does not the whole effort constitute a denial of the biblical teaching which regards all of these – biblically defined – as taking place at the time of conversion? It is strange that men who strongly repudiate many of the unscriptural elements in the so-called 'charismatic movement' or earlier Pentecostalism or even the earlier 'Higher Life' movement actually espouse a theology that in essence amounts to the same thing – that being 'in Christ' is not sufficient, that there must be some further crisis experience in order for the Christian to receive all that God intends for him, and that there are as a result two categories of Christians, those who have

---

12 John W. Sanderson, *The Fruit of The Spirit* (Grand Rapids: Zondervan, 1972), p. 10.

13 Sanderson, *Fruit of the Spirit*, p. 10.

attained this second level and those who have not. Kenneth L. Gentry has documented the affinities between the teaching of those who advocate a second crisis experience of dedication, lordship or discipleship and that of the 'Higher Life' movement of the late nineteenth and early twentieth centuries;[14] its similarity to certain aspects of 'charismatic' teaching is also evident.

2) Suggested correctives for evangelical preaching and evangelism. These questions lead to the further question: 'What must we do to restore the biblical pattern of proclaiming and confessing Jesus as Lord?' The present writer offers the following suggestions.

(a) Evangelicals must preach the apostolic gospel in its fullness. That means proclaiming the resurrection, exaltation and lordship of Jesus Christ as well as His death. It is difficult, in the light of what we have seen in Acts, to imagine the apostles preaching the latter apart from the former; and yet our modern tendency is to do so, emphasizing the death of Jesus while ignoring His exaltation. Geoffrey Wilson has well said that 'no preaching which fails to do justice to Christ's present sovereignty is faithful to the authoritative pattern laid down in the New Testament'.[15] The gospel includes *all* the 'good news' of what God has wrought through Jesus Christ, including the installation of Jesus as God's appointed King to rule on God's behalf and the deliverance of humans from the dominion of sin as well as from its penalty. The latter means that the biblical gospel announces and challenges the human presumption of autonomy from God.

(b) Evangelicals must give due emphasis to the necessity and meaning of acknowledging Jesus as Lord. In evangelism this means that we must not dilute the biblical demand for

---

14 Gentry, 'The Great Option', pp. 78-79; *Lord of the Saved*, pp. 95-97. See also Paul Schaefer, 'An American Tale,' in Horton, *Christ the Lord*, pp. 149-77.

15 Geoffrey B. Wilson, *Romans: A Digest of Reformed Comment*, rev. ed. (Edinburgh: Banner of Truth Trust, 1977), p. 178.

repentance (Acts 17:30), nor must we fail to explain the significance of the confession of Jesus' lordship (Rom. 10:9; see the earlier section on the meaning of the confession). That is, the confession of Jesus' lordship implies no less than the renunciation *in principle* of personal autonomy, a feature of the biblical message which must not be ignored. This approach may result in fewer 'decisions', but it will promote genuine conversions.

(c) Evangelicals need to reformulate some of their teaching concerning the Christian life. In particular, it would be conducive to a more biblical approach to revise that teaching which deals with the various 'crisis experiences' through which Christians may pass. It would seem that a more biblical terminology than that which is commonly used could be developed. Kenneth Prior makes a helpful attempt to do so in his volume, *The Way of Holiness*.[16] He suggests that while some supposed experiences of a 'second blessing' may actually amount to initial conversion, other experiences (popularly described by the various terms mentioned above, including 'making Christ Lord of one's life') may be regarded as perhaps one or another of the following: recovery from backsliding, the discovery of some neglected scriptural truth, a sudden awareness of the cost of discipleship, gaining 'full assurance' of one's salvation, experiencing God's special guidance or exercising certain gifts of the Holy Spirit. On the whole this seems an eminently more scriptural approach than that of emphasizing the necessity of some such experience as 'making Christ Lord', 'dedication', 'discipleship', etc., as is commonly done.

(d) Evangelicals must offer a living demonstration of that to which they call their hearers – a willing acknowledgment of the authority of Jesus Christ as Lord. It is only when our words are supported by our actions that they will carry conviction and power. It must be true of us even as we press the truth upon others: Jesus is Lord.

---

16   Kenneth F. W. Prior, *The Way of Holiness* (London: InterVarsity, 1967), pp. 85-96.

2. Evangelical Christians should view Scripture as an expression of the authority of Jesus Christ as Lord.

Evangelical circles have seen in recent years some serious 'slippage' in their uniform adherence to a robust affirmation of the historic Protestant and evangelical doctrine of Scripture. One potential antidote for this slippage is to recognize that the Bible (the whole of it, not merely the New Testament) carries the authority of Jesus the risen Lord. The argument for this proposition proceeds as follows (for a more detailed elaboration of this argument, see Appendix 3):

1. Jesus appointed apostles to share and exercise His authority.

2. The apostles were specifically commissioned to bear witness to the redemptive acts of God accomplished through Messiah Jesus.

3. The apostles were promised the assistance of the Holy Spirit for the carrying out of this specific ministry of witness.

4. The apostles delivered an authoritative witness to the saving events divinely wrought through Messiah Jesus.

5. The authoritative apostolic witness to Jesus was eventually reduced to written form.

6. A portion of the authoritative apostolic witness to Jesus involved Jesus' teaching.

7. Jesus in His teaching affirmed the authenticity of the Old Testament writings and the historicity of Old Testament events.

8. Christians cannot faithfully confess Jesus as Lord while rejecting His testimony to the Old Testament or while rejecting the authority of the apostolic testimony in the New Testament.

It would seem that nothing less than affirmation of the full authority of the Bible is required of faithful adherence to the confession of Jesus' lordship.

3. Evangelical Christians should approach all of life in light of the lordship of Jesus Christ.

The lordship of Jesus Christ may be expressed in the individual Christian's personal life and in the Christian community's corporate life.

1) The lordship of Jesus is to be honored in the individual Christian's personal life. The New Testament contains exhortations such as the one found in Colossians 3:17: 'And whatever you do, in word or deed, *do everything in the name of the Lord Jesus,* giving thanks to God the Father through him.' This exhortation may be understood as intended to govern both the personal and community aspects of the Christian life, for Paul in the preceding verses has mentioned obligations which can be fulfilled only on the individual and personal level (3:1-8), as well as those which pertain to the Christian community with its interpersonal relationships (3:9-15) and its corporate worship (3:16). The phrase 'in the name of the Lord Jesus' likely means something like 'in acknowledgment of his authority' or 'in obedience to him'. Thus Calvin explains that Paul concludes the preceding more general portion of the exhortations of this letter 'in a summary way, that life must be regulated in such a manner, that whatever we say or do may be wholly governed by the authority of Christ, and may have an eye to his glory as the mark.' Further, 'we shall fitly comprehend under this term the two following things – that all our aims may set out with invocation of Christ, and may be subservient to his glory.'[17] It seems, then, that Calvin would have us understand that the phrase 'in the name of the Lord Jesus' involves subjection to the authority of Jesus the exalted Messiah, invocation of His blessing, and seeking His glory in all that we do.

Similarly, commentator Herbert Carson notes that the exhortation of Colossians 3:17 reflects 'the main theme of the Epistle, namely the pre-eminence of Christ'. Carson continues:

> His sovereignty embraces every aspect of life, not only the so-called 'sacred' but also the secular. To *do all in the name of the Lord Jesus* means to live and act as those who bear His name, and so to seek to live worthy of Him. It means also to act as those for whom he is Lord, and this involves obedience to His will. It means reliance upon Him, for the name speaks

---

17   John Calvin, 'Commentary on the Epistle to the Colossians,' in *Calvin's Commentaries: Commentaries on the Epistles of Paul the Apostle to the Philippians, Colossians, and Thessalonians,* trans. John Pringle (reprint ed.; Grand Rapids: Baker, 2005), XXI: 218.

of the person .... There is however no hint that such a life of obedience is to be conceived in terms of duty, but rather of 'thanksgiving'.[18]

Carson's analysis may be used to conveniently distinguish distinct elements implied in the exhortation.

The Christian is to recognize that Jesus is Lord over all of life. As Carson reminds us, the lordship of Jesus is comprehensive. The Christian should refuse the separation of life into compartments labeled 'sacred' and 'secular'. Jesus' lordship extends to the entire life of the Christian believer: not only his or her immediate relationship with God, but one's marriage and family life, one's work life, one's finances, one's leisure activities – the whole of life is to be subsumed under the lordship of Jesus Christ. Anything in any sphere of the Christian's life that is contrary to the ethic of the New Testament needs to be brought under Jesus' lordship by an act of repentance and reformation.

The Christian is to live so as to bring honor to the name of the Lord Jesus. 'To live and act as those who bear His name' means for the Christian to recognize that he or she is always a representative of the Lord Jesus, and thus to avoid any attitudes or behaviors which would bring dishonor to Him. 'Walk in a manner worthy of the calling to which you have been called' is the way Paul put it in Ephesians 4:1.

The Christian is to live in active submission to Jesus' lordship. As Carson put it, recognizing Jesus' lordship 'involves obedience to His will'. The operative idea in 'lordship' is 'authoritative ownership' (see Appendix 1), which means that the Christian is to live in obedient submission to the one who is now his or her Lord, Jesus the Messiah. The Christian is one who has been 'bought with a price', so that 'you are not your own' (1 Cor. 6:19-20). Jesus Himself said, 'If you love me, you will keep my commandments' (John 14:15).

The Christian is to live in conscious reliance upon the Lord Jesus. 'The name speaks of the person,' and Jesus said, 'apart from me, you can do nothing' (John 15:5c). It is the power of

---

18 Herbert M. Carson, *The Epistles of Paul to the Colossians and Philemon: An Introduction and Commentary*, Tyndale New Testament Commentaries (Grand Rapids: Eerdmans, 1960), pp. 91-92.

the risen Lord Jesus, imparted to believers through the Holy Spirit, which enables the Christian to live in the way that has been described. Paul desired to 'know him and the power of his resurrection' (Phil. 3:10).

The Christian is to live in thankfulness to God through the Lord Jesus. Paul concludes his exhortation in Colossians 3:17 with a call to thankfulness. Christ 'suffered once for sins, the righteous for the unrighteous, that he might bring us to God' (1 Pet. 3:18), and it ought to be a matter for profound thanks on the part of the Christian that he or she has been brought into fellowship with the holy God through the intercession of the Lord Jesus and has been made to be God's own beloved child. Nothing else in the universe can compare to this high privilege, and possessing everything else without it counts for nothing. Here is ground for thankfulness indeed.

2) The lordship of Jesus is to be honored in the Christian community's corporate life. Paul called the Corinthian congregation to disciplinary action in the name of the Lord Jesus: 'When you are assembled in the name of the Lord Jesus and my spirit is present, with the power of our Lord Jesus ....' (1 Cor. 5:4). New Testament scholar David Garland notes, in the midst of an extensive discussion of this passage, that Paul 'wishes to instill in them a sense of responsibility for exercising discipline under the lordship of Christ'.[19] This suggests that Paul understood that Christian congregations are to carry out their corporate life under Christ's lordship. We have observed earlier in this study that after Christ's ascension, His lordship was exercised in the churches through the apostles as His appointed representatives and through the writings embodying the apostolic tradition, which writings have become our New Testament. All this confers on Christian congregations both the right and the responsibility to carry on their own corporate life under the lordship of Christ as expressed through the New Testament Scriptures. While this is a vast topic, and views will differ in various ecclesiastical traditions, yet it is appropriate to point out that all areas of corporate congregational life rightly come under the purview of the Lordship of Jesus, the

---

19   Garland, *1 Corinthians*, p. 169.

Head of the church. The New Testament contains patterns and standards of congregational life related to membership, leadership, worship, fellowship and community life, ministry, and discipline. All these are to be brought under the lordship of Christ as exercised through the New Testament.

Within the Christian fellowship to which this writer belongs, the Southern Baptist Convention, it would appear that there is much room for growth in submission to the Lord Jesus in congregational life. A recent observer, Tom Ascol, has written, 'according to statistical analysis, SBC churches still have an overwhelmingly large percentage of members who give no signs of spiritual life.' He continues, 'At some point the question needs to be humbly yet forcefully asked, 'What difference does it make if we have an inerrant Bible if we are not willing to believe what it teaches and do what it says?' Ascol goes on to make a pointed application:

> Either Christ is Lord of the church, or He is not. If He is, then local churches have no choice but to follow His clear teaching about how churches are to function. Historically, Baptists have been champions of this principle and have been the vanguard of advocating regenerate church membership and church discipline. The sad but incontrovertible fact is that most Southern Baptist churches give only lip service to these teachings of Christ, if they regard them at all.[20]

The arena in which Christ's lordship is to be most evident is in the lives of His people and His churches. Is it any wonder that an unbelieving world refuses to give heed to the message of the gospel when those who are to exemplify Christ's lordship before a watching world fall so far short?

3) A Telling Testimony. A recent and compelling testimony to the significance of this issue is to be found in a scholarly review of 'Jesus studies' by Craig Keener. Keener is a contemporary New Testament scholar who in his youth was a professed atheist and who rejected Christianity.[21] He informs us that

---

20 Tom Ascol, 'The Other Resurgence', *The Founders Journal*, Issue 71 (Winter 2008), pp. 2, 3.

21 Keener's story is told in Appendix 8 of Craig S. Keener, *The Historical Jesus of the Gospels* (Grand Rapids: Eerdmans, 2009), pp. 379-88.

'my primary objection to Christianity in particular was that Christians did not seem to take it seriously.' The basis for this stance was his observation that 'eighty percent of people in my country [the USA] claimed to be his followers, yet most of them apparently lived as if it made no difference for their lives.' Keener drives home his argument as follows:

> Much of western Christendom does not proceed as if the Jesus of the Gospels is alive and continues to reign in his church. In practice, a gulf remains between their affirmation of Jesus' resurrection and their *living as if he is humanity's rightful lord*, so that a theological affirmation does not translate into their experience.

Keener informs his readers that he came to Christian faith through an encounter with 'the risen Christ in an unsolicited and unexpected personal experience', and that he came to understand that 'the reality of Jesus rises or falls not on how successfully his professed followers have followed his teaching, but on Jesus himself.' [22] Nevertheless, Keener's testimony is striking, making the telling point that Christians' failure to live as an expression of the lordship of Jesus was the crucial issue in their failing to commend the Christian faith to him. How many times could such a story be repeated by others?

III. Application to Western Culture

For purposes of this study the 'West' will be understood as Europe, the United States of America, and their cultural derivatives. This region of the globe inherited the cultural heritage of the ancient Hebrews, Greeks and Romans, along with the Germanic influences received during the Middle Ages. The region was nominally Christian until the Reformation of the sixteenth century, when reformers such as Martin Luther, Huldreich Zwingli, John Calvin, Anabaptist groups, Thomas Cranmer, John Knox and others sought to restore the Christian faith to its biblical foundations, and were to greater or lesser degrees successful. However, a competing tradition was already present in the West, and it

---

22 Citations from Keener, *The Historical Jesus of the Gospels*, pp. 387, 384 (emphasis added), p. 385.

expressed itself forcefully in the developments known as the 'Enlightenment'.

1. Beginning with the 'Enlightenment', Western culture adopted what became a systematic rejection of the Bible as divine revelation.

The Reformation period of religious turmoil and warfare prompted some European thinkers to seek a more moderating approach philosophically and politically. That influence, combined with the results of the so-called scientific revolution (which began contemporaneously with the Reformers), led to a European intellectual movement known as the 'Enlightenment' (roughly 1650-1800). One of the goals of Enlightenment thinkers was the development of a 'rational religion', one which measured up to the criteria established by human reason apart from the aid of divine revelation recognized as such, and some preferred freedom from the constraints of religion altogether. About the same time there arose a new approach to the Bible, originating perhaps with a Dutch Jewish thinker, Baruch Spinoza (1632-77). This new approach sought to view the Bible as any other ancient literature, as merely a product of its human authors without the influence of divine inspiration. This approach to the Bible came to dominate intellectual circles and universities in the West until by the twentieth century the authority of the Bible as divine revelation was recognized by only a relatively small minority of the population of Europe, with a somewhat larger representation in the United States.

This briefest of summaries of the Enlightenment can be fleshed out somewhat more fully by noting some of the intellectual influences connected with its origins and effects.[23]

1) Loss of transcendental truth: Nominalism. A medieval philosophical movement known as Nominalism denied the reality of transcendental truth (that is, anything beyond human observation). This helped to fuel the scientific revolution,

---

23 The summary outline that follows is adapted from Graeme Goldsworthy, *Gospel-Centered Hermeneutics: Foundations and Principles of Evangelical Biblical Interpretation* (Downers Grove, IL: IVP Academic, 2006), pp. 120-22.

which was based on human observation or experience, and thus was empirical in method.

2) Placing of man at the center: Descartes. French philosopher René Descartes (1596-1650), attempting to find an intellectual starting point that was undeniable, famously said, 'I think, therefore I am'. As stated by Graeme Goldsworthy, 'Descartes' dictum ... expressed a starting point of complete subjectivity and autonomy.'[24] Man himself was made the starting point in the search for truth.

3) Bold assertion of human autonomy: Kant. While Descartes may have assumed human autonomy, the philosopher Immanuel Kant (1724-1804) boldly asserted it. Kant defined the Enlightenment as 'the movement by which man emerges from the state of inferiority which made it impossible for him to use his reason without submission to the direction of others', including God.[25] Man was to dare to be independent of all external authority, even that of God Himself.

These components of Enlightenment thought shaped that movement as a revolt against God – the God of the Bible (the only God given serious consideration in the West). In asserting human autonomy Western thought was issuing a declaration of independence from the God of the Bible and His revelation. Thus Western thought and the resulting secular culture recapitulated the primal sin of the original humans in the Garden of Eden: the effort to establish human autonomy over against God, and specifically the rejection of God's revelation (the epistemological foundation) concerning the nature of things (metaphysics) and the proper bounds of human freedom and behavior (ethics).

2. The West has descended into a philosophical and cultural abyss, the only way out of which is recognition of the rule of God expressed in the lordship of Jesus Christ.

The American thinker Richard Weaver has described the logical and practical consequences of this philosophical revolution in the West:

---

24   Goldsworthy, *Gospel-Centered Hermeneutics*, p. 122

25   Jacques de Senarclens, *Heirs of the Reformation* (London: SCM, 1963), p. 35, cited in Goldsworthy, *Gospel-Centered Hermeneutics*, p. 122.

The denial of universals [nominalism] carries with it the denial of everything transcending experience. The denial of everything transcending experience means inevitably – though ways are found to hedge on this – the denial of truth. With the denial of objective truth there is no escape from the relativism of 'man the measure of all things'.

Concludes Weaver: 'Thus began ... a feeling of alienation from all fixed truth',[26] leading, he might have added, to a pervasive mood of despair. Weaver, writing more than sixty years ago, here identified some of the central features of 'postmodernism' before that term had been popularized.

The only legitimate way out of this pit is the one which the modern West seems to find most distasteful: acknowledgment of the authority of the God of the Bible and of His historical self-disclosure, culminating in the redemptive work and present lordship of Jesus Christ. The West finds this distasteful, for it would require modern man to relinquish his cherished assertion of autonomy. The primal sin of humanity is never far from us.

IV. Application to Theological Liberalism

Something similar could be said of the movement of revisionist theology known as Theological Liberalism. This was a movement of the early nineteenth century in continental Europe which spread to Britain and the United States later in the century.

1. Theological liberalism partook of the spirit of the 'Enlightenment'

Goldsworthy identifies 'three parallel aspects' that led 'to the Protestant liberalism of the nineteenth century'.[27]

1) Schleiermacher's view of religious consciousness. Friedrich Schleiermacher (1768-1834) was a German theologian who sought to combine biblical revelation and natural theology. He posited that the Bible was not a divine revelation but

---

26 Richard M. Weaver, *Ideas Have Consequences* (Chicago: University of Chicago Press, 1948), p. 4.

27 Summarized and adapted from Goldsworthy, *Gospel-Centered Hermeneutics*, pp. 123-25.

a record of religious experience, and that the common element in all religious experience was the consciousness of being dependent on God or being in relation with God. Jesus was merely a human being who possessed a heightened sense of dependence on God; redemption is His modeling this sense and thus passing it on to others.

2) Kant's view of moral consciousness. In the view of philosopher Kant religion is a means of restoring man's original disposition to do good. 'Kant moralizes the Christian faith in a way that makes biblical religion hardly more than an instrument to serve morality. This moral obligation is the striving of man after the good whereby we save ourselves', accomplished through the imitation of Jesus.[28]

3) The rise of historicism. Several influences coalesced into an outlook known as Historicism. Historicism was not the result of any new discovery or the development of a new historical methodology. Rather it was a philosophical orientation which saw innate historical forces as providing the explanation of all events and of human culture, as determining the beliefs of all people, and as involving everything human (including belief systems) in a process of continuous development and change. When applied to the Christian faith this meant that Jesus was a mere man and a decidedly non-supernatural historical figure, the Bible is a solely human book and Christian beliefs are subject to constant evolution.[29]

As a result of such influences theological liberalism emerged as a movement which revised or modified all Christian doctrines, bringing them into essential conformity with the outlook of the Enlightenment, including the elimination of the supernatural and the assertion of human autonomy. The latter is demonstrated in the comment by a noted liberal

---

28 Goldsworthy, *Gospel-Centered Hermeneutics*, pp. 123-24.

29 This definition of historicism is dependent on Grant Wacker, *Augustus H. Strong and the Dilemma of Historical Consciousness* (Macon, GA: Mercer University Press, 1985), p. 16; for its rise, see pp. 33-42. For a treatment of one Christian scholar's response to historicism, see Terry A. Chrisope, *Toward a Sure Faith: J. Gresham Machen and the Dilemma of Biblical Criticism, 1881-1915* (Fearn, Ross-shire, Great Britain: Christian Focus, 2000).

theologian, Henry Sloan Coffin: 'Liberalism is opposed to external authority because it obstructs free response to the truth ....'[30] In other words, the authority of the Bible (an 'external authority') is rejected because it treads on the freedom of human beings to determine for themselves what is true and what is not; that is, it violates human autonomy.

2. **The only hope for a recovery from theological liberalism is a return to the authority of the Bible as an expression of the lordship of Jesus Christ.**

Theological liberalism has shown itself to be a transitional and unstable compound. Eventually it evolves into something that is not recognizably Christian, as evidenced by the condition of the 'mainline' liberal denominations in the United States and elsewhere, which are committed to little or none of the intellectual content of historic Christianity. This is the case because theological liberalism, it might be argued, is not Christian in the first place. This was the argument of J. Gresham Machen in his 1923 book *Christianity and Liberalism*. There he maintained that 'modern liberalism not only is a different religion from Christianity but belongs in a totally different class of religions.... the liberal attempt at reconciling Christianity with modern science has really relinquished everything distinctive of Christianity.'[31] Machen's verdict has been affirmed by more recent scholars: 'J. Gresham Machen was right. What we have in the Enlightenment tradition of criticism is nothing less than another religion that supplants biblical faith.'[32] The further comment of Harrisville and Sundberg on Machen will form a fitting conclusion to this study:

---

30 Henry Sloan Coffin, 'The Scriptures', in *Liberal Christianity: An Appraisal* (New York, 1942), p. 234, quoted in Wilbur M. Smith, *Therefore Stand: A Plea for a Vigorous Apologetic in the Present Crisis of Evangelical Christianity* (Boston: W. A. Wilde, 1945), p. 130. The entire quotation presented by Smith shows Coffin's complete commitment to the principles of historicism.

31 J. Gresham Machen, *Christianity and Liberalism* (reprint ed; Grand Rapids: Eerdmans, 1956), p. 7.

32 Roy A. Harrisville and Walter Sundberg, *The Bible in Modern Culture: Theology and Historical-Critical Method from Spinoza to Kasemann* (Grand Rapids: Eerdmans, 1995) , p. 268.

The external grounding of the Christian proclamation in the narrative integrity of the biblical record is the core of Machen's argument. The New Testament proclaims the Lordship of Jesus Christ. One may affirm this proclamation or deny it. What cannot be done is to transform it or resymbolize it into something else. To do so is an act of arbitrary subjectivity. Further, it is the unethical manipulation of the common understanding of inherited religious language that denies the perspicuity of scripture. Historical criticism is no 'science' if it ignores the 'facts' of what the Bible says.[33]

The only way out of the impasse for theological liberalism is to relinquish its claim to autonomous knowledge and submit itself to what the Bible says. And what the Bible says is that 'Jesus is Lord'. One day all humanity will be compelled to acknowledge this reality.

---

33   Harrisville and Sundberg, *The Bible in Modern Culture*, p. 270.

APPENDICES

Appendix 1:

The Meaning of the Title 'Lord' (kyrios)

The foundation for a study of the lordship of Jesus Christ and its implications must be laid in an examination of the meaning and use of the Greek word *kyrios*, the word which is commonly translated 'Lord' when applied to Jesus in the New Testament.[1]

The noun *ho kyrios* is the substantive form of the adjective *kyrios*, which when used of persons means 'having power or authority over', and which in turn derives from another noun, *to kyros*, meaning 'supreme power, authority'.[2] The idea of legitimacy attaches to the authority or power represented by *kyrios* (both the adjective and the noun) so that it refers to an authority which lawfully, validly and legitimately belongs to the one who possesses it. '*Kyrios* always contains the idea of legality and authority',[3] and thus sometimes stands in contrast to *despotes* (also meaning 'master' or 'lord'), which may carry overtones of high-handedness. *Despotes* speaks of the possession or exercise of power in fact, while *kyrios* emphasizes the legitimacy and

---

1 The following summary is based on the article on *kyrios* by W. Foerster and G. Quell in G. Kittel and G. Friedrich, eds., *Theological Dictionary of the New Testament*, trans. and ed. Geoffrey W. Bromiley, 10 vols. (Grand Rapids: Eerdmans, 1964-76), 3:1039-98; and that on 'Lord' by H. Bietenhard in Colin Brown, gen. ed., *The New International Dictionary of New Testament Theology* (Grand Rapids: Zondervan, 1975-78), 2:508-20; and supplemented by additional sources. The Kittel and Brown dictionaries will hereinafter be referred to as *TDNT* and *NIDNTT* respectively.

2 Henry George Liddell and Robert Scott, *A Greek-English Lexicon*, rev. Henry Stuart Jones, with supplement (Oxford: Oxford University Press, 1968), pp. 1013-14.

3 *NIDNTT*, 2:510.

authority of the power exercised. The root idea of *kyrios* is thus legitimate authority, a fact which will be borne out by the following brief survey of the ancient use of the word. We may conveniently divide our treatment historically according to classical usage (including Hellenistic), Old Testament usage (in the Septuagint) and New Testament usage.

I. The classical and Hellenistic usage of *kyrios*

In classical usage *ho kyrios* first appears with a fixed sense in the early fourth century B.C., where it has two distinct meanings: 'the lawful owner of a slave', and 'the legal guardian of a wife or girl'; both reflect the idea of 'one who has full authority'.[4] The word had only limited use in the Attic (literary) dialect, but there it derived from the adjective 'a restriction to legitimate power of disposal which is never wholly lost in the *koine* ('common dialect').[5] In the *koine, kyrios* is often used interchangeably with *despotes,* but a distinction may still be discerned: '*Kyrios* is the one who can dispose of something or someone, *despotes* the one who owns something or someone.'[6] As the New Testament era nears, the more *kyrios* tends to displace *despotes*; it is the more flattering term.

In the realm of religion, although the term *kyrios* is sometimes applied to the gods, the Greeks generally did not regard their gods as possessing lordship, except perhaps in limited spheres. The reason is that the Greek gods were not personal creator-gods, and thus evoked no corresponding human response of submission. The gods were, like men, subject to fate, not the lords of fate. 'At root, man has no personal responsibility towards these gods, nor can they personally encounter man with punishments'; gods and men 'are organically related members of one reality, and their mutual relation cannot be described in terms of *kyrios* and *doulos* ("lord" and "slave").'[7]

In the East, however, the religious situation was different. For the inhabitants of Egypt, Syria and Asia Minor 'the gods

---

4   *TDNT,* 3:1042-43.

5   *TDNT,* 3:1043.

6   *TDNT,* 3:1045.

7   *TDNT,* 3:1048.

are the lords of reality. Destiny is in their hands.'[8] They are creator-gods, they can intervene in the world and in human affairs, and man is responsible to them. 'They are the lords of destiny and the lords of men',[9] and are treated as such by their human subjects. This basic difference between Greece and the East paved the way for a broader application of *kyrios* to the gods during the Hellenistic period.

As the use of the Greek language spread over the Mediterranean world during the Hellenistic period (from about 323 B.C. to the New Testament era), the application of *kyrios* to the gods became relatively more prevalent in the East than it was in Greece, although Foerster remarks that '*kyrios* never became widespread as a predicate of the gods',[10] and he finds no instance of it (except for *kyrios* with the genitive, 'lord of ...') prior to the first century B.C. Its local use in various places 'corresponded to native, non-Greek usage'[11] – that is, it simply reflected the local idiom.

There are two features of this application of *kyrios* to the gods which are of special interest to our present investigation. In the first place, *kyrios* 'is particularly used in expression of a personal relationship of man to the deity ... and as a correlate of *doulos* inasmuch as the man concerned describes as *kyrios* the god under whose orders he stands.'[12] Secondly, the gods to whom *kyrios* is most commonly applied are those in whom the attribute of 'dominion over nature and destiny is most impressively present'.[13] Thus there is present in this usage the idea of the power and authority of the god who is termed *kyrios*, as well as the implication of a personal relationship involving submission of the worshipper to his god.

The attributes of power and authority also attach to positions of rulership in the human political sphere, and *kyrios* was eventually applied to them as well. This is observable in

---

8   *TDNT,* 3:1048.

9   *TDNT,* 3:1049.

10   *TDNT,* 3:1051.

11   *TDNT,* 3:1051

12   *TDNT,* 3:1052.

13   *TDNT,* 3:1052.

the first centuries B.C. and A.D., as political rulers both in the East and in Rome are termed *kyrios* (for example, the Roman emperors Augustus, Caligula, Nero and Domitian; the Palestinian rulers Herod the Great, Agrippa I and Agrippa II; and the Queen of Upper Egypt).[14] It is a matter of dispute whether this title implied the divinity of the ruler, a question which lies beyond the scope of the present discussion.[15] It is sufficient for our purpose to note that *kyrios* was used of those who in the human sphere occupied positions of legitimate authority and power.

II. The Old Testament usage of *kyrios*

In the Septuagint *kyrios* occurs over 9,000 times. Three major aspects of its occurrence are of particular interest for the present discussion.

First, *kyrios* is used to translate various Hebrew and Aramaic words which refer to men. The most common of these is *adon* (lord), which is often used as a polite form of address (Gen. 19:2; 32:4) but which perhaps also often implied the superior position of the one addressed or referred to (e.g., when used of kings and other rulers, Gen. 47:25; throughout 2 Sam., 1 Kings 1, etc.). Sometimes *adon* (and thus *kyrios*) refers directly to a position of rulership (Gen. 45:8, 9; Ps. 105:21). *Kyrios* also translates several other words which refer to positions of authority: *gebir*, 'master' (Gen. 27:29, 37); *baal*, 'owner' (Judg. 19:22, 23); and the Aramaic *shallit*, 'ruler' (Dan. 4:17, Theodotion's version [4:14 in Aramaic]); and *mara*, 'lord', used both of God (Dan. 2:47; 5:23, Theodotion) and men (Dan. 4:19, 24, Theodotion [4:16, 21 in Aramaic]).

Second, *kyrios* is used many times to translate *adon* when the latter refers to God. It is used alone (Gen. 18:27; Ps. 113 [114, Heb.] : 7) and in combination with other titles and names of God (Isa. 28:22; Amos 9:5; Zeph. 1:9). As a name for God *kyrios* is a strict translation of the Hebrew only in such cases

---

14   *TDNT,* 3:1054-58; *NIDNTT,* 2:510-11.

15   For a treatment of this question see Oscar Cullmann, *The Christology of the New Testament,* trans. Shirley C. Guthrie and Charles A. M. Hall, rev. ed. (Philadelphia: Westminster Press, 1963), pp. 195-99.

where it represents *adon*. The two words are roughly equivalent in that both mean 'lord', implying rightful authority and power.

In the third place, *kyrios* is used most often in the Septuagint (some 6,156 times) to represent *YHWH*, the proper name of God. In these instances, Bietenhard points out, it is not a strict translation but 'an interpretative circumlocution'; it stands for 'all that the Hebrew text implied by the divine name', namely, that 'Yahweh is Creator and Lord of the whole universe' and 'the God of Israel, His covenant people'. Further, 'By choosing *kyrios* for Yahweh the LXX Greek text also emphasized the idea of legal authority. Because Yahweh saved his people from Egypt and chose them as his possession, he is the legitimate Lord of Israel. As Creator of the world he is also its legitimate Lord with unlimited control over it.'[16]

It is thus evident that the use of *kyrios* in the Septuagint is consistently colored by the implication of legitimate power and authority, whether the term is applied to God or to men.

III. The New Testament usage of *kyrios*

In the New Testament there are two levels of common usage of *kyrios*, the secular and the religious, both of which continue to maintain the idea of legitimate power and authority, which was originally inherent in the word.[17]

In the secular usage *kyrios* can mean the 'owner' of something, for example, a vineyard (Matt. 20:8), a house (Mark 13:35), or a colt (Luke 19:33). This meaning passes easily into that of 'lord' or 'master', 'one who is in a position of authority',[18] for instance, of the harvest (Matt. 9:38) or the sabbath (Mark 2:28) – though in fact both these references have religious significance, since they apply to God and to Jesus respectively. *Kyrios* can also denote the owner or master of a slave or servant (*doulos* – as in John 13:16, Matt. 10:24;

---

16 For the preceding three paragraphs, *NIDNTT*, 2:512.

17 I. Howard Marshall also provides a brief overview of the ways *kyrios* is used in the New Testament, *Jesus the Saviour*, pp. 198-99.

18 Frederick William Danker, ed., *A Greek-English Lexicon of the New Testament and other Early Christian Literature*, p. 577. Abbreviated as BDAG.

18:31; Eph. 6:5 and several other New Testament passages). The vocative form *kyrie* is commonly used by slaves in addressing their masters (Matt. 13:27; 25:20, 22, 24; Luke 14:22). *Kyrios* is used to designate a person of high or superior position, such as a husband in contrast to his wife (1 Pet. 3:6), a father (Matt. 21:29-30, various readings), or a civil official (Matt. 27:63). This usage shades into *kyrie* as a form of polite address, equivalent to the English 'sir'. It is used in addressing Jesus as well as others (Matt. 25:11; John 4:11; 12:21; 20:15; Acts 16:30).

Kyrios is more commonly used in the New Testament, however, in a religious sense. It often refers to God, either as used by the New Testament writers directly (Luke 1:6, 28) or, as is frequently the case, in quotations from the Old Testament (Mark 12:36; Acts 3:22; Rom. 9:28-29). This use of *kyrios* is simply a continuation of Septuagint usage, and is intended to imply all that was meant by the Hebrew *YHWH*.

But it is in reference to Jesus that *kyrios* finds its most distinctive use in the New Testament.[19] The term is applied to Him throughout the book, but we may approach the matter historically by dividing the career of Jesus into two periods – that before His resurrection, and that after it. This is not an arbitrary division, nor one of mere convenience, for it has considerable theological significance. It is during the period following Jesus' resurrection that *kyrios* becomes, as Geerhardus Vos puts it, the 'specific designation of the exalted Saviour'.[20] It is thus with this period, and with the application of *kyrios* to the exalted Jesus, that the present study is primarily concerned. But neither can the earlier period be ignored, for with respect to the use of *kyrios* in reference to Jesus there seems to be a good deal of continuity between the two. That is, during the earthly life of Jesus, *kyrios* was applied to Him in such a way as to imply recognition of His divine person and Messianic office.

---

19 Marshall provides a survey of the application of the term *kyrios* to Jesus in the Gospels as well as the rest of the New Testament, *Jesus the Saviour*, pp. 199-200.

20 Geerhardus Vos, *The Self-Disclosure of Jesus*, ed. Johannes G. Vos (Phillipsburg, NJ: Presbyterian and Reformed, 1978), p. 118.

A demonstration of this would require a full treatment of the use of *kyrios* in the Gospels, which is beyond the scope of the present study. A brief survey must suffice to indicate the pertinent lines of thought. *Kyrios* is applied to Jesus in three ways in the Gospel accounts. First, the Gospel writers themselves (as distinct from personages within the Gospels) use *kyrios* of Jesus, either directly in the narrative (Luke 7:13 and often in Luke; seldom in John; hardly at all in Matthew and Mark) or in Old Testament quotations (probably Mark 1:3). Second, persons within the narrative speak of Jesus as 'Lord' or 'the Lord' (Luke 1:43; 19:34), including Jesus Himself, directly (Luke 6:5; 19:31) and in parables (Mark 13:35). Third, persons in the narrative address Jesus as 'Lord' (Matt. 8:2, 25, etc.).

Geerhardus Vos draws the following conclusions concerning these three modes of usage: (i) The Gospel writers themselves attach 'a higher and richer significance to the name *kyrios* beginning with the resurrection',[21] as indicated by their infrequent use of that title before the resurrection and their more frequent use of it afterwards. (ii) When persons within the Gospel narrative refer to Jesus as a third person using *kyrios* ('the Lord' etc.) there occurs in many cases 'a real anticipation of the subsequent usage',[22] that is, as a Christological title (Luke 1:43; 2:11; 6:5 and parallels; 19:31 and parallels, 20:41-44 and parallels). (iii) When the vocative *kyrie* is used in addressing Jesus it is often 'a real precursor of the standard designation of the Saviour from the apostolic age onwards .... It recognizes His Messianic character and, at times at least, His divine nature and dignity as reflected in His Messiahship' (Matt. 7:21; 8:21; 26:22; Luke 5:8).[23]

Vos' conclusions may be regarded as generally valid, although the evidence in support of the first point does not seem to be as strong as he supposes. The other two, however, are based on sounder evidence, and indicate that *kyrios* as applied to Jesus in the Gospels to a large degree anticipates the usage that later became common among Christians.

---

21 Vos, *Self-Disclosure*, p. 121.

22 Vos, *Self-Disclosure*, p. 127.

23 Vos, *Self-Disclosure*, p. 135.

Vos goes on to make two further observations which have a bearing on our present study. The first is that the evidence for the lordship of Jesus in the Gospels is not limited to the use of particular words (e.g. *kyrios*). That evidence extends rather to the 'general structure of the relation of the disciples to Jesus in the record .... The absolute things asked of the disciples, the unqualified duty to follow – to forsake all others for Jesus' sake, including even the dearest of earthly relationships.... – all this demands for its ultimate ground His unique Lordship as recognized even at that time.'[24] Such a relationship manifests the essence of lordship, and as we shall have opportunity to observe, is qualitatively no different from all which obtains between Jesus and believers following His exaltation.

Second, Vos notes that 'the presence of one stable element from beginning to end marks the continuity in the history of the conception' of Jesus' lordship in the New Testament, that is, 'the element of *authoritative ownership*',[25] which serves as the ground for the absolute demands made on the disciples of Jesus. This idea is present both before and after the resurrection and serves to demonstrate the basic meaning of divine lordship in the New Testament, particularly as exercised by Jesus.

---

24 Vos, *Self-Disclosure*, pp. 135-36.

25 Vos, *Self-Disclosure*, p. 136, emphasis added.

Appendix 2:

John Murray on the Hypostatic Union[1]

1. Theanthropic constitution. From the time of conception in the womb of the virgin, and for ever, the second Person of the Godhead is God–man. This identity did not suffer dissolution even in death. The death meant separation of the elements of his human nature. But he, as the Son of God, was still united to the two separated elements of his human nature. He, as respects his body, was laid in the tomb and, as respects his disembodied spirit, he went to the Father. He was buried. He was raised from the dead. He was indissolubly united to the disunited elements of his human nature. When he was raised from the dead, human nature in its restored integrity belonged to his person, and it was in that restored integrity that he manifested himself repeatedly to his disciples and to various other persons, including more than five hundred at one time. It was in this human nature that he ascended to heaven and sat down at the right hand of God. It is as God–man he is exalted and given all authority in heaven and in earth. It is in human nature that he will return, and as God–man he will judge the world. The elect will be conformed to his image, and it is as the firstborn among many brethren that he will fulfill the Father's predestinating design (Rom. 8:29; cf. Phil. 3:21). The thought of ceasing to be the God–man is, therefore, alien to all that the Scripture reveals respecting his own glory and the glory of those for whose sake he became man.

---

1   From John Murray, *Collected Writings*, 2:139-40.

2. Economic subordination. By the incarnation and by taking the form of a Servant, the Son came to sustain new relations to the Father and the Holy Spirit. He became subject to the Father and dependent upon the operations of the Holy Spirit. He came down from heaven, not to do His own will, but the will of the Father who sent him (cf. John 6:38). As the Father had life in himself, so gave he to the Son to have life in himself (cf. John 5:26). It is in this light that we are to interpret Jesus' statement, 'The Father is greater than I' (John 14:28). It is our Lord's servanthood that advertises this subordination more than any other office. As servant he was obedient unto death (cf. Phil. 2: 7, 8).

Manifold were the activities of the Holy Spirit. By the Spirit he was begotten in Mary's womb. With the Spirit he was endued at the baptism in Jordan. By the Spirit he was driven into the wilderness to be tempted of the devil. In the power of the Spirit he returned to Galilee. By the Spirit he cast out demons. In the Holy Spirit he rejoiced and gave thanks (cf. Luke 10:21). Through the eternal Spirit he offered Himself and fulfilled the climactic demand of his commission (cf. Heb. 9:12). According to the Spirit he was constituted the Son of God with power in the resurrection (cf. Rom. 1:4). By virtue of this, Christ is 'life-giving Spirit' (1 Cor. 15:45), and Paul can say, 'The Lord is the Spirit' (2 Cor. 3:17). He is given the Spirit without measure (cf. John 3:34).

3. Mediatorial investiture. The authority with which he is invested as a result of his obedience unto death must be distinguished from the authority and government that he possesses and exercises intrinsically as God the Son. The latter is intrinsic to his deity (cf. Matt. 28:18; John 3:35; Acts 2:36; Eph. 1:20-23; Phil. 2:9-11; 1 Pet. 3:22). This authority and sovereignty is universal and all-inclusive. How it is related to the sovereignty that is intrinsic we cannot tell. Here is another aspect of the duality that exists all along the line in the mystery of the incarnation. The duality in this instance consists in the coexistence of the exercise of prerogatives belonging to him in virtue of his Godhood and of prerogatives which were bestowed upon him as Mediator and Lord. Mystery enshrouds this duality for us, but may we not deny the co-existence or the distinctions involved.

Appendix 3:

Scripture as an Expression of Jesus' Authority

The argument summarized in Chapter 11 may be elaborated as follows:

2. Evangelical Christians should view Scripture as an expression of the authority of Jesus Christ as Lord.

a) *Jesus appointed apostles to share and exercise His authority.* According to Matthew 10:1 Jesus 'called to him his twelve disciples and gave them *authority* over unclean spirits, to cast them out, and to heal every disease and every affliction', and also authorized them to 'go to the lost sheep of the house of Israel. And proclaim as you go, saying the kingdom of heaven is at hand' (10:6-7). The term translated 'authority' is *exousia*, 'the right to control or command, *authority, absolute power, warrant*'.[1] Jesus 'gave' the apostles authority, suggesting an extension of His authority by which He Himself was doing these very same things He commissioned them to do. That is, ultimately it was Jesus' authority which the apostles exercised, and it was at His command and in His behalf that they exercised it. It was not an independently originated and exercised authority which the apostles possessed but one that derived from Jesus Himself.

This is in keeping with the meaning of the word 'apostle' (*apostolos*), which (or an equivalent Aramaic term) Jesus applied to the twelve: 'he appointed twelve (whom *he also named apostles*) so that they might be with him and he might send them out to preach and have authority to cast out demons' (Mark 3:14-15). Later, after the death and resurrection of Jesus,

---

1   BDAG, p. 353.

'the death of Jesus leaves the disciples at a loss, but the risen Lord constitutes them a community and renews the commission. The apostles are now witnesses of the resurrection.... They become his authoritative representatives.'[2] As stated by New Testament scholar Herman Ridderbos, 'Christ established *a formal authority structure to be the source and standard for all future preaching of the gospel*' – and that authority structure was the apostolate of the first century.[3] This corresponds also with Jesus' statement in Matthew 28:18-20 in which, after His resurrection, He claimed 'all *authority* in heaven and on earth', then authorized the apostles to make disciples on His behalf and promised them His continuing presence (which also implied the continuance of His presence with the church after the deaths of the apostles, but not necessarily the continuation of their office).

b) *The apostles were specifically commissioned to bear witness to the redemptive acts of God accomplished through Messiah Jesus.* Acts 10:39-43 quotes Peter as saying to the household of Cornelius:

> And *we are witnesses of all that he [Jesus] did* both in the country of the Jews and in Jerusalem. They put him to death by hanging him on a tree, but God raised him on the third day and made him to appear, not to all the people but *to us who had been chosen by God as witnesses,* who ate and drank with him after he rose from the dead. And *he commanded us to preach to the people and to testify* that he is the one appointed by God to be judge of the living and the dead. To him all the prophets bear witness that everyone who believes in him receives forgiveness of sins through his name.

Peter evidently is referring to the apostles as those who had been appointed as witnesses and proclaimers of the mighty acts of God in Jesus. Ridderbos points out that by virtue of the fact that God chose these witnesses, 'in that way the apostolate was actually a part of God's redemptive activity in the fullness

---

2 TDNT-Abridged, p. 72; see this entire article, pp. 67-75.

3 Herman Ridderbos, *Redemptive History and the New Testament Scriptures,* 2nd rev. ed., transl. H. De Jongste, rev. Richard B. Gaffin, Jr. (Phillipsburg, NJ: Presbyterian and Reformed, 1988), p. 13, emphasis his.

of time.... According to Peter, the apostles are to give an authoritative and exclusive testimony in the world; they are to vouch for the truth and significance of Christ's redemptive acts.'[4]

c) *The apostles were promised the assistance of the Holy Spirit for the carrying out of this specific ministry of witness.* Jesus promised to the apostles both before His death (Matt. 10:18-20; Mark 13:11//Luke 21:13-15; John 14:26; 15:26-27; 16:13-15) and after his resurrection (Acts 1:8) that they would be enabled and empowered by the Holy Spirit to bear the witness which they were commissioned to deliver. Especially significant in the current discussion is Jesus' word in John 14:25-26: 'These things I have spoken to you while I am still with you. But the Helper, the Holy Spirit, whom the Father will send in my name, he will teach you all things and bring to your remembrance all that I have said to you.' The remembrance of Jesus' teaching (as well as His deeds) and its passing on to others would be a central component of the apostles' witness to Him, and thus is related to Jesus' later word in Acts 1:8: 'But you will receive power when the Holy Spirit has come upon you, and you will be my witnesses....'

Furthermore, it is most significant that Jesus Himself is portrayed as an active agent, along with the Father, in the sending of the Holy Spirit. When Jesus warned the apostles that they would face persecution and prosecution from hostile rulers He encouraged them that an appropriate response would be granted to them (Mark 13:11a, b); in Mark's account, it is said that 'it is not you who speak, but the Holy Spirit' (13:11c), while in Luke, Jesus says '*I will give you* a mouth of wisdom' (Luke 21:15). This suggests that the Holy Spirit would work in the apostles at the instigation of Jesus Himself.

Shortly afterward, when Jesus told the apostles about the coming of the Holy Spirit, He portrayed Himself as just as fully involved in that bestowal as the Father: '*I will ask* the Father, and he will give you another Helper, to be with you forever, even the Spirit of truth' (John 14:16-17); 'But the Helper, the Holy Spirit, whom the *Father will send in my name....*'

---

4   Ridderbos, *Redemptive History and the New Testament Scriptures*, p. 13.

(John 14:26); 'But when the Helper comes, whom *I will send you* from the Father, the Spirit of truth, who proceeds from the Father, he will bear witness about me. And you also will bear witness' (John 15:26-27). This impression is confirmed when the Holy Spirit descends on the apostles on the Day of Pentecost and Peter attributes the granting of the Spirit to the exalted Lord Jesus: '*Being therefore exalted at the right hand of God*, and having received from the Father the promise of the Holy Spirit, *he has poured out this* that you yourselves are seeing and hearing' (Acts 2:33); the subject of this sentence is Jesus, whom 'God has made ... both Lord and Christ....' (2:36).

These texts demonstrate not only that Jesus as exalted Lord was an active agent in the bestowal of the Holy Spirit, but also that the giving of the Spirit and the resulting witness of the apostles were integral elements in the history of redemption, not merely ancillary elements. The death and resurrection of Jesus would have their intended consequences only if the message about Him were definitively and authoritatively set forth and delivered to the nations by His appointed representatives, the apostles. 'It is evident, then, that the New Testament itself inseparably unites the central events of redemption on the one hand and their announcement and transmission on the other. *The announcement of redemption cannot be separated from the history of redemption itself.*'[5]

d) *The apostles delivered an authoritative witness to the saving events divinely wrought through Messiah Jesus.* That the apostles did indeed deliver the witness they were commissioned to deliver is indicated in Hebrews 2:2-4. After referring to the message 'declared by angels' (the Mosaic Law), the writer refers to the 'great salvation' accomplished by Jesus, saying, 'It was declared at first by the Lord [Jesus], and *it was attested to us by those who heard*, while God also bore witness by signs and wonders and various miracles and by gifts of the Holy Spirit distributed according to his will.' The word translated 'attested' is *bebaioo*, meaning 'to put something beyond doubt, *confirm*,

---

5   Ridderbos, *Redemptive History and the New Testament Scriptures*, p. 15, emphasis his.

establish', in this context suggesting '*the saving message was guaranteed to us*' 'as of something legally validated'[6] by those who heard [Jesus], that is, the apostles. Ridderbos thus claims that the term implies that 'the redemption first announced by the Lord was *authenticated in a legally binding way* by the apostles who heard it.' Thus, 'their word is the revelatory word; it is the unique, once-and-for-all witness to Christ to which the church and the world are accountable and by which they will be judged.'[7] If this understanding is correct then the apostles delivered a message which legally obligates those who hear it to respond appropriately; it is as if humankind has been served a divinely-sent legal notice. And behind it is the authority of Him who will be 'judge of the living and the dead', the Lord Jesus Himself (Acts 10:42).

e) *The authoritative apostolic witness to Jesus was eventually reduced to written form.* Ridderbos observes that there are indications already in the New Testament itself that there was a recognized need for authoritative writings to embody the apostolic tradition and to preserve it for posterity, and that such writings, when they came into existence, were viewed as possessing not only apostolic authority but also the status of Scripture. Paul evidently regarded the tradition which he had received from other apostles (that is, for example, information about the institution of the Lord's Supper, to which he refers here) as coming nevertheless 'from the Lord [Jesus]' (1 Cor. 11:23), and thus as carrying the Lord's authority.[8]

This view of apostolic authority as embodying the exalted Lord Jesus' authority is carried over into Paul's writings and is claimed by Paul. Thus Paul could write to the Corinthian Christians: 'If anyone thinks that he is a prophet, or spiritual, he should acknowledge that *the things I am writing to you are a command of*

---

6 BDAG, p. 173.

7 Ridderbos, *Redemptive History and the New Testament Scriptures*, p. 15, emphasis his.

8 See Ridderbos's argument concerning tradition (especially apostolic tradition) in the New Testament in *Redemptive History and the New Testament Scriptures*, pp. 15-21: 'As apostolic tradition, it is the word of the living Lord; it is the authoritative word from Christ about Christ' (pp. 20-21).

the Lord [Jesus]' (1 Cor. 14:37). Likewise, Paul could command the Thessalonian believers to submit to his written words: 'So then, brothers, stand firm and hold to the traditions that you were taught by us, either by our spoken word or *by our letter*' (2 Thes. 2:15). Paul could also require that his letters be read in public congregational gatherings, just as the Old Testament Scriptures were: 'And *when this letter has been read among you*, have it also read in the church of the Laodiceans; and *see that you also read the letter from Laodicea*' (Col. 4:16).

When the facts of Jesus' earthly life came to be written down it was as embodying apostolic tradition, as Luke demonstrates in his prologue. He states that he intended to 'compile a narrative of the things that have been accomplished among us, just *as those who from the beginning were eyewitnesses and ministers of the word have delivered them to us*' (Luke 1:1-2; the word translated 'delivered' here is *paradidomi*, which in such a context has become virtually a New Testament technical term, 'to pass on to another what one knows, of oral or written tradition, *hand down, pass on, transmit, relate, teach*'[9]). By the time Paul wrote 1 Timothy, he could quote verbatim the words of Jesus as related in Luke 10:7 as 'Scripture' (1 Tim. 5:18). And in 2 Peter 3:2, 'the commandment of the Lord and Savior through your apostles' is placed on the same level as 'the predictions of the holy prophets' (presumably the Old Testament prophets; see 2 Pet. 1:19-21), while in 2 Peter 3:15-16 the letters of 'our beloved brother Paul' are placed on a par with 'the other Scriptures'. It is thus apparent that the writings embodying the apostolic tradition were from a very early time intended to carry, and in fact did carry, apostolic authority, which is no less than the very authority of the exalted Lord Jesus Himself.[10]

f) *A portion of the authoritative apostolic witness to Jesus involved Jesus' teaching.* As the quotation of Jesus' words from the Gospel of Luke in 1 Timothy 5:18 illustrates, and as Paul's reference to the explicit teaching of Jesus concerning marriage

---

9   BDAG, p. 762.

10   Ridderbos develops this line of thought further in *Redemptive History and the New Testament Scriptures*, pp. 22-24.

and divorce in 1 Corinthians 7:10-11 shows, the teaching of Jesus constituted a substantial point of interest and a good deal of the content of the tradition about Jesus that was passed on in the early church. That teaching of Jesus, which itself was authoritative, was passed on in an authoritative way by the apostles who were aided by the Holy Spirit sent by the exalted Lord Jesus for this very purpose (John 15:26). Similarly, Jesus expected the content of His teaching to be passed on to those who would later become disciples through the word of the apostles: 'teaching them to observe all that I have commanded you' (Matt. 28:20), which commission was accompanied by the promise, 'And behold, I am with you always, to the end of the age.' It is perhaps to be understood here that the continuing presence of the risen Lord with His representatives (through the Holy Spirit) would ensure their faithful communication of His teaching. That teaching of Jesus would eventually be fixed in written form in the four gospels of the New Testament.

g) *Jesus in His teaching affirmed the authenticity of the Old Testament writings and the historicity of Old Testament events.* In the authoritative record of Jesus' authoritative teaching, there is to be found a full affirmation of the Old Testament and its teaching. Specifically, Jesus affirmed the authenticity of Old Testament writings with respect to their authorship and the historicity of Old Testament events with respect to their occurrence.

(1) *Jesus affirmed the claimed authorship of Old Testament writings.* Jesus made abundant use of the Old Testament in His earthly teaching ministry. As He did so He affirmed the authorship of specific Old Testament writings (often denied or rejected by modern negative biblical scholarship) by referring to their authors, often in a way which was more than a mere accommodation to conventional views of authorship in His time. He identified four authors specifically by name.[11]

(i) *Moses.* For example, when Jesus cleansed a leper, He told the man, 'go, show yourself to the priest and offer the

---

11 Adapted from Robert P. Lightner, *The Saviour and the Scriptures* (Philadelphia: Presbyterian and Reformed, 1966), pp. 45-46.

gift that *Moses commanded*' (Matt. 8:4). When He engaged the Sadducees in discussion about the resurrection of the dead He said, 'But that the dead are raised, even *Moses showed*, in the passage about the bush' (Luke 20:37). He claimed that 'If you believed *Moses*, you would believe me; for *he wrote of me*. But if you do not believe his writings, how will you believe my words?' (John 5:46-47). Several other times Jesus assigned authorship of the Pentateuch (the first five books of the Old Testament) to Moses (Matt. 19:7-8; Mark 10:3; John 7:19, 22-23) and made other references to Moses which lack of space forbids recounting here.

(ii) David. The argument of Jesus in Matthew 22:41-46 (//Mark 12:35-37; Luke 20:41-44) depends upon the authorship of Psalm 110 by David (which is claimed in the title of that psalm). Jesus' point is that '*David, in the Spirit, calls* [Messiah] *Lord*', therefore Messiah must be more than merely David's son. Jesus' entire argument falls to the ground if David, the greatest king of Israel, to whom the messianic promise was made (2 Sam. 7), were not the author of Psalm 110. R. T. France has observed concerning this passage:

The argument may thus be seen to rest upon three premises, that the speaker in Psalm 110 is David, that the person addressed by Yahweh in verse 1 is the Messiah, and that the use of the term *adonai* ('my lord') implies the superiority of the one so described. Without any one of these premises the argument would be invalid.[12]

Thus Jesus emphatically affirmed the Davidic authorship of Psalm 110.

(iii) Isaiah. Jesus quoted from the book of Isaiah several times, sometimes mentioning the author by name. In explaining His use of parables as a judgment on unbelief, Jesus quoted Isaiah 6:9-10, introducing the citation thus:

---

12 R. T. France, *Jesus and the Old Testament: His Application of Old Testament Passages to Himself and His Mission* (Downers Grove, IL: Inter-Varsity, 1971), p. 102. France discuses the validity of these premises in an excursus, pp. 163-69.

'Indeed, in their case the *prophecy of Isaiah* is fulfilled that says...' (Matt. 13:14) and then proceeds with the quotation. On another occasion, when denouncing the Pharisees and scribes, He said, 'You hypocrites! Well did *Isaiah prophesy* of you, when he said ...' and followed with a citation of Isaiah 29:13 regarding vain worship (Matt. 15:7-9).

(iv) Daniel. In His final apocalyptic discourse Jesus said, 'So when you see the abomination of desolation *spoken of by the prophet Daniel*, standing in the holy place' (Matt. 24:15), followed by instructions to His disciples. The allusion is apparently to Daniel 9:27, which says, 'And on the wing of abominations shall come one who makes desolate'. Jesus mentioned the person of Daniel and not just the writing which bears His name.

The significant aspect of all these citations for the present purpose is that Jesus affirmed the authorship of these Old Testament writings by those who are named as authors in the writings themselves. These happen to be just some of those writings whose claimed authorship is most vigorously denied by much modern scholarship based on naturalistic assumptions.

(2) *Jesus affirmed the historicity of many of the central elements of the Old Testament narrative.* In the course of His teaching Jesus referred to many events described in the Old Testament. Robert Lightner[13] has reproduced a table developed by W. E. Vine listing the Old Testament events referred to by Jesus, which is adapted for use here:

Event Recorded in New Testament

Creation of humans	Gen. 1:27; 2:24; 5:2	Matt. 19:4
Murder of Abel	Gen. 4	Matt. 23:35
Times of Noah	Gen. 7	Matt. 24:37

---

13 Lightner, *The Saviour and the Scriptures*, p. 98.

The Flood	Gen. 7	Luke 17:27
Days of Lot	Gen. 13	Luke 17:28
Destruction of Sodom	Gen. 19	Luke 17:29
Word of God to Moses	Exod. 3:6	Matt. 22:32
Rite of circumcision	Gen. 17; Lev. 12:3	John 7:22
Giving of the Law	Exod. 20	John 7:19
Commandments of the Law	Exod. 20:12-16	Matt. 19:18
Law concerning leprosy	Lev. 14	Mark 1:44
Lifting up of the serpent of bronze	Num. 21:9	John 3:14
Profanation of the Sabbath by priests	Num. 28:9-10	Matt. 12:5
David's eating of the bread of Presence	1 Sam. 21	Matt. 12:3-4
Glory of Solomon	1 Kings 10	Matt. 6:29
Queen of Sheba's visit to Solomon	1 Kings 10	Matt 12:42
Famine in the days of Elijah	1 Kings 17	Luke 4:25
Sending of Elijah to widow of Sidon	1 Kings 17	Luke 4:26
Healing of Naaman by Elisha	2 Kings 5	Luke 4:27

Stoning of Zechariah	2 Chron. 24:20-21	Matt. 23:35
Jonah's message to Nineveh	Jonah 3:4-5	Matt. 12:41
Daniel's prophecy of abomination	Dan. 9:27	Matt. 24:15

Lightner points out that Jesus' arguments in citing these passages often depend on the reality of these events: 'the entire validity of His arguments stands or falls upon the actual objective historicity of the events He refers to.' Lightner concludes, correctly it would seem, that Jesus' 'citations of these historical events ... places His divine stamp of approval upon the authenticity of the events and the authority of the record which contains them.'[14]

h) *Christians cannot faithfully confess Jesus as Lord while rejecting His testimony to the Old Testament or while rejecting the authority of the apostolic testimony in the New Testament.* It remains for us to offer this conclusion: the confession of Jesus as Lord would seem to require of Christians:

(i) Recognition of Jesus' authority and teaching as the starting point for an evangelical view of Scripture;

(ii) Submission to Jesus' teaching on all matters, including the authority of the Old Testament as involving its authenticity and historicity;

(iii) Submission to apostolic authority and testimony as exercised through the New Testament writings as an extension of Jesus' own authority;

(iv) Acknowledgment of the authority of the Lord Jesus Himself as that which ultimately lies behind and certifies the entire Bible.

It may not be intellectually fashionable or respectable to adopt positions which Jesus took with respect to the authority, historicity and authorship of the Bible; it is certainly out of line with much modern scholarship. But it is not fashionable in our world to acknowledge Jesus as Lord in the first place. Yet it must be

---

14 Lightner, *The Savior and the Scriptures*, pp. 99, 97.

maintained that one cannot consistently confess Jesus as Lord and reject what He taught concerning anything, including the Bible. For the confessing Christian, Jesus' lordship must be observed here as well as in everything else. And the converse is also true: to reject or deny Jesus' authority and teaching with respect to the Old Testament and as further expressed through the apostles is to reject His lordship and to assert one's own personal autonomy; it must be considered as no less than an act of rebellion.

Bibliography

Abbott, T.K. *A Critical and Exegetical Commentary on the Epistles to the Ephesians and to the Colossians,* International Critical Commentary. Edinburgh: T. & T. Clark, 1897.

Abbott-Smith, G. *A Manual Greek Lexicon of the New Testament,* 3rd ed. Edinburgh, U.K.: T & T Clark, 1994.

Aland, Kurt, Black, M., Martini, C. M., Metzger, B. M., and Wikgren, A., eds. *The Greek New Testament,* 3rd ed. New York: American Bible Society, 1975.

Alexander, Joseph Addison. *A Commentary on the Acts of the Apostles,* 2 vols. in 1, reprint ed. London: Banner of Truth, 1963.

Berkhof, Louis. *Systematic Theology,* reprint ed. Edinburgh: Banner of Truth Trust, 1958.

Bettenson, Henry, ed. *Documents of the Christian Church.* 2nd ed. London: Oxford University Press, 1963.

Bird, Michael F. 'What Is There between Minneapolis and St. Andrews? A Third Way in the Piper–Wright Debate.' *Journal of the Evangelical Theological Society* 54.2 (June 2011) 299-309.

Bock, Darrell L. *Acts.* Baker Exegetical Commentary. Grand Rapids: Baker, 2007.

_____. *Luke.* Baker Exegetical Commentary. Grand Rapids: Baker, 1994.

Broadus, John A. 'Commentary on the Gospel of Matthew' in Alvah Hovey, ed., *An American Commentary on the New Testament,* 7 vols. Valley Forge: American Baptist Publication Society, 1886, Vol. 1.

Bromiley, Geoffrey W. *Theological Dictionary of the New Testament,* edited by Gerhard Kittel and Gerhard Friedrich, translated by

Geoffrey W. Bromiley, abridged in one volume. Grand Rapids: Eerdmans, 1985.

Brown, Colin, gen. ed. *The New International Dictionary of New Testament Theology*, Translated from the German *Theologisches Begriffslexicon zum Neuen Testament*, 3 vols. Grand Rapids: Zondervan, 1975-78.

Bruce, F. F. *The Epistle of Paul to the Romans*, Tyndale New Testament Commentaries. Grand Rapids: Eerdmans, 1963.

_____. *The Epistle to the Ephesians*. Westwood, N.J.: Fleming H. Revell Co., 1961.

_____. *Jesus: Lord and Savior*. Downers Grove, IL: InterVarsity, 1986.

Calvin, John. *Institutes of the Christian Religion*, trans. Henry Beveridge. London: James Clarke, 1953.

Carson, D. A. *The Sermon on the Mount: An Evangelical Exposition of Matthew 5–7*. Grand Rapids: Baker, 1978.

Chafer, Lewis Sperry. *Systematic Theology*, 8 vols. Dallas: Dallas Seminary Press, 1947.

Collins, C. John. *Genesis 1-4: A Linguistic, Literary, and Theological Commentary*. Phillipsburg, NJ: Presbyterian and Reformed, 2006.

Cranfield, C. E. B. *A Critical and Exegetical Commentary on the Epistle to the Romans*, International Critical Commentary, 2 vols. Edinburgh: T. & T. Clark, 1975, 1979.

Cullmann, Oscar. *The Christology of the New Testament*, Translated by Shirley C. Guthrie and Charles A. M. Hall, rev. ed. Philadelphia: Westminster Press, 1963.

_____. *The Earliest Christian Confessions*, translated by J. K. S. Reid. London: Lutterworth Press, 1949.

Culver, Robert Duncan. *Systematic Theology: Biblical and Historical*. Geanies House, Fearn, Ross-shire, UK: Christian Focus, 2005.

Danker, Frederick William. *A Greek–English Lexicon of the New Testament and other Early Christian Literature*. 3rd ed. Chicago: University of Chicago Press, 2000.

Dodd, C. H. *The Apostolic Preaching and Its Developments*, reprint ed. New York: Harper & Row, 1964.

Douglas, J. D., et al., eds., *The New Bible Dictionary*. Grand Rapids: Eerdmans, 1962; 3rd ed., Leicester, England: InterVarsity, 1996.

Dunn, James D. G. *Christianity in the Making*, vol. 2: *Beginning from Jerusalem*. Grand Rapids: Eerdmans, 2009.

France, R. T. *The Gospel of Matthew*. New International Commentary on the New Testament. Grand Rapids: Eerdmans, 2007.

_____. *Jesus and the Old Testament: His Application of Old Testament Passages to Himself and His Mission*. Downers Grove, IL: InterVarsity, 1971.

_____. *Matthew*. Tyndale New Testament Commentary. Grand Rapids: Eerdmans, 1985.

Franzmann, Martin H. *Follow Me: Discipleship According to Saint Matthew*. St. Louis: Concordia, 1961.

Freedman, David Noel, ed. *Anchor Bible Dictionary*. New York: Doubleday, 1992.

Garland, David E. *1 Corinthians*, Baker Exegetical Commentary. Grand Rapids: Baker, 2003.

Gentry, Kenneth L. *Lord of the Saved: Getting to the Heart of the Lordship Debate*. Phillipsburg, NJ: Presbyterian & Reformed, 1992.

_____. 'The Great Option: A Study of the Lordship Controversy.' *Baptist Reformation Review* 5 (Spring 1976): 49-79.

Ginter, Marlene, and Traz, Karen. 'Is Jesus Christ the Lord of Your Life?' *Baptist Herald*, February 1978, p.12.

Grudem, Wayne. *Systematic Theology: An Introduction to Biblical Doctrine*. Grand Rapids: Zondervan, 1994; 2000 reprint.

Guthrie, Donald. *New Testament Theology*. Downers Grove, IL: InterVarsity, 1981.

A Handy Concordance to the Septuagint, reprint ed. London: Samuel Bagster & Sons, 1970.

Harrison, Everett F. 'Must Christ Be Lord To Be Savior? No.' *Eternity*, September 1959, p.14.

_____. 'Romans' in Frank E. Gaebelein, ed., *The Expositor's Bible Commentary*, 12 vols. Grand Rapids: Zondervan, 1976-, 10: 1-171.

_____. *A Short Life of Christ*. Grand Rapids: Eerdmans, 1968.

Hassler, Andrew. 'Ethnocentric Legalism and the Justification of the Individual: Rethinking Some New Perspective Assumptions.' *Journal of the Evangelical Theological Society* 54.2 (June 2011), 311-27.

'Have You Made the Wonderful Discovery of the Spirit-FilledLife?' Campus Crusade for Christ, 1966.

Hendriksen, William. *Exposition of Ephesians*, New Testament Commentary. Grand Rapids: Baker Book House, 1967.

————. *Exposition of Philippians*, New Testament Commentary. Grand Rapids: Baker Book House, 1962.

Hodge, Charles. *A Commentary on Romans*, reprint ed. London: Banner of Truth Trust, 1972.

————. *Commentary on the Epistle to the Ephesians*, reprint ed. Old Tappan, NJ: Fleming H. Revell Co, n.d.

Hodges, Zane. *Absolutely Free!* Grand Rapids: Zondervan, 1989.

Hoehner, Harold W. *Ephesians: An Exegetical Commentary.* Grand Rapids: Baker Academic, 2002.

Hoeksema, Herman. *Reformed Dogmatics.* Grand Rapids: Reformed Free Publishing Association, 1966.

Horton, Michael, ed. *Christ the Lord: The Reformation and Lordship Salvation.* Grand Rapids: Baker, 1992.

Hughes, Philip Edgcumbe. *A Commentary on the Epistle to the Hebrews.* Grand Rapids: Eerdmans, 1977.

Hughes, Philip Edgcumbe. *Paul's Second Epistle to the Corinthians*, New International Commentary on the New Testament. Grand Rapids: Eerdmans, 1962.

Hurtado, Larry W. 'Lord.' Gerald F. Hawthrone et al., eds., *Dictionary of Paul and His Letters.* Downers Grove, IL: InterVarsity, 1993; pp. 560-69.

————. *Lord Jesus Christ: Devotion to Jesus in Earliest Christianity.* Grand Rapids: Eerdmans, 2003

Kittel, Gerhard, and Friedrich, Gerhard, eds. *Theological Dictionary of the New Testament*, translated and edited by Geoffrey W. Bromiley, 10 vols. Grand Rapids: Eerdmans, 1964-76.

Ladd, George Eldon. *A Theology of the New Testament.* Grand Rapids: Eerdmans, 1974.

Lange, John Peter. *Commentary on the Holy Scriptures: Critical, Doctrinal and Homiletical,* translated and edited by Philip Schaff, 24 vols. in 12, reprint ed. Grand Rapids: Zondervan, 1960.

Lewis, C. S. *Mere Christianity. An Anniversary Edition of Three Books: The Case for Christianity, Christian Behavior, and Beyond Personality,* ed. and with an Introduction by Walter Hooper. New York: Macmillan, 1981.

Liddell, Henry George, and Scott, Robert. *A Greek–English Lexicon.* Revised by Henry Stuart Jones, with supplement. Oxford: Oxford University Press, 1968.

_____. *A Lexicon: Abridged from Liddell and Scott's Greek–English Lexicon.* Oxford: Oxford University Press, 1966.

Lightfoot, J.B. *Saint Paul's Epistle to the Philippians.* London: Macmillan, 1891.

Lightner, Robert P. *The Saviour and the Scriptures.* Philadelphia: Presbyterian and Reformed, 1966.

Lloyd-Jones, D. Martyn. *Great Doctrines of the Bible,* vol. 2, *God the Holy Spirit,* 3 vols. in one. Wheaton, IL: Crossway, 2003.

_____. *Romans: An Exposition of Chapter 6.* London: Banner of Truth Trust, 1972.

MacArthur, John F. Jr. *Faith Works: The Gospel According to the Apostles.* Dallas: Word, 1994.

_____. *The Gospel According to Jesus.* Grand Rapids: Zondervan, 1988, 1994.

Malone, Fred A. *The Baptism of Disciples Alone: A Covenantal Argument for Credobaptism Versus Paedobaptism* 2nd ed. Cape Coral, FL: Founders Press, 2007.

Mangalwadi, Vishal. *Missionary Conspiracy: Letters to a Postmodern Hindu.* Carlisle, Cumbria, UK: OM Publishing, 1998.

Marshall, I. Howard. *The Gospel of Luke: A Commentary on the Greek Text,* New International Greek Testament Commentary. Grand Rapids: Eerdmans, 1978.

_____. *Jesus the Saviour: Studies in New Testament Theology.* Downers Grove, IL: InterVarsity, 1990.

_____. *New Testament Theology: Many Witnesses, One Gospel.* Downers Grove, IL: InterVarsity, 2004.

Martin, R. P., *Carmen Christi: Philippians 2:5-11 in Recent Interpretation and in the Setting of Early Christian Worship.* Cambridge: Cambridge University Press, 1967.

Metzger, Bruce M. 'The Ascension of Jesus Christ.' *Historical and Literary Studies: Pagan, Jewish, and Christian.* Grand Rapids: Eerdmans, 1968.

_____. *The New Testament: Its Background, Growth, and Content.* Nashville: Abingdon, 1965.

Moo, Douglas J. *The Epistle to the Romans.* New International Commentary on the New Testament. Grand Rapids: Eerdmans, 1996.

Morris, Leon. *The Apostolic Preaching of the Cross*, 3rd ed. Grand Rapids: Eerdmans, 1965.

_____. *The Gospel According to John.* New International Commentary on the New Testament. Grand Rapids: Eerdmans, 1971.

Motyer, J. A.. *Philippian Studies: The Richness of Christ.* Chicago: Inter-Varsity Press, 1966.

Moule, C. F. D., *The Origin of Christology.* Cambridge: Cambridge University Press, 1977.

Moulton, W. F., and Geden, A.S., eds. *A Concordance to the Greek New Testament*, 4th ed., edited by H. K. Moulton. Edinburgh: T. & T. Clark, 1963.

Mounce, Robert H., *The Essential Nature of New Testament Preaching.* Grand Rapids: Eerdmans, 1960.

Mounce, William D., gen. ed. *Mounce's Complete Expository Dictionary of Old & New Testament Words.* Grand Rapids: Zondervan, 2006.

Murray, Iain H. *Evangelicalism Divided: A Record of Crucial Change in the Years 1950 to 2000.* Edinburgh: Banner of Truth, 2000.

Murray, John. *Collected Writings of John Murray,* 4 vols. Edinburgh: Banner of Truth, 1976-82.

_____. *Epistle to the Romans,* New International Commentary on the New Testament, 2 vols. in 1. Grand Rapids: Eerdmans, 1959, 1965.

_____. *Principles of Conduct.* Grand Rapids: Eerdmans, 1957.

_____. *Redemption Accomplished and Applied*. Grand Rapids: Eerdmans, 1955.

Needham, David C. *Birthright: Christian Do You Know Who You Are?* Portland, OR: Multnomah Press, 1979.

Nestle, Eberhard, and Aland, Kurt and Barbara, *Novum Testamentum Graece*, 27th ed. Stuttgart: Deutsche Bibelgesellschaft, 1993.

Neufeld, Vernon H. *The Earliest Christian Confessions*. Grand Rapids: Eerdmans, 1963.

New American Standard Bible. Philadelphia: A. J. Holman Company, 1973.

Niehaus, Jeffrey J. 'An Argument against Theologically Constructed Covenants.' *Journal of the Evangelical Theological Society* 50/2 (June 2007) 259-73.

_____. 'Covenant and Narrative, God and Time.' *Journal of the Evangelical Theological Society* 53/3 (September 2010) 535-59.

_____. 'Covenant: An Idea in the Mind of God.' *Journal of the Evangelical Theological Society* 52/2 (June 2009) 225-46.

Nicoll, W. Robertson, ed. *The Expositor's Greek Testament*, 5 vols., reprint ed. Grand Rapids: Eerdmans, 1967.

O'Brien, Peter T. 'Colossians.' D. A. Carson et al., eds., *New Bible Commentary*, 4th ed. Downers Grove, IL: IVP Academic, 1994.

_____. *The Epistle to the Philippians: A Commentary on the Greek Text*. Grand Rapids: Eerdmans, 1991.

Ortlund, Dane C. 'Justified by Faith, Judged according to Works: Another Look at a Pauline Paradox.' *Journal of the Evangelical Theological Society* 52/2 (June 2009): 323-39.

Osborne, Grant R. *The Hermeneutical Spiral: A Comprehensive Introduction to Biblical Interpretation*. Downers Grove, IL: InterVarsity, 1991.

Packer, J. I. *Knowing God*, reprint ed. Downers Grove, IL: InterVarsity, 1993.

Piper, John. *The Future of Justification: A Response to N. T. Wright*. Wheaton, IL: Crossway, 2007.

Prior, Kenneth F.W. *The Way of Holiness*. London: Inter-Varsity Press, 1967.

Rahlfs, Alfred, ed. *Septuaginta*, 2 vols., 9th ed. Stuttgart: Wurttembergische Bibelanstalt, 1971.

Reisinger, Ernest C., *What Should We Think of 'The Carnal Christian'?* Edinburgh: Banner of Truth Trust, n.d.

Reymond, Robert L. *A New Systematic Theology of the Christian Faith*, 2nd ed. Nashville: Thomas Nelson, 2002.

_____. *Jesus, Divine Messiah: The New Testament Witness.* Phillipsburg, NJ: Presbyterian and Reformed, 1990.

Ridderbos, Herman. *The Coming of the Kingdom*, trans. H. de Jongste, ed. Raymond O. Zorn. Philadelphia: Presbyterian and Reformed, 1962.

_____. *Paul: An Outline of His Theology*, transl. John Richard De Witt. Grand Rapids: Eerdmans, 1975.

_____ *Redemptive History and the New Testament Scriptures*, 2nd revised ed, translated by H. De Jongste, revised by Richard B. Gaffin, Jr. Phillipsburg, NJ: Presbyterian and Reformed, 1988.

Robertson, O. Palmer. *The Christ of the Covenants*. Phillipsburg, NJ: Presbyterian and Reformed, 1980.

_____. *The Israel of God: Yesterday, Today, and Tomorrow.* Phillipsburg, NJ: Presbyterian and Reformed, 2000.

Robinson, J. Armitage. *St. Paul's Epistle to the Ephesians*. London: James Clarke & Co.

Ryrie, Charles Caldwell. *Balancing the Christian Life*. Chicago: Moody Press, 1969.

_____. *So Great Salvation*. Wheaton, IL: Victor, 1989.

Sanderson, John W. *The Fruit of the Spirit*. Grand Rapids: Zondervan, 1972.

Sauer, Erich. *The Dawn of World Redemption: A Survey of Historical Revelation in the Old Testament*. Grand Rapids: Eerdmans, 1953.

Schaeffer, Francis A. *Genesis in Space and Time: The Flow of Biblical History*. Downers Grove, IL: InterVarsity, 1972.

Schaff, Philip, ed. *The Creeds of Christendom*, 3 vols, 6th ed. Grand Rapids: Baker, 1985 [1931].

Schreiner, Thomas R. *1, 2 Peter, Jude*. New American Commentary. Nashville: Broadman & Holman, 2003.

_____. *Romans*. Baker Exegetical Commentary. Grand Rapids: Baker, 1998.

Schreiner, Thomas R., and Caneday, Ardel B. *The Race Set Before Us: A Biblical Theology of Perseverance and Assurance.* Downers Grove, IL: InterVarsity, 2001.

Scruton, Roger. *Modern Philosophy: An Introduction and Survey.* New York: Penguin, 1994.

Seifrid, Mark. 'The Near Word of Christ and the Distant Vision of N. T. Wright.' *Journal of the Evangelical Theological Society* 54.2 (June 2011) 279-97.

Shedd, W. G. T. *Dogmatic Theology*, 3 vols., reprint ed. Grand Rapids: Zondervan, 1969. 3rd ed., ed. Alan W. Gomes. Phillipsburg, NJ: Presbyterian and Reformed, 2003.

Stott, John R. 'Must Christ Be Lord To Be Savior? Yes.' *Eternity*, September 1959, p. 15.

Van Groningen, Gerard. *Messianic Revelation in the Old Testament*, 2 vols. Eugene, OR: Wipf and Stock, 1997.

Verbrugge, Verlyn D. *New International Dictionary of New Testament Theology: Abridged Edition.* Grand Rapids: Zondervan, 2000.

Vos, Geerhardus. *Biblical Theology: Old and New Testaments.* Edinburgh: Banner of Truth, 1975.

_____. *Redemptive History and Biblical Interpretation: The Shorter Writings of Geerhardus Vos,* ed. Richard B. Gaffin, Jr. Phillipsburg, NJ: Presbyterian and Reformed, 1980.

_____. *The Self-Disclosure of Jesus,* ed. Johannes G. Vos. Phillipsburg, NJ: Presbyterian and Reformed Publishing Co., 1978.

Wagner, C. Peter. 'Who Found It?' *Eternity*, September 1977, pp 13-19.

Warfield, Benjamin Breckinridge. *Perfectionism,* ed. Samuel G. Craig. Philadelphia: Presbyterian and Reformed, 1974.

Westcott, Brooke Foss, *Saint Paul's Epistle to the Ephesians,* reprint ed. Minneapolis: Klock & Klock, 1978.

Wilson, Geoffrey B., *Romans: A Digest of Reformed Comment,* rev. ed. Edinburgh: Banner of Truth Trust, 1977.

Wright, N. T. *The Resurrection of the Son of God.* Minneapolis: Fortress, 2003.

_____. *What Saint Paul Really Said: Was Paul of Tarsus the Real Founder of Christianity?* Grand Rapids: Eerdmans, 1997.

Zerwick, Max, and Grosvener, Mary. *A Grammatical Analysis of the Greek New Testament*, 5th ed. Rome: Editrice Pontificio Istituto Biblico, 1996.

Subject Index

Scripture Index

345

Christian Focus Publications
publishes books for all ages

Our mission statement –

STAYING FAITHFUL

In dependence upon God we seek to impact the world through literature faithful to His infallible Word, the Bible. Our aim is to ensure that the Lord Jesus Christ is presented as the only hope to obtain forgiveness of sin, live a useful life and look forward to heaven with Him.

REACHING OUT

Christ's last command requires us to reach out to our world with His gospel. We seek to help fulfil that by publishing books that point people towards Jesus and help them develop a Christ-like maturity. We aim to equip all levels of readers for life, work, ministry and mission.

Books in our adult range are published in three imprints:

Christian Focus contains popular works including biographies, commentaries, basic doctrine and Christian living. Our children's books are also published in this imprint.

Mentor focuses on books written at a level suitable for Bible College and seminary students, pastors, and other serious readers. The imprint includes commentaries, doctrinal studies, examination of current issues and church history.

Christian Heritage contains classic writings from the past.

Christian Focus Publications Ltd,
Geanies House, Fearn, Ross-shire,
IV20 1TW, Scotland, United Kingdom.
www.christianfocus.com